Excavations in Akhmīm, Egypt

Continuity and change in city life from late antiquity to the present

First Report

Sheila McNally
and
Ivančica Dvoržak Schrunk

BAR International Series 590

1993

I0091878

Published in 2019 by
BAR Publishing, Oxford

BAR International Series 590

Excavations in Akhmīm, Egypt

© The authors individually and the Publisher 1993

The authors' moral rights under the 1988 UK Copyright,
Designs and Patents Act are hereby expressly asserted.

All rights reserved. No part of this work may be copied, reproduced, stored,
sold, distributed, scanned, saved in any form of digital format or transmitted
in any form digitally, without the written permission of the Publisher.

ISBN 9780860547600 paperback
ISBN 9781407348919 e-book

DOI https://doi.org/10.30861/9780860547600

A catalogue record for this book is available from the British Library

This book is available at www.barpublishing.com

BAR Publishing is the trading name of British Archaeological Reports (Oxford) Ltd.
British Archaeological Reports was first incorporated in 1974 to publish the BAR
Series, International and British. In 1992 Hadrian Books Ltd became part of the BAR
group. This volume was originally published by Tempvs Reparatvm in conjunction
with British Archaeological Reports (Oxford) Ltd / Hadrian Books Ltd, the Series
principal publisher, in 1993. This present volume is published by BAR Publishing,
2019.

BAR
PUBLISHING

BAR titles are available from:

BAR Publishing
122 Banbury Rd, Oxford, OX2 7BP, UK
EMAIL   info@barpublishing.com
PHONE +44 (0)1865 310431
FAX   +44 (0)1865 316916
www.barpublishing.com

TABLE OF CONTENTS

LIST OF DRAWINGS

Drawings were done by Peter Donaldson, Pieter Brouke, Michael C. Nelson, and Scott Karakas.

LIST OF PLATES

Photographs were made by Peter Donaldson, George Parker, and other mission members.

ACKNOWLEDGEMENTS

We are deeply grateful to the many people who have made this work possible.

We are indebted to the Egyptian Antiquities Organization for permitting, supervising, and facilitating our work at every level. In addition to past kindness from Drs. Viktor Girgis, Ahmed Kadri and Shehata Adam, we have recently benefited from the warm encouragement of the present director, Dr. Mohammed Ibrahim Bakr. We thank Dr. Fahmy Abd el-Alim, General Director of the Islamic and Coptic Antiquities, for his assistance. Dr. Ali al-Kholi, General Director of the Pharaonic Antiquities, has also been most helpful. The former head of the local inspectorate, Mme Amina al-Gamal, oversaw our activities not only with competence, but with a cheerfulness that made our stay easier and more enjoyable.

The former director of the Islamic Museum in Cairo, Dr. Abd el-Rauf Ali Yussef, was in the past and still continues to be ready with practical and scholarly assistance. We also owe much to the efficiency and kindness of the present director, Mme Nam'it Abou Bakr. All the curators and other staff have been unfailingly helpful.

His Holiness Pope Shenouda most graciously received our mission in 1978 and gave us his advice, encouragement, and blessing.

The present Brother Samuel of Deir el-Suriyan, then Sameh Adley, architect for the Coptic Patriarchate, eagerly opened many doors, working for and with us.

We cannot possibly list, but we do most happily remember, all the people in Sohag and Akhmim who contributed so much to the pleasantness and effectiveness of our stay. We thank particularly Samuel Mina of the Bank of Alexandria in Sohag. The able and diligent local workmen were efficiently supervised by Rais Anwar of Quft and his cohorts. The young women and men cheerfully spent many hours cataloguing the pottery. We will not name here all those who worked for us in the field and in the laboratory, but we can assure them that their efforts are well remembered. We also benefited from the hospitality of the weaving school in Akhmim, during most of our stay ably directed by Joke van Neerven.

We thank all scholars who made it possible for us to work in Egypt, who aided us practically and intellectually without stint and without ever reminding us of our status as newcomers. We owe a special debt to George Scanlon, always so warmly encouraging both in Cairo and in the United States, and to Donald Whitcomb and Janet Johnson who helped us during research visits to the University of Chicago. Our gratitute also goes to William Y. and Nettie Adams who came to Minnesota to look at our pottery and textiles and share their expertise. Michael Bates wrote preliminary notes on our coins after their cleaning by the Islamic Museum. In recent years, Mieczyslaw and Elizabeth Rodziewicz worked very hard on our material during their term in Minnesota, and provided unsurpassable hospitality in Egypt.

We thank all the team members mentioned in Chapter Two. From the first season when we were very understaffed, we remember the seemingly tireless efforts of Michael Berger and Jerome Schaeffer, as well as Ralph Mitchell, the student, now sadly and prematurely deceased, whom George Scanlon generously sent to help us in classifying glazed ware. In the later seasons, we wish to express particular gratitude to Peter Donaldson who worked so meticulously not only to supervise but to record in word, drawing, and photography, making a contribution far beyond any one imaginable "job description."

Special thanks go to May Trad, who took us to Akhmim in the first place, found for us what became the main excavation site, and has never ceased to help in so many ways.

We thank the staff of the American Research Center in Egypt. Paul Walker greeted our first inquiries with enthusiasm, and made our first efforts not only possible but pleasant. Subsequent directors James Allen, Robert Wenke, and Nannette Pyne facilitated work. The present Director in New York, Terry Walz, has been more than helpful as we prepared this document and considered further plans. Of course we cannot think of the Center in Cairo without remembering the welcoming presence of Mme. Atteya Habachi. It is a continuing joy to have known her. Mme Amira Khattab continues to provide friendly efficiency.

Chicago House in Luxor often made us welcome. We will always treasure the memory of Martha Bell's hospitality. Lanny Bell's resourcefulness and knowledge smoothed out many difficulties.

In the United States, the students mentioned in Chapter Two worked long, hard, and well on computerization, pottery recording, and draughting. This massive computer project would never have been feasible without the commitment of Peter Patton, then head of the University of Minnesota's Computer Center and Acting Director of the Center for Ancient Studies: He was an early and dedicated advocate of uses of the computer by scholars in the humanites. Many patient people strove to work out the computer system, and to educate us in its operation. Among these we owe particular, inexpressible but pleasant debts of gratitude to Tom Rindflesch and John Arndt for their long term contributions. Both gave many years of patience, ingenuity, humor, and imagination.

Guy Gibbon, professor of Anthropology, took a deep interest in the project, offering valuable advice on publication, and continuing to participate in plans for future work.

We thank all our colleagues in the Department of Classical and Near Eastern Studies at the University of Minnesota for their willingness, even enthusiasm in answering questions and putting up with impositions. Most particularly we thank the Department Chair, George Sheets, and the secretaries, Jan Philibert and Judy Scullin.

Funding for the overseas portions of this project came from the National Endowment for the Humanities, an anonymous donor, and the Graduate School of the University of Minnesota. The Graduate School continued to give liberal support for the preparation of this volume.

Chapter 1

THE SITE

Akhmīm lies roughly 450 kilometers south of Cairo and 200 kilometers from Luxor, if distance is measured along the river, or along the road and railroad that now follow it. The Nile makes a deep bend, flowing northeast to southwest. Akhmīm, although on the "east" bank, lies north of the river, at the southern edge of a fertile plain stretching fom the river to the Arabian plateau (Maps 1, p. 17; 2, p. 18).[1]

City life in Akhmīm has continued without interruption from ancient times to the present. Both in and around the city, evidence from the earliest to latest periods overlaps and can be disentangled only with difficulty, testifying to continuity in land usage and building practices. Much has been written about the continuity in Egyptian life fostered by its distinctive geography, by the unifying force of the Nile, and the isolating forces of the deserts, rapids and sea. Implicit in any description of long term development are questions of the amount of stability and change in populations, practices, and ideas: the degree to which changes effected specific classes or society as a whole, and the degree to which change occurred internally or was imposed from without.

This summary is divided into five parts. The first two, Neolithic and Pharaonic, saw largely indigenous development. Then a long term interaction with an outside culture began, and continued through the Graeco-Roman and Late Antique periods. Late Antique has been distinguished from the earlier Graeco-Roman period because of the amount known about it, and its relevance to this project. After Late Antiquity the second long-term foreign interaction begins, initiated by the Islamic conquest. The subsequent centuries are described as one phase, the Islamic, because study has so far been insufficient to allow greater distinctions.

We are fortunate in the existence of three major projects concerned with the Pharaonic or and Greco-Roman material: those of Naguib Kanawati, of the Egyptian Archaeological Service, and of the German Archaeological Institute. I am especially indebted to Kuhlmann's masterly analysis and summary of early sources, including the sometimes bewildering

descriptions of Nineteenth Century scholars (Kuhlmann 1983).

Neolithic

We know there was Neolithic settlement somewhere in the area, but not whether it was at the site of the present city. In the late Nineteenth Century Robert Forrer found pre-dynastic slate palettes and related materials in the neighborhood of a late Roman (Coptic) cemetery to the northwest (near Dayr al-Shuhadā, see Map 2; Forrer 1893, 1901, Kuhlmann 1982, 1983, 56-57). A collection of finds seen in 1978 in a school in Akhmīm and now dispersed included fine Neolithic pottery from the vicinity.

Pharaonic

In the Pharaonic period the city became the capital of the ninth nome of Upper Egypt, the nome of the god Min, an ithyphallic deity. An inscription from the Twelfth Dynasty includes the first mention of this capital, called Hnt-Mnw (Fischer 1964 110–11, with alternate form; for forms of the name see also Gauthier 1905).[2]

Early in this century Gauthier assembled mentions of the city and of the nome from Pharaonic into Islamic times (Gauthier 1905, 1912, 1914). He thoroughly reviewed evidence for the physical area and organization of the nome. He described it as running on both sides of the Nile, with the largest tract between the Nile and the eastern mountains, and as bounded by the sixth, seventh, eighth, tenth and eleventh nomes. His description integrates evidence from various periods, since he argues that the boundaries remained relatively stable over time, although some changes did occur, especially between Pharaonic and Greco-Roman times. Later scholars have thought the nome was smaller than he suggested, questioning specifically how far its territory extended on the opposite, west bank of the Nile, and to the south on the east bank. The core area emerges geographically clear and unchanging. It is the triangular plain on the east bank of the Nile created where the river loops away from the Arabian plateau, first turning southwestward, along the site of the city itself, and then turning back northeastward toward the cliffs near the village of Najᶜ al-Sawāmᶜa Sharq (Map 2).

Until very recently, archaeological evidence for the Pharaonic period came almost entirely from outside

---

[1] Kuhlmann (1983, 4) links its fertility in part to the directions from which flood waters spread over this plain. He indicates how Akhmīm may have exploited peculiarities of its geographical position first in agriculture, when its fertility may have given rise of the cult of Min, and then later in developing textile and stone working industries. In addition to the geographic features he mentions, it has also been suggested that the river bend creates humidity, advantageous for the retting of flax.

[2] The city was sometimes referred to by a distinct name, Jpw, sometimes as Hnt-Mnj: scholars usually regard these as interchangeable, but Kuhlmann (1983, 9–13) believes that they were originally two sites that later coalesced.

the city itself. To the northeast lie three large areas of tombs. Two are cliff sites usually called by the names of nearby villages: the al-Salamunī cliffs about six kilometers north of Akhmīm, and the al-Hawawish cliffs about six kilometers to the east. Another cemetery is to be found in the valley closer to the village of al-Hawawish itself (about three kilometers from Akhmīm), near the Neolithic finds and the Late Roman cemetery already mentioned (Map 2). Kuhlmann designates the northernmost cliffs near al-Salamunī as C, the cliffs near al-Hawawish as B, and the nearer site as A (1982, 351–52; 1983, 52–53, fig. 14).[3]

All three sites contain Pharaonic graves, and A and C also contain graves of other periods. The richness of these graves aroused in scholars of the later Nineteenth Century an enthusiasm that soon turned to despair. In the 1880's Maspero initiated a thorough investigation. By his authority but in his absence, a rapid and far-reaching excavation took place:

> "Je laissai à Akhmīm un de nos réis, Khalil-Sakkar...quinze jours ne s'étaient pas écoulés qu'il avait ouvert vingt tombeaux, renfermant près de huit cents momies. ...C'est vraiment une ville, dont les habitents se comptent par milliers et se lèvent tour à tour à notre appel, sans que le nombre paraisse en diminuer depuis deux ans" (1893, 215).

Rais Khalil worked near al-Hawawish (at Kuhlmann's site A). He found graves ranging from the sixth dynasty through the Graeco-Roman period (Maspero 1893). At the more northerly site, al-Salamunī, Old Kingdom graves were identified. Schiaparelli said there were also New Kingdom tombs there, but Kuhlmann sees no evidence to support that (Schiaparelli 1885, Kuhlmann 1983, 83–84). In 1913–14, Whittemore excavated a group of Eighteenth Dynasty graves, as well as some later ones, in the northern area, near the village of Naj[C] al-Sawām[C]a Sharq (Whittemore 1914, Bourriau and Millard 1971).

The large scale discoveries at which Maspero rejoiced quickly led to illegal excavations on a still larger scale and to Akhmīm's development as a major center for trade in illegal antiquities. Traveling along the Nile in 1886 Petrie noted

> "At Ekhmim there had been great expectations two or three years before of results from a large and undisturbed cemetery of all periods; but a French Consul was put there (without any subjects to represent), and he raided and stripped the place under Consular seal, which could not be interfered with" (Petrie 1932, 80).

Several years later, Bouriant laments

> "Il y a cinq ans, vous vous le rappelez, vous faisiez donner le premier coup de pioche dans la nécropole d'Akhmīm. Les résultats ont été

merveilleux....Aujourd'hui c'est un veritable pillage qu'il est impossible de reprimer" (1889, 140).

Petrie's villain, the French consul, was one M. Frenay, a miller. Others, such as Wallis Budge and Charles Wilbour, found him far more satisfactory. These two men traveled to and fro over the years, the former on behalf of the British Museum, the latter amassing a private collection much of which later came to the Brooklyn Museum. Both followed developments with an enthusiasm occasionally mixed with disgust for the newfangled efforts of officials to spoil their fun. In 1884, Frenay told Wilbour "of Khalil's great success, and how all Ekhmeem was agog to dig" (Wilbour 1936, 300). In 1886, "At Akhmīm (Budge) found a very fine collection in the hands of a Frenchman who owned a flour mill in Cairo, and he caused the police to be entertained at supper whilst he and I conducted our deal for Coptic manuscripts" (Budge 1920, vol. 1, 135; for the manuscripts, see below p.8). Both men bought numerous antiquities at Akhmīm, which had become a center for trade not limited to objects actually found there. They also bought elsewhere objects said to have come from Akhmīm.[4]

Maspero's investigations yielded inscriptions ranging from Pharaonic through Graeco-Roman times, published by Bouriant (1884, 368–82; 1886, 123–24; 140–43). Coffins from al-Hawawish were published by Lacau (1904–6: now restudied by Kanawati, see below). Stelae and other finds from Akhmīm in various museums were gathered together by Porter and Moss (1937, vol. 5, 17-26).[5]

In the cliffs behind al-Salamunī and al-Hawawish, the despoiled tombs themselves remain. Kuhlmann, reviewing the early accounts and revisiting the sites, has described five Pharaonic types at the cliffs near al-Hawawish and one Old Kingdom type at al-Salamunī (Kuhlmann 1983, B 1–5, pp. 65–71; C–1, pp. 75–77). Between 1979 and 1988 Naguib Kanawati studied the rock-cut tombs of al-Hawawish (Kanawati 1980–89), providing a heartening demonstration of how much careful study can recover from ravaged sites. He found paintings, pottery and other small finds, and inscriptions that allowed him to identify tomb owners and their ranks, and to date the tombs. They all fall between the Fifth and the Twelfth Dynasties. Their owners include seven governors and two viziers, clear evidence of the nome's importance during that period. Kanawati also gathered data on many objects (statues, coffins, architraves, etc.) removed from al-Hawawish to the Cairo Museum, and to many museums abroad. In many cases he could match them to the tomb from which

---

[3] Kuhlmann thinks some confusion crept into Maspero's publication in the use of the term al-Hawawish, and so he prefers to call the cliff cemetery there Bayl al-Madina. I am not following him because of Kanawati's continued use of the older nomenclature (Kanawati 1980–89).

[4] For an example of the resultant confusion in provenience, see Kuhlmann 1983, 22 note 81: Wilbour acquired the Brooklyn torso of Meket-Aton from a dealer in Akhmīm. Had it been brought there from el-Amarna, or does it indicate an Amarna-period cult center in Akhmīm? For the continuation of this situation to the present day as far as papyri are concerned, see Turner 1980, 51.

[5] For several inscriptions relating to a builder from Akhmīm, see Gaballa 1981.

they originally came. He found indications that a rock-cut temple might lie in the area (Kanawati 1980, 6; cf. Kuhlmann's discussion of evidence for a necropolis temple 1983, 12-13, 21).

The most impressive rock-cut structure at al-Salamunī is the rock-cut temple of Min. Lepsius first described this impressive "Grotto of Pan." Kees and von Bissing visited it again in the winter of 1912-13. Between 1979 and 1981 the German Archaeological Institute studied the temple, and their work continues to the present day (see the yearly reports in *AA*). The Pharaoh Ay constructed the temple at the very end of the Eighteenth Dynasty. A high priest substantially refurbished it at an unknown date, and it continued in use through the Graeco-Roman periods (Lepsius 1849, 1:162–65; Kees 1914; Kuhlmann 1979).

Ay's inscription on the temple indicates he refurbished Akhmīm generally. His interest in the site increases the possibility that he and his family, who play such intriguing roles in the Amarna period and reaction, may have come from Akhmīm (Kuhlmann 1979, 187; cf. Kees 1949). An inscription at the temple contains a Greek name that Kuhlmann has reinterpreted as referring to a consort of the Fourth Century Pharaoh Nectanebo I. It indicates an important early contact with Greece (Kuhlmann 1981).

During the New Kingdom quarries were opened in the al-Salamunī cliffs, and Kuhlmann suggests that the worship in the temple was connected with the quarrying activity (Kuhlmann 1981, 279; 1983, 85-86.

Ancient writers (Herodotus II, 91) and especially medieval Arab geographers (Kamāl 1926–51) alluded to important temples standing in the city itself. The early European travelers however found only scattered remnants (e.g., Pococke 1743; references collected by Kuhlmann 1983, 20-40). Dating specific remains presents problems. Kuhlmann sees evidence for the existence of a temple by the First Dynasty, and for temple building in the Sixth Dynasty of the Old Kingdom as well as during the Middle and New Kingdoms (Kuhlmann 1983, 20–23).

In the 1183 AC, Ibn Ǧubayr passed through Akhmīm on his way to Mecca, and described a great temple he saw there. In 1799 Saint-Genis saw blocks belonging to this structure that confirmed Ibn Ǧubayr's account of its impressive size (Saint-Genis 1821, 4. 47). On the basis of these two sources, Sauneron thought the temple might have been Pharaonic, judging it to have been the equal of the Late Period temples of Edfu, Dendera or Philae, and even to rival some New Kingdom construction (Sauneron 1952, 135 and passim). Kuhlmann draws different conclusions about details of the structure (Kuhlmann 1983, 34–37).

Sauneron spoke of existing remains of a temple at the northwest of the city begun in the Pharaonic period, and a temple at the southeast dating to the Roman period (Sauneron 1952). Kuhlmann (1983) identifies more "ruin fields," and makes a noble effort to bring order out of conflicting evidence from ancient sources, recent travelers, and present-day remains. In 1978, only one

well-defined foundation, in a sports ground north of the city, remained to be seen,[6] as well as numerous spolia scattered through the town. Among the latter was a column drum reused as a mill stone, as Saint Genis had also seen in 1791 (Saint-Genis 1821, 4, 47).

In the last decade, Pharaonic monuments have come to light in two more places. In 1981, excavations for an apartment building on the outskirts of the city itself uncovered the remains of a temple built by Rameses II, excavated by the Egyptian Antiquities Service (Yaḥyā Ṣalāḥ Ṣabr al-Maṣrī 1983; Kuhlmann 1983, 16–17, fig. 3, p. 17). Fragments of a statue of the king, and a better preserved statue of his daughter Meritamun were found. In 1991 the construction of a post office stopped when workers came upon two more statues, one of them again of Rameses II. These statues both extend out of the building site under a Muslim cemetery. So far it has not been possibly to uncover them completely, or determine their surroundings.

Graeco-Roman

Gauthier's description of the nome (1905, 1912, 1914) includes Graeco-Roman references found in sources that included inscriptions, papyri, and mummy labels. More have been published since.

A number of Greek and Roman writers mention Akhmīm. The most notable are Herodotus in the Fifth Century B.C., Agatharkides in the Second Century B.C., Diodorus Siculus in the First Century B.C., Strabo (First Century B.C. to First Century A.C.), Pliny the Elder in the First Century A.C., Plutarch and Ptolemy in the Second Century A.C., the *Antonine Itinerary*, and the Sixth Century Stephan of Byzantium.

Herodotus (2, 91) calls the city by a Greek version of its Egyptian name, χεμμις . He says that during his travels in Egypt he found this city unique because of its ties to Greece. The ties surprised him and continue to puzzle modern scholars. Townspeople told him that they worshipped the Greek hero Perseus. They supported their statement with a story about the hero's sandal print, and a description of the games celebrated in the Greek manner to honor him. Herodotus briefly describes the sanctuary of Perseus.

Scholars usually assume that he had identified Min, chief god of the nome, with Perseus, but recently Lloyd has suggested that Horus was meant (Lloyd 1969, 82–83). Some explain the identification with Perseus as a linguistic error (e.g., Sauneron 1962, summary of opinions Lloyd 1969, 81–82). Others deny that there could be a linguistic explanation, and look for some underlying relationship between Greek and Egyptian deities (e.g., Morenz 1963, summary Lloyd 1969, 82–83). Bernand points to parallels between Min and

---

[6] Although it is apparently the foundation called Pharaonic by Sauneron, nothing about it seemed to us incompatible with a later date. Uncertainty as to its period led the Antiquities Service to withdraw permission for us to investigate it and its surroundings.

Hermes (1977, 233–41). Castiglione suggests that Herodotus' account arose out of an attempt to explain a monument in the form of a sandal print, like those still surviving elsewhere in Egypt (1966). Sethe thought that Egyptian attempts to explain representations of a pole-climbing ceremony honoring Min might have led to Herodotus' belief that games were celebrated (Sethe 1899, Castiglione 1966, 43 note 10; cf. Lloyd's disagreement 1969, 83). Bernand, like Lloyd, believes the games existed.[7]

Whatever Herodotus' sources, several modern authors take seriously his view that Akhmīm had some unusual link with Greek culture. Lloyd carries that argument furthest. He thinks Herodotus must have spoken with people who were in fact of Greek descent, but so assimilated that Herodotus took them for Egyptians.

Later Greek writers sometimes call the city by a version of the indigenous name Herodotus uses, and sometimes give it a new Greek one, Panopolis. Herodotus' mention of Perseus never recurs. Instead, the god Min is identified with Pan.[8] Diodorus Siculus cites the name as an indication of the importance of Pan to the Egyptians, and gives us both versions: "the inhabitants of (Egypt)...have also named a city after him in the Thebaid, called by the natives Chemmo, which when translated means city of Pan" (I.18.2).[9] Just a little later Strabo notes its antiquity, and its contemporary importance in the building and textile industries (17.1.42): "and then (one comes) to Panopolis, an old settlement of linen-workers and stone-workers"[10] At about the same time Pliny the Elder renders the name in Latin letters, Panopolis (*Nat Hist* 5.11.61). In the Second Century A.C. the geographer Ptolemy called the nome χεμμο. His sentence on the extent of the nome (4.5.32) provides one of Gauthier's main sources.[11] Plutarch *de Isis et Os.* 356, 14 speaks of "the Pans and Satyrs who lived in the region around Chemmis."[12] The *Antonine Itinerary* indicates the continuing importance of the city. In the Sixth Century A.C. Stephan of

Byzantium described a statue of Pan still surviving there.[13]

Inscriptions supplement the authors by recording the worship of Pan, and also indicate royal and imperial building activity. Both inscriptions at the al-Salamunī cliffs (Lepsius 1849, Kuhlmann 1979) and the Trajanic inscription from a temple in the city (Letronne 1842, Kuhlmann 1983, 42-44, figs. 8-11) invoke Pan. Inscribed rocks in the Wadi Bīr al-ᶜAin, west of al-Salamunī (Map 2) provide a particularly interesting source for the study of religious amalgamation and continuity. Many of the inscriptions there, like groups at other sites in the eastern desert, mention Pan (Bernand 1977: Kuhlmann 1983, 7-8, Pls. 7–12, 15).[14] Most are Ptolemaic, others Roman. Several, written by hunters, speak of assembling a collection of animals. Bernand suggests such a collection would have been connected with one of the temples, and that the whole area around the rock may have been particularly sacred to Pan. Inscriptions to Pan also occur at quarries in the area (Bernand 1977, 42).[15]

Bernand accepts Lesquier's contention that the Pan worshipped here and at other places between the Nile and the Red Sea is not only or even dominantly a god of fertility, but also a god of quarries, of mountains and of travelers (Bernand 1972, 94–96).[16] A route to the Red Sea ran either out of this Wadi, or through a declivity to

---

[7]He cites a Diocletianic papyrus from Oxyrrhynkos that refers to the Paneia, but rejects as a falsification a reference to these games in an inscription on a tanned piece of calfskin: "Les Paneia d'Égypte ont bien existé, mais c'est un papyrus, non ce faux sur peau qui nous les fait connaitre" (1977, 237, 241). Kanawati has found pictures of bull fights watched by spectators in Pharaonic tombs, and relates them to this account of games (Kanawati 1989).

[8] The identity of Ḫnt-Mnw, Chemmis, and Panopolis rests on inscriptions including mummy labels, and a list of bishoprics, Gauthier 1905, 45-46; Grohmann 1959, Beilage 1.

[9]Loeb translation. καλουμενην μεν υπο των εγχωριων Χεμμω, μεθερμηνευομενην δε Πανος πολιν.

[10] Loeb translation: (to) Πανων πολις, λινουργων και λιθουργων κατοικια παλαια 17.1.41

[11]Ptolemy (*Geog* 4.5 32) calls the site χεμμομεγα, χεμμς, χιμμ-, πανοσπολις

[12]Loeb translation: περι Χεμμιν.

---

[13]Πανος πολις, [πολις] Αιγυπτια. εστι δε και του Θεου αγαλμα μεγα ωρθιακος το αιδοιον εις επτα δακτυλους, επαιρει τε μαστιγας τη δεξια Σεληνην, ης ειδωλον φασιν ειναι τον Πανα. ο πολιτης Πανοπολιτης 500, 10

[14] Bernand quotes the various travelers, beginning with Lucas in 1714, whom the eerie landscape of this Wadi impressed: Maspero and Bouriant, directed by Frenay's local informants, were the first to note the inscribed rock. Maspero speaks movingly of the religious continuity shown by graffiti ranging from the New Kingdom to the present. The inscriptions were collected and published by Bouriant, Sayce, Lefebvre, and Preisigke before being restudied by Bernand in his general research into the cult of Pan in Egypt.

[15]Borkowski discusses the quarries in connection with the professions of Late Antique house owners in Panopolis (1975, 78-79).

[16]Bernand quotes Lesquier: "Ce Pan n'a rien du chèvre-pied hellénique. C'est le dieu de Panopolis (Akhmīm), l'égyptien Min, divinité de la fécondation. Panopolis était la ville des carriers [reference to Strabo]; et ce sont les tailleurs de pierre qui ont amené son culte à leur suite, non seulement dans les carrières les plus voisines de Coptos et donc de Panopolis, mais sur toutes les routes qui de la Thébaïde conduisent au désert. Le dieu 'sauveur,' 'qui exauce les prières,' [references to inscriptions] y était devenu le protecteur des voyages, ευοδος. Pourquoi les Grecs d'Égypte avaient-ils assimilé Pan à ce Min? Sans doute parce que l'un et l'autre étaient des montagnards. En Grèce Pan habite les grottes des hauts sommets, et la montagne du nome Panopolite (Gebel Toukh) est nommée dans les graffittes démotiques lieu où Min sejourne et se repose." He argues that the ichthyphallicism of the Egyptian fertility god also warded off danger to travelers and those who worked in quarries and mines (Lesquier 1918, 284 -85).

the south: Kuhlmann points out that it can only have been passable by people on foot (Kuhlmann 1983, 6-7).

The Graeco-Roman graves opened in the early 1880s were briefly described by Maspero (1893, 218–19). Bouriant published Ptolemaic stelai from the cemeteries (1884: 368–82; 1886, 140–43, which he considered "d'une importance exceptionelle pour l'etude de la religion égyptienne aux dernieres epoques" (1884, 381). Kuhlmann has described some of the surviving tomb types: at al-Salamunī, types C–2 (late Ptolemaic?); C–3 and C–4 (Roman); near the village of al-Hawawish, A–1 and A–2 (A-3, Christian) (Kuhlmann 1983, 79–81, 61–62). Earlier scholars thought some of the Late graves at al-Salamunī might be reused New Kingdom tombs, but Kuhlmann rules out that possibility (Kuhlmann 1982, 352–53; 1983, 75)

Some of these tombs that are cut into the al-Salamunī cliffs contain paintings. Ceiling paintings, which have survived better than wall paintings, include numerous zodiacs. A few tombs contain striking combinations of Greek and Egyptian motifs. Early in this century Rubensohn stressed the importance of one example in which Egyptian deities appear together with representations of marble panels and of garlands, "weil sie bisher das einzige Beispiel ist, in dem sich griechischer Einfluss in der malerischen Ausschmückung eines aegyptischen Grabes geltend macht" (Rubensohn 1906, 130). Rostovtzev published a plan and schematic sketch of one tomb painted with wreaths and decorated panels (1914, 494–95, figs. 92, 93). He mentioned photographing a second one (Rostovtzev 1919, 147–48). After the Second World War, von Bissing published his notes and his wife's watercolors of tombs he had seen on two much earlier trips. In addition to general descriptions of the topography, he described in detail: a) one tomb visited in 1897 in the al-Salamunī cliffs, and b) three seen in 1913 near the al-Hawawish area.[17] He again comments on the combination of Greek and Egyptian characteristics. One Judgment scene contains both Greek and Egyptian furnishings, and von Bissing suggests that an "Egyptian" may be serving a "Roman" (1946/47, 5).[18] He compares the paintings that imitate marble wall veneer with Alexandrian examples and First Style in Pompeii, and also with remains in the Roman chapel at Luxor now dated to the time of Diocletian. Dates suggested earlier for these decorations need to be reexamined in light of today's knowledge of Roman painting. Von Bissing had been unable to find again the tomb he had seen in 1897. He believed it had been destroyed, but in 1981 Peter Grossmann rediscovered it, and it is now protected.

Eighteenth and Nineteenth Century travelers also saw several Graeco-Roman carvings and inscriptions in and on the outskirts of the town itself. The texts indicate building activity at Akhmīm in the reigns of Nectanebo I, the Ptolemies, and several Roman emperors (e.g. Pococke 1743, Sonnini 1800, Lepsius 1849, Champollion le Jeune 1909: all gathered by Kuhlmann 1983).[19] Pococke, Sonnini, and Champollion noted with particular interest a stone carved with both a zodiac and an inscription. Nestor l'Hôte found the zodiac carving completely buried, but the inscription remained legible and was fully published by Letronne (Nestor l'Hôte 1840, 86–88; Letronne 1842, Kuhlmann 1983, figs. 8–11). The inscription records the completion in A.D. 109 of a Trajanic addition to a temple of Pan/Min and Triphis.

By the Third Century a number of public buildings can be documented in Akhmīm. Bowman points out that there were three sets of baths, the windows of which were glazed by the government; a gymnasium, a praetorium, a theater, and bakeries, as well as the παλατιον nearby (Bowman 1992, 500, 502). A Third or Fourth Century A.C. city register lists numerous temples (see below p.8). In the 1980s numerous Graeco-Roman fragments were still to be found built into houses in the city, and others had been taken to the Antiquities Department in Suhāj.

Late Antique

In Late Antiquity Akhmīm reached a peak of productivity. It was in the forefront of Christian religious development, a strong center of late pagan philosophy and religion, of magical practice, and possibly of Gnostic thought. It was manufacturing fine textiles with both Christian and pagan motifs.

Already by the late Third Century there was a sizable Christian community in Akhmīm, and many legends tell of the martyrs here during Diocletian's persecution (Timm 1984, vol. I: 80-81).

Pachomius, the founder of the Christian monasticism, came from just south of Akhmīm. In the first half of the Fourth Century A.D. he founded nine monasteries, including three in or near Akhmīm. According to Rousseau :

"A defensible chronology would run as follows: the community at Tse, 'in Tkahšmin' (i.e., the present Akhmīm Panopolis), under Pesso (Greek *Life* 1, 83; Sahidic *Life* 5, 52); then that of Panopolis, otherwise

---

[17]Slight differences exist between Rubensohn's, Rostovtzev's, and von Bissing's plans and elevations, but either they refer to the same tomb or there was a well-defined convention.

[18]Sauneron discusses the furnishings from another point of view in his article on the "cauldron of Sohag." (Sauneron 1983, 160–64). The painting, and the rites Sauneron discusses probably help to explain the cauldron vision of Zosimus.

[19] Champollion's account is among the fullest: "Au nord et dans un bas-fond rempli par l'inondations, sont de grandes masses calcaires sans sculptures, à l'exception d'un bloc au milieu de bassin, et qui portait sur une des faces un tableau sculpté représentant un roi faisant un acte d'adoration....je reconnus que le roi en adoration était Ptolémmée alexandre, que la divinité adorée était Amen-Hor-Ammon-Générateur, celui qu'en effet les Grecs ont considéré comme *Pan*, et dont la statue est très fidèlement décrite dans Étienne de Byzance, article *Panopolis*....Plus au nord-est, deux énormes blocs, sur l'un desquels est une inscription grecque (the inscription of Trajan)..." (Champollion le Jeune 1909, 145–46).

unnamed, 'near' the city, under Samuel (Greek *Life* 1, 81, 83; Sahidic *Life* 5, 54); and finally that at Tsmine, in the 'vicinity of the city of Šmin,' under Petronius...who was given some responsibility for "the other two monasteries near him (Greek *Life* 1, 83; Bohairic *Life* 57)" (Rousseau 1985, 163, footnotes inserted into text)..[20]

When Lefort looked for the sites of some of Pachomius' foundations, he did not investigate the area around Akhmīm (1939).

Gauthier lists references to these and to the other, more southerly, Pachomian monasteries that lay within the broad boundaries he sets for the Panopolite nome (see also Timm 1984 vol. 1, 84-85). He also notes the existence of other monasteries in the neighborhood (For the monasteries existing today, Meinardus 1965; Timm 1984 vol. 1, 88; vol. 2: 636-37; 639-42, 653-57, 660-61, 675, 676, 713-14, 733-34, 795-96, 808-10; Samuel 1990). Several on the east side of the river might also be the Pachomian foundations: Sabra (Gauthier 1905, 97) built in the name of the archangel Michael; Dayr al-Ḥadīd (96–97) and, most interesting, Dermadoud or the Monastery of the Seven Mountains (95–96) in the Wadi Bīr al-ᶜAin (see Map 2).

The last has sometimes been thought to be the place to which the patriarch Nestorius, suspected of heresy, was banished and where he died about 450–51. The story of his death in or near Akhmīm appears first in the Thirteenth Century. We know he was in Panopolis some years earlier, but not what happened to him later (Nestorius 1905; Gauthier 1905, 84–86; 1912, 120, cf. Munier 1940).[21]

A name that may be Nestorius (not, of course, necessarily the patriarch) has been found among the inscriptions nearby (most recently, Wagner 1982, 347, note 2). Monks added inscriptions to the Wadi, some on the famous rock mentioned above, some elsewhere (Kuhlmann 1983, fig. 1). Two prayers, one wholly in Greek and one that begins in Greek and ends in Coptic, have been dated to the Sixth or Seventh Century by the letter forms (Wagner 1982). They show that monks in this part of Upper Egypt continued to use Greek as well as Coptic at least until the Islamic conquest.[22]

Several structures remain at Dermadoud, as well as much late Roman pottery. Grossmann has identified one of the best preserved structures as a cistern (Kuhlmann 1983, Pl. 14; Samuel 1990, 70). In 1714 Lacy, the first modern European visitor, met hermits still living here (Bernand 1977, 8). Kuhlmann looked in vain for cave dwellings (Kuhlmann 1983, 9: he thinks only a small number of hermits can ever have lived there.)

Gauthier also included within the nome of Akhmīm the two important monasteries across the river, the White and Red monasteries, Dayr al-Abyaḍ and Dayr al-Aḥmar. Even if they were not within its governmental district, they were certainly important to its life. The White Monastery, founded in the mid Fourth Century, achieved great power under the Abbot Shenoute in the Fifth Century. In one manuscript of his *Life*, its inhabitants are numbered as 2200 monks and 1800 nuns (Besa 1983, pp. v, 5).[23] It collected and produced numerous texts, becoming a major source for Panopolitan papyri. The Red Monastery is less well documented, but probably similar in date (Meinardus 1965, 293–94; Timm 1984 vol. 2, 601-34, 639-42; Mahmoud ali Mohamed and Grossmann 1991).

The strength of pagan religion, Greek culture, and possibly Gnostic thought in Akhmīm led to confrontations with the monks in both the Fourth and the Fifth Centuries. In the time of Pachomius, a debate occurred between monks and philosophers from the city. One account sets a mild tone: "Who would bring olives from elsewhere to sell them in Panopolis," the philosophers inquired, and were answered "We are the salt, we have come to salt you." Other (possibly later) versions are more acrimonious (Rousseau 1985, 164–69: Büchler 1980, 143–45).[24]

Who were the opponents? Büchler agrees with Robinson's contention that the questions raised between the two groups were "thoroughly Gnostic," but Rousseau thinks it hard to distinguish between pagan and Gnostic speculation (Büchler 1980, 143–45; Rousseau 1985, 164–66).[25] Rousseau nonetheless agrees that Gnosticism probably flourished at Akhmīm (see especially 166, note 4 with full bibliography). Colin Roberts advanced this view on the basis of Kahle's list of early Coptic manuscripts:

"There is a quite remarkable predominance of Gnostic texts, mostly of the fourth, some of the fifth century in the sub-Akhmīmic dialect;...Panopolis then may have been a centre of Gnosticism analogous to whatever centre further south preserved the Najᶜ Ḥammādi codices

---

[20] Problems about the number and chronology of the foundations near Akhmīm have arisen because of discrepancies between the Greek and Coptic *Lives*, discussed by, among others, Amelineau 1893, Chitty 1957, Vielleux 1968, Coquin 1979); the sources are summarized by Büchler (1980, 115-21) and Rousseau (1985, 38-48, chart on 42 traces development).

[21] In the Thirteenth Century Abū Ṣaliḥ says Nestorius was at Akhmīm seven years, and was buried there, although giving the wrong century (Abū Ṣaliḥ 1895, 239-40). Local tradition holds that he was buried at the north of the kom. Timm (1984 vol. 1, 82) mentions traditions that Athanasius and Sebellus were also in exile at Panopolis.

[22] Evidence for Greek, Coptic and Arabic in use in the secular realm in the Eighth Century comes from a manuscript concerning tax relief (Grohmann 1938, discussed below).

---

[23] The numbers are exaggerated, but Hahn (1991) presents arguments for the community's vast size, as well as its great political importance.

[24] Note the variant cited by Borkowski, who uses it to discuss production and processing of olives in the nome (Borkowski 1975, 71-72).

[25] "The garden of Ptolemagrius" in Akhmīm may indicate an innovative form of pagan religion that contributed to monasticism (Welles 1946).

and contrasting perhaps with Oxyrrynchus" (Roberts 1979, 70).

The writings of the Alchemist Zosimus of Panopolis may also reflect the range of stimuli available in the late Third or early Fourth Century city. "He was a man of strong spiritual urges and little conventional scholarship, who moved in an eclectic milieu compounded of Platonism and gnosticism together with Judaism and... the 'oriental' wisdom of Hermes and Zoroaster." (Fowden, 1986, 120)[26]

In the Fifth Century, violent confrontations were initiated by the irascible abbot of the White Monastery, Shenoute. Born near Akhmīm, Shenoute was the earliest figure to write exclusively in the Coptic language, the new form of ancient Egyptian, in preference to Greek. He spent much of his time combating rampant paganism, and his biography attests to the vigor of Copts on the one hand, and of Pagan culture on the other. His biographer Besa mentions instances of the continuity of pagan rites in a temple and a house in or near Akhmim (Besa 1983, chs. 81, 83–84, 88, pp. 65, 86, 67–68 On Shenoute, most recently van der Vliet 1993, p.16 below)

Relationships between beliefs may not always have been so exclusionary. Textiles with Dionysiac and Christian themes were used in the same grave in the early Fifth Century (Willers 1993, p. 16 below). In the same century, Akhmīm produced one of the major literary figures of Late Antiquity, the poet Nonnus.[27] The forty-eight books of his poem on Dionysus display an encyclopedic familiarity with Greek literature, and some knowledge, rare in the East but shared by other Panopolite poets, of Latin. Nonnus is also said to have rendered the Gospel of St. John into verse. Scholars used to think he had probably converted to Christianity between the two productions, but now think it possible that he wrote the *Dionysiaka* after the verse Gospel, and saw no opposition between the two.[28] Nonnus worked in Alexandria, but may well have acquired his learning in Akhmīm, since we have more evidence that pagan learning flourished there.

Other poets from Panopolis who flourished in the Fifth Century include Cyrus and Pamprepios. Cameron notes characteristics the Panopolitans shared with other Egyptian poets of the period: they were pagans (or at least steeped in pagan learning, see note 26), they knew Latin as well as Greek, they wrote on contemporary rather than mythological subjects, and they

sought their fortunes outside Egypt, teaching or holding positions at court (Cameron 1965).[29]

The papyri add earlier evidence of cultivated, creative pagans. A Fourth Century man named Panodoros may have had a school of philosophy (diatribe) with a temple of Persephone in its courtyard (Borkowski 1975, 25). Aurelius Ammon wrote a classification of philosophers (Willis 1978). His brother Harpocration had a distinguished career abroad (Browne 1976; Willis 1979, cf. Fowden 1986, 174)

Rémondon argued that the final pagan resistance to Christianity in Egypt involved class warfare.

"Nous saisissons sur le vif les attaches des intellectuels païens avec la province égyptienne, plus spécialement avec le Haute-Egypte: ils se recrutent dans l'aristocratie de Panopolis et de Thèbes, dans les classes aisées qui peuvent apprendre et lire le grec, tandis que les milieux populaires, plus purement coptes, suivent volontiers Schenoudi et ses émules...." "Le paganisme est une survivance si tenace que certains Egyptiens ont vraisemblablement dû devenir musulmans sans passer par le christianisme "(1952, 67, 72).

He thought these hostilities might have gone further. Imperial support for the monks might have caused disaffection in the pagan upper classes causing them to favor the incursions of Blemmyes from the south. Later, on the eve of the Islamic conquest, a band of brigands and Ethiopian slaves active near Akhmīm (John of Nikiou, ch. 97) might also reflect pagan unrest (Rémondon 1952, 73-75).

There is little evidence for these views. As already noted, aristocratic scholars were not always pagan. Many pagans served the court well.[30] The pagans attacked by Shenoute were not necessarily upper class.[31] So far, there is no evidence for pagan institutions in Akhmīm after the Fifth Century. The statue of Min/Pan survived to the Sixth century (see note 13) precisely because Shenoute had driven out its demons..

The papyrological evidence is still unfolding. Many manuscripts have reached, and continue to reach, diverse European and American libraries through diverse paths.

A large group of papyri including religious texts, and all manner of reused secular documents from Panopolis, survived at the White Monastery outside

---

[26]Fowden (1986) surveys the evidence for his life and thought (120-126), and considers the plausibility of his relationship to Panopolis (173-74).

[27]Collart and Stegeman discuss the skimpy evidence for Nonnus' life (Collart 1930b, 1–7; Stegemann 1930, 206–9).

[28]On the compatibility of belief in the two texts, see Bowersock c.1990, 40-44; Livrea 1989 1-35; Vian 1988. C. Sherry (1991) argues that Nonnus did not write the verse paraphrase. See now also Gelzer 1993, p.16 below.

[29]Cameron later changed his view of Cyrus (Cameron 1982, 239; cf. Gregory 1975) and stressed the compatibility of pagan and Christian learning in phrases cited by Bowersock (c.1990, 62-66)

[30]One major pagan scholar (not from Akhmīm) fought in the Byzantine army against the Blemmyes. For him, loyalty to Constantinople continued a great tradition: He wrote an epic poem describing the struggle "as a great battle of Hellenism over the barbarians" (Bowersock c. 1990, 61-62, citing Livrea's edition).

[31]Although Shenoute may have been concerned to protect the poor against abuse by the rich as well as to protect the faithful against heresy, see Timbie 1986; cf. Wipszecka 1988.

7

Suhāj. They had been apparently shut away in a small room and more or less forgotten for centuries. Some reached European collections in the Eighteenth and early Nineteenth Centuries, but "personne ne put voir de ses propres yeux la cellule-bibliothèque du Monastere Blanc avant J. Maspero (pour autant qu'il l'ait réellement vue) en 1883." (Orlandi 1972)

> "Un hasard heureux a permis à la Bibliothéque nationale d'acquérir environ quatre mille feuillets de parchemin, contentant des fragments d'ouvrages rédiges en dialecte copte-thébain....Les livres incomplets, les feuilles détachées des bibles hors d'usage, des évangéliares ou des recueils d'homélies en usage dans le couvent, étaient entassés pêle-mêle sur le sol d'une cellule situé derriéere le choeur, dans une tour de refuge ne communiquant avec le corps de l'église que par un passage secret des plus étroits" (Maspero 1892, 1).

Tito Orlandi is now trying to reconstruct the contents of the original library(Orlandi 1972, 1986). Some Panopolitan papyri were purchased for the French Institute in Cairo by Maspero and Amélineau in the 1880s (Coquin 1979). Bouriant purchased another group, which have been since 1887 in the Bibliothéque Nationale (Supplement grec 1099, Fonds copte 135). Maspero later published the Coptic fragments of the Old Testament (1892). The Greek pieces were studied by Wilcken and others but were first fully published by Collart, who drew attention to the literary texts, i.e., an epitome and glossary of Homer, excerpts from Hesiod, Euripides, the Palatine Anthology, as well as to the administrative documents (Collart 1930a).[32] Budge purchased Coptic manuscripts for the British Museum from Frenay in Akhmīm (see above).

Two Panopolitan papyri from the White Monastery in the Chester Beatty Library in Dublin (Skeat 1964) have been called "our most important source of evidence for the military and civil administration in Upper Egypt in the reign of Diocletian." (Bowman 1978, 25) Skeat published them in 1964. Skeat reconstructed two rolls that had been cut up and reassembled to form a codex for recording tax receipts. One roll contained copies of letters sent in A.D. 298 by the strategos of Akhmīm, and the other of letters received in A.D. 300 by (the same? or another) strategos.

At the Twelfth International Congress of Papyrology, Hagedorn could still say that "hardly two dozen" administrative papyri were known from Akhmīm (Hagedorn 1970, 208, partial list in note 4), as a prelude

to his announcement that Cologne had acquired about 30 more. Scholars at the Fourteenth Congress discovered that the University of Cologne and Duke University had acquired parts of one family's archive. The two universities subsequently arranged for cooperative research.[33] Willis (1978) gives literature up to that time. He lists five distinct groups of Panopolitan papyri, published or in the process of publication: (1) the new group, (2) the Youtie-Hagedorn project, (3) the Beatty rolls, (4) the city register in Geneva and Berlin worked on by Martin and Borkowski, and (5) papyri in Vienna being studied by Sijpesteijn (Youtie, Hagedorn, and Youtie 1971a and b, 1973; Martin 1962, Borkowski 1975).

Other papyri of unknown provenience may be attributed to Panopolis on the basis of the dialect (Lacau 1911) and for other reasons: Turner (1980, 52–53) gives reasons for believing that a large group of manuscripts in several collections originated in Panopolis, but also points out the difficulties of precisely establishing provenience.[34] The attribution would enlarge Panopolis' position in the period.

A "Panopolitan standard type" has been identified for codices manufactured in the late third and early fourth centuries, comprising one documentary and from three to six Christian texts (Gascou 1989, 81-83).

A city register drawn up in the early Fourth Century adds more concrete detail to our picture of the city (Martin 1962, Borkowski 1975).[35] Streets are irregular, houses may be on small alleys or at angles, some are in ruins but some new ones have just been

---

[32]These purchases aroused the indignation of other seekers: Wilbour on his visit in 1890 recorded that "Mr. Frenay (the miller, consul, and antiquities dealer, see above)... told us the Abbe Amélineau tried to burgle the White Monastery...after drugging the monks. Frenay afterwards bought most of the library for the National Library" (1936, 561). In 1887, "He (Frenay) told me (Budge) that it was he who had sold to Maspero all the Coptic papyri and manuscripts which the Louvre had acquired during the last few years....Thus I learned at first hand that the Director of the Service of Antiquities bought and disposed of antiquities, and exported them.... " (1920, vol. 1, 135).

[33]"...Professor G.M. Browne and I in uncoordinated papers announced the separate acquisition by the University of Cologne and Duke University of papyri constituting an archive of documents deriving from an important family in Panopolis spanning the last decade of the Third Century and the first half of the fourth....To Cologne had fallen some 30 papyri, mostly larger in size, while Duke's share comprised some 500 fragments,...through the statesmanship of Professor Ludwig Koenen it was arranged that the two collections would exchange lesser fragments in order that all parts of each divided document might be reunited in either of the two collections. This procedure is still in progress. But when Professors Koenen, Brown, John Oates and I spread the two groups side by side at the Duke Library during a memorable week in November 1975, it became clear that substantial parts of most of our documents are still missing, and are likely to have found their way elsewhere." (Willis 1978, 140).

[34]He included the Bodmer Papyri, and Roberts followed him, "If, as seems very probable, Panopolis was the provenance of the Bodmer papyri, it may well have been a centre where pagan, Orthodox, and Gnostic cultures all flourished." (Roberts 1979, 89) Robinson has argued against this attribution, and gained Turner's agreement (Robinson 1986, 2-3).

[35]This roll exists as two sets of fragments, one in Geneva and one in Berlin. Martin's attribution of the Geneva fragments by internal evidence has been borne out by the Panopolitan names in the Berlin segments. Borkowski, however, argues that the date must be raised from c. 250, proposed by Martin, to 298–330. Martin's date was based on names, Borkowski's on paleography (1975, 13).

8

built. Inhabitants are identified by trades—jeweler, carpenter, etc., and those practicing similar trades tend to live in the same neighborhoods. Borkowski charts thirty-three professions, the number of people, possessions, and ateliers for each (1975, 44–46).· Personal names include Greek, Egyptian, and Latin elements, with the Egyptian strongly predominating. Probably the population is largely indigenous, but the use of mixed Egyptian-Greek words in names suggests a thorough Hellenization (Martin 1962).

The register lists nine ιεπον (temples, although Pelletier thought they might be altars, Borkowski 1975, 25–26) situated along city streets. Three names of divinities appear in the fragments: one of Ammon, one of the Good Demon, and one of Persephone. If Martin (1962, 65) is right in explaining Persephone as the equivalent of the local deity Triphis, then both were associated with fertility. The cult of Persephone Triphis shows again how the cultures had intermingled.

An εκκλεσια, probably a building, is mentioned, as well as deacons (Borkowski 1975, 75, 69). Timm notes references to two or three churches in Akhmīm and five monasteries on in its neighborhood in Late Antiquity (Timm 1984, vol. 1, 84–85).

Kuhlmann argues that there must have been substantial Byzantine building in Akhmīm. He points out that later writers mention that marble columns were taken from Akhmīm on several occasions, and that marble was only used in Egypt in Byzantine times (Kuhlmann 1983, 32–33). The buildings would presumably be churches and possibly other official structures. Intermittent evidence for soldiers stationed in or near the city exists from the time of Diocletian to the Sixth Century (Timm 1984, vol. 1, 84).

Long a center of textile manufacture, Akhmīm produced some of the finest tapestry weaving of its time. The official and unofficial digging that took place in the Nineteenth Century produced a wealth of Coptic materials, notably textiles. Most of these came from the cemetery beside the monastery of Dayr al-Shuhadā, also known as Dayr al-Wustānî, northeast of the city (see Map 2). Robert Forrer undertook a rapid but thorough search for textiles in that cemetery in the early 1890s (Forrer 1891a, 1891b, 1893, 1895; Frauberger 1895; Kuhlmann 1983, 55–56; Timm, 1984 vol. 1, note 47 pp. 95–96 gives a partial list of publications).

The textiles Forrer gathered came from Christian graves, from which numerous stelae also survive (Timm 1984, vol. 1, p. 90 and pp. 92-93 notes 20-23, including other epigraphic material).

Other textiles from Akhmīm attest to the persistence of enthusiasm for pagan myths, particularly those relating to Dionysos. The specific way in which two fine examples show the Triumph of Dionysos reflects ideas also found in the *Dionysiaka*, where Nonnus calls Dionysos the "light-bringer," and one who wins salvation by triumphing over obstacles (Lenzen 1960, esp. 22–23; see also Allen 1990, 16).

The city register shows three weavers (καθημενιτενς) owned houses in Late Antique Panopolis.

Most weavers, Borkowski argues, would not own houses (Borkowski 1975, 44, 46). Most weaving may have been carried out in the home, as were many other crafts (Wipszycka 1965, 56; 1971, 221; Husson 1983, 84-86), and as weaving is today. Other arrangements were possible. Wipszycka cites one papyrus that may indicate a weaving factory at Akhmīm belonging to the strategos (1965, 86). A Fourth Century lease suggests simple, flexible arrangements (McGing 1990: The papyrus is in the Chester Beatty Library in Dublin, and has no inventory number). A linen weaver leases a workshop and two looms, so presumably the whole workshop held four looms, and could be a modest room, probably in a house.[36] The most puzzling fact about this workshop is that it was located in the παρεμβολε των χριστιανων, which McGing suggests (among other possibilities) may have been a name of a "sort of Christian quarter in the town" (1990, 120, cf. Youtie 1971a, 24; Timm 1984 vol. 1, 82). An Islamic inscription (see below p.10) also mentions a weaving factory.

Islam

The nomes were renamed but not basically reshaped as pagi in the Late Roman period, and then by Islamic divisions, kuras (Grohmann 1959). At the end of the Roman period, Akhmīm was also the center of a Christian diocese. It probably retained its political position after the Islamic Conquest in the Seventh Century, since it was still the capital of a province in the Fourteenth Century. The Arabic province was larger than the original nome (Gauthier 1905, 43, 94; see also Grohmann 1938 note 96 p. 92). It is included in the "Description of Egypt" written in A.D. 1376 but based on a cadastre of 1315 (published by Silvestre de Sacy: Abd al-Laṭif 1810). Grohmann has cited any mentions in Greek, in Coptic, and by Arab chroniclers (1959).

A papyrus in the Egyptian Library provides a glimpse into the administration of this area about a century after the conquest.[37] A complaint had been made to an official with an Arab name that another administrator, also with an Arab name, had collected taxes unfairly. The headmen of the area, all with Coptic names, were called together and signed a declaration saying that they had not been oppressed. "It is not possible to ascertain whether this acquittal of the accused official was justified by the evidence, or the result of threatened penalties" (Grohmann 1938, 70; see also Maccoul 1985). The document has a Coptic text signed by the Coptic officials, a Greek summary, and a shorter Arabic one. The Coptic and Greek texts were written by

---

[36]Whether the workshop was independent, or a room in a house, is not stated, but another weaving workshop attested in papyri was a room in a house containing another workshop and two more rooms (P.Neph.48.10-11, McGing 1990, 118).

[37]Dated by the Arabic script to "the first half, or , at the latest, the third quarter of the second century of the Hiǧra" Grohmann 1938, 86.

Jacob of Panopolis, and the Arabic by another scribe: both hands are of high quality (Grohmann 1938, 67).

Up to the time of the Conquest, the two crafts mentioned by Strabo, stone masonry and weaving, were clearly flourishing. The stone masonry seems to have stopped with the conquest, here and elsewhere. The older products were prized however. In the second half of the Eighth Century, Roman buildings were destroyed and spoils taken to Mecca.

> "Al-Mahdi (Abbasid caliph from 775–85) brought these marble columns from Egypt and Syria. The majority of them came from the city of Akhmīm, a province of Egypt: now (i.e. 1577) it is a fully destroyed city, which counts among the oldest cities of the country of Egypt and is rich in marble. The best marble and the finest carved and worked capitals were sent to Cairo and other cities. It is said that the majority of the marbles used in the Holy Mosque (of Mecca) were brought from there."[38]

This demolition did not signify general ruin in the city. Textile production flourished under the new regime. Two post conquest products, one conservative and one innovative, document the spread of the Arabic language, and, in one case, of Islamic religion, into Upper Egypt.

The conservative piece is a fragment of silk medallion with a pattern of two shooting Amazons, a pattern used from the Third Century on. This example incorporates a quotation from the Koran, "God is sufficient for me," part of the ninth surah, verse 129, pointing to a Muslim weaver, not just a Muslim patron (Grube 1962, 78).[39]

The innovative piece is a rug to cover a cushion. The technique is called weft-cut pile, apparently invented by local artisans to imitate rugs from Turkestan that, like many oriental rugs, have knotted piles. The technique seems to be new, to please a new clientele. The importance of cushions also increased as Arab customs replaced Roman ones (Goitein 1983, 108-109). An Arabic inscription runs around the border, again showing

Arabic in use in the factory. The inscription says: "In the name of god, Benediction from God, from what has been made in the factory of Akhmīm. Year two hundred and three," i.e., 818/819, two centuries after the Conquest (Kuhnel 1960).

Two centuries later, Tenth Century Arab geographers find Akhmīm flourishing. Al-Maqdisi (985) says there are not many towns in Egypt, because a town must have a mosque: Akhmīm does. It is a prosperous place. (Kamāl 1926–51, 669–70 or. p. 201, 193–95). In 997/387 Ibn Zoulaq may be the first to praise the antiquities (Yūsuf Kamāl 1926–51, fol.26v–27v, 685r).. He also notes the continued existence of monasteries there.

Later Arab geographers continue to mention the marvels of Akhmīm. Specific descriptions begin in the Twelfth Century. By that time the city lay on a well-traveled pilgrim and trade route to the Red Sea (Kuhlmann 1983, 25, note 101).[40]

No bishops' names are known for the first decades after the Arab conquest (Timm 1984, vol. 1, 85) but then the bishopric reappears. In the Thirteenth Century Abū Salih sees Akhmīm as a center of Coptic religion. He says there are seventy churches in or near the city (Timm 1984, vol. 1, 89). He describes the White Monastery, which he calls the Monastery of Saint Sinthius, in great detail. In the neighborhood of Akhmīm he mentions the Monastery of Aṭ-Ṭair (the Birds), citing two authors who tell strange tales about the behavior of birds there (17);[41] the Monastery of the Seven Mountains (19); the Monastery of al-Karkas (20); the Monastery of Ṣabrah and the Monastery of Abû Abshâdah (22).[42]

---

[38]My translation of Kuhlmann's quote from Al-I^c lām bi-a^c lām balad Allāh (mašğid) al-ḥarām by Qutb ad-Dīn an-Nahrawālī, (a Sixteenth Century source) ed. F. Wüstenfeld, Leipzig 1857, III, 109 cited in Kuhlmann 1983, 32.

[39]In the Metropolitan Museum, Ca. no. 51.57. The full surah runs: "But if they turn back, say: Allah is sufficient for me, there is no God but Him, on Him do I rely, and He is the Lord of the mighty power." The attribution of this and other "Zacariou Silks" to Akhmīm is probable, not certain. Grube argues that they continued to be manufactured from the Third until the Tenth Century without notable change. He says they are "of extraordinarily pure graeco-roman design and it is therefore quite problematic to identify patterns that would have to be earlier, as it will be very difficult to securely date silks that show a stronger degree of abstraction of decline of quality in the design to a later period (1962, 80)." The same caution about stylistic dating must apply to other crafts as well.

---

[40]Besides Ibn Ğubayr, discussed above, Kuhlmann quotes two other Twelfth Century writers, al-Idrisi and al-Mazini; two from the Thirteenth Century, Yaqut Ar-Rumiand Al-Qazwini; three from the Fourteenth, Al-Disaq, Ibn Fadlallah, Ibn Baṭṭūṭa; and three from the Fifteenth, Abn Duqmaq, Al-Qalqasandi, al-Maqrizi.

[41]"This monastery is ancient, stands far above the Nile, and has a flight of steps to it cut in the rock. It stands opposite to Sammallût." (Two authors tell of how birds thrust their heads into a cleft there until one of them dies.) The author, upon whom may god have mercy, adds: 'this is one of the things that have long ceased to happen.' " (1895, 310-11; see Timm 1984 vol. 1, 87-88).

[42]"This monastery stands at the entry of seven valleys, and stands high between high mountains, and the sun rises upon it two hours later than generally on account of the height of the mountain, at the foot of which it stands; and when there are yet two hours before sunset the inhabitants think the sun has already set and the night has begun, and they kindle lights. Near this monastery there is a spring of water at the exit overshadowed by a willow, and this spot where the monastery of the Willow stands is called Wâdî 'l-Mulûk (Valley of the Kings), because there a plant grows called Mulúkah, like the raddish, by which water is coloured of a deep red, and it is used by chemists. Above this monastery stands

> 20. The Monastery of al-Karkas, on a mountain, and hewn in its side; and there is no approach to it, but the ascent is by incisions cut in the rock, and by them alone

In the Fourteenth Century Ibn Baṭṭūṭa says:

"Thence I journeyed to the town of Ikhmim, which is a place, solidly built and of imposing appearance. It is built of stones, and in the interior there are sculptures and writing of the ancients, which is not understood in these days, and images of the spheres and stars. They assert that it was built when the Flying Eagle was in the sign of the Scorpion. It contains also images of animals and other things, and the people tell a number of fanciful stories, over which it is not necessary to linger, on the subject of these images. There was at Ikhmim a man known as the Preacher, who ordered the destruction of one of these berbas and built a college with its stones" (Ibn Baṭṭūṭa 65, 1958, 103–4).[43]

This is the century when the administrative description was written (published by De Sacy, see above).

In the next century al-Maqrizi said that a great temple in Akhmim had just been destroyed. He recounts tales about it, and says that many magicians continue to live at Akhmim. He may mention two churches in the city.[44]

By the Sixteenth Century Leo Africanus and Qutb ad-Din an-Nahrawā (see note 31) both spoke of the city as fully destroyed.

The vigor of its Coptic traditions can be seen however in the construction between the late Sixteenth and the Nineteenth Century of numerous monasteries and churches: Most of these conform to a distinct local type first recognized by Sameh Adley, now Brother Samuel of the Syrian Monastery (McNally 1991, Samuel 1990, 69-80).

The early European travelers found intriguing remnants of the grand architecture. They describe a prosperous city, still engaged in its ancient activity of weaving, still with a strong Coptic minority, apparently accepting missionaries--first Roman Catholic and then Presbyterian--a foreign Arab sheikh, and inquisitive antiquarians with equanimity or indifference. Maspero said "...derriere ces premiers plans modernes, une vieille cité égyptienne s'entend, indolente et silencieuse" (1893–98, 214).

The coming of the railway on the opposite bank of the Nile changed the city's status. As traffic moved from the river first to rail and now to road, Suhāj grew and Akhmim stagnated. The market for its age old industry declined. Today there are said to be 500 hand weavers still left, as well as a weaving factory. In the last few years, the city has grown in size and population.[45] Massive new building around the urban core is transforming the city's appearance, bringing new prosperity, while destroying many remnants of the past.

ADDENDUM

The Abegg Stiftung has recently discovered that an early fourth century tapestry depicting an initiate into Dionysiac mysteries, and a later fourth century silk strip representing scenes from the life of the Virgin Mary had both been wrapped around the same body in a grave thought to be in the area of Akhmim. The burial probably took place early in the Fifth Century. The interpretation of the find is still proceding.

The discovery stimulated a conference on relationships between Christians and pagans in Late Antique Egypt, the papers from which have just been published. They include a summary of the textile evidence, with previous bibliography, by Dietrich Willers, discussion of Nonnos of Panopolis in the essay by Thomas Gelzer, and discussion of Shenute in the essay by van der Vliet. The references are given at the end of the Bibliography, on p. 16.

---

can it be reached. Between the Monastery of the willow spring and the Monastery of al-Ḳarḳas there is a journey of three hours, and below the Monastery of al-Ḳarḳas is a well of fresh water surrounded by Bân trees.

21. The Monastery of Ṣabrah, east of Ikhmîm, is named after an Arab tribe named the Ṣabrah, and dedicated to the angle Michael; but there is only one monk there.

[43]Gibb comments: "(Akhmîm's) ancient temple (berba) is described in all medieval works, although it was already in ruins by this time, chiefly because it was associated with Hermes the Great.... It is noteworthy that Ibn Baṭṭūṭa doesn't mention any of the other berbas in Upper Egypt, even at Luxor...."(Ibn Baṭṭūṭa. 1958). al-Idris mentions this connection, Kuhlmann 1983, 2; Timm 1984, vol. 1, 92. On connections with Hermes, see also Bernand 1977.

[44]Timm (1984, vol. 1, 89) says these must be in the city proper, and therefore cannot be monasteries as Meinardus had held.

---

[45]*Webster's New Geographical Dictionary* (1988) gives population figures based on the 1966 census as 44,800. The *New Encyclopaedia Britannica* (1990) gives an estimate as of 1986 of 70,602.

BIBLIOGRAPHY

Ābd al-Laṭīf. 1810. *Relation de l'Égypte par Abd-Allatif, medecin de Bagdad, suivie de divers extraits d'écrivains orientaux, et d'une État des provinces et des villages de l'Égypte dans le XIVe. siecle.* Translated and annotated by Antoine Isaac Silvestre de Sacy. Paris: Dreuttel and Würtz.

Abū Saliḥ, al-Armanī. 1895. *The Churches and Monasteries of Egypt and Some Neighboring Countries: attributed to Abu Salih, the Armenian.* Translated by B.T. Evetts with added notes by Alfred J. Butler. Oxford: Clarendon Press.

Allen, Susan Heuck. 1990. "Dionysiac Imagery in Coptic Textiles and Later Medieval Art," The Classics in the Midle Ages: *Papers of the Twentieth Annual Conference of the Center for Medieval and Early Renaissance Studies.* ed. Aldo s. Bernardo and Saul Levin.

Amélineau, Émile. 1893. *La géographie de l'Égypte à l'époque copte.* Paris: Imprimerie nationale.

Bernand, André. 1972. *De Koptos à Kosseir.* Leiden: E.J. Brill.

Bernand, André. 1977. *Pan du désert.* Leiden: E.J. Brill.

Besa. 1983. *The Life of Shenoute.* Introduction, translation and notes by David N. Bell. Kalamazoo: Cistercian Publications.

Bissing, Friedrich Wilhelm Freiherr von. 1946/47. "Aus römischen Gräbern zu Achmim (Panopolis) in Oberägypten." *JDAI* 61/62:1–16.

Bissing, Friedrich Wilhelm Freiherr von. 1950. "Tombeaux d'époque romaine à Akhmîm." *Annales du Service des Antiquites de l'Égypte* 50:547–76.

Borkowski, Zbigniew. 1975. *Une description topographique des immeubles à Panopolis.* Warsaw: Państwowe Wydawn.

Bouriant, Urbain. 1884. "Mission dans la Haute-Égypte (1884–1885)." In *Mémoires publiés par les membres de la Mission archéologique française au Caire* 1:367–82. Paris.

Bouriant, Urbain, 1886. "Petits Monuments" *Recueil de travaux relatifs à la philologie et à l'archéologie égyptiennes et assyriennes* 8:140–43.

Bouriant, Urbain. 1889. "Notes de voyage." *Recueil de travaux relatifs à la philologie et à l'archéologie égyptiennes et assyriennes* 11:123–49.

Bourriau, Janine and Anne Millard. 1971. "The Excavation of Sawāma in 1914 by G.A. Wainwright and T. Whittemore." JEA 57: 28–57.

Bowersock, Glen Warren. c. 1990. *Hellenism in Late Antiquity.* Ann Arbor: University of Michigan Press.

Bowman, Alan K. 1978. "The military occupation of Upper Egypt in the reign of Diocletian." *Bulletin of the American Society of Papyrologists* 15:25–38.

Bowman, Alan K. 1992. "Public Buildings in Roman Egypt." *JRA* 5: 495-503.

Browne, Gerald M. 1975. "A Panegyrist from Panopolis." *Proceedings of the Fourteenth International Congress of Papyrologists* 29–33. London: EES.

Browne, Gerald M. 1976. "Property belonging to Aurelia Senpasis and Aurelius Petearbeschinis." *Collectanea Papyrologica: Texts Published in Honor of H.C. Youtie.* ed. A.H. Hanson. 2:489–500. Bonn: R. Habelt.

Browne, Gerald M. 1977. "Harpocration Panegyrista." *Illinois Classical Studies* 2:184–96.

Büchler, Bernward. 1980. *Die Armut der Armen.* Munich: Kosel-Verlag GmbH & Co.

Budge, E.A. Wallis. 1920. *By Nile and Tigris, a narrative of journeys in Egypt and Mesopotamia on behalf of the British Museum between the Years 1886 and 1913.* London: J. Murray.

Cameron, Alan. 1965. "Wandering Poets: a Literary Movement in Byzantine Egypt." *Historia* 14: 470–509.

Cameron, Alan. 1982. "The Empress and the Poet: Paganism and Politics at the Court of Theodosius III," Later Greek Literature, Yale Classical Studies 27 (1982) 217-89.

Castiglione, László. 1966. "Hérodote II 91." *Mélanges offerts à Kazimierz Michaiłowski.* 41–49. Warsaw: Państwowe Wydawnictwo Naukowe.

Champollion le Jeune, J.F. 1909. *Lettres et Journaux de Champollion le Jeune.* Selected and edited by H. Hartleben. 2:144–50, 151 *Bibliothèque Égyptologique* 31.

Chitty, Derwas J. 1957. "A Note on the Chronology of the Pachomian Foundations." *Studia Patristica* 2:379–85. Berlin: Akademie Verlag.

Chuvin, P. 1986. "Nonnos de Panopolis entre paganisme et christianisme," *Bull. de l'Assoc Bude* 45: 387-96.

Collart, Paul. 1930a. *Les papyrus grecs d'Achmîm à la Bibliothèque Nationale de Paris.* Cairo: IFAO.

Collart Paul. 1930b. *Nonnos de Panopolis: Études sur la composition et le texte des dionysiaques.* Cairo: IFAO.

Coquin, René-Georges. 1979. "Un complément aux *vie Sahidiques de Pachôme*: le manuscript IFAO, copte 3." *BIFAO* 79:209–47.

De Meulenaere, Herman. 1988. "Prophètes et danseurs panopolitains à la Basse Époque." *BIFAO* 88:41-50.

Gascou, Jean. 1989. "Les codices documentaires égyptiens." *Les Debuts du Codex.* ed. Alain Blanchard. Turnhout, Brepols.

Fischer, Henry George. 1964. *Inscriptions from the Coptite Nome, Dynasties VI to XI. Analecta Orientalia* 40. Rome: Pontificum Institutum Biblicum.

Forrer, Robert. 1891a. *Die Gräber und Textilfunde von Achmim-Panopolis.* Strassburg i/E: E. Birkhäuser.

Forrer, Robert. 1891b. *Römische und byzantinische Seiden-Textilien aus dem Gräberfelde von Achmim-Panopolis.* Strassburg i/E.: E. Birkäuser.

Forrer, Robert. 1893. *Die frühchristlichen Alterthümer aus dem Gräberfelde von Achmim-Panopolis (nebst analogen unedirten Funden aus Köln, etc.).* Strassburg i/E.: Lohbauer.

Forrer, Robert. 1895. *Mein Besuch in el-Achmim. Reisebriefe aus Aegypten.* Strassburg i/E.: F. Schlesier.

Forrer, Robert. 1901. *Über Steinzeit-Hockergräber zu Achmim, Naqada etc. In Ober-Ägypten und über europäische Parallelfunde. Achmin Studien* 1. Strassburg: K.J. Trubner.

Fowden, Garth. 1986. *The Egyptian Hermes: a historical approach to the late pagan mind.* Cambridge, New York: Cambridge University Press.

Frauberger, Heinrich. 1895. *Antik und frühmittelalterlichen Fussbekleidungen aus Achmim-Panopolis.* Dusseldorf: S. Geibel & Co. in Altenburg.

Gaballa, G.A. 1981. "Harnakht, Chief Builder of Min." *Annales du Service des Antiquites de l'Égypte* 64:7–14.

Gauthier, M. Henri. 1905. "Notes géographiques sur le nome Panopolite." *BIFAO* 4:39–101.

Gauthier, M. Henri. 1912. "Nouvelles notes géographiques sur le nome Panopolite." *BIFAO* 10:89–130.

Gauthier, M. Henri. 1914. "Index aux notes géographiques sur le nome Panopolite." *BIFAO* 11:49–63.

Goitein, Solomon D. 1983. *A Mediterranean society: the Jewish Communities of the Arab World as Portrayed in the documents of the Cairo Geniza.* IV Berkeley: University of Californai Press. 47-82.

Gregory, Timothy E. 1975. "The Remarkable Christmas Homily of Kyros Panopolites." *GRBS* 16: 317-24.

Grohmann, Adolf. 1938. *Arabic Papyri in the Egyptian Library.* III. Cairo, Egyptian Library Press.

Grohmann, Adolf. 1959. *Studien zur historischen Geographie und Verwaltung des frühmittelalterlichen Ägypten.* Vienna: R. M. Rohrer.

Grube, Ernst. J. 1962. "Studies in the Survival and Continuity of Pre-Muslim Traditions in Egyptian Islamic Art.." *Journal of the American Research Center in Egypt.* 1: 75-97.

Hagedorn, Dieter 1970. "Papyri aus Panopolis in der Kölner Sammlung." In *Proceedings of the Twelfth International Congress of Papyrologists.* Toronto: A.M. Hackert.

Hahn, Johannes. 1991. "Hoher Besuch im Weissen Kloster: Flavianus, Praeses Thebaidis, bei Schenute von Atripe." *ZPE* 87:248-252.

Ibn Baṭṭūṭa. 1958. *The Travels of Ibn Baṭṭūṭa, AD 1325–54.* Translated and annotated by H.A.R. Gibb from the text edited by D. Defremery and B.R. Sanguinetti, 64–65. Cambridge, England: Hakluyt Society, Cambridge University Press.

John of Nikiou. 1883. *Chronique de Jean, Évêque de Nikiou.* Translated by H. Zotenberg. Paris: Imprimerie nationale.

John of Nikiou. 1971. "Die Arabische Eroberung Aegyptens nach Johannes von Nikiu." Franz Altheim and Ruth Stiehl, *Christentum am Roten Meer.* Berlin, New York: Walter de Gruyter. 1: 356-89.

Jullien, (P.) Michel. 1901. "A la recherches de Tabenne et des autres monasteres fondes par Saint Pachom." *Études des Pères jésuites.* 89:238–58.

Kamāl, Yūsuf, Prince, ed. 1926–51. *Monumenta cartographica Africae et Aegypti.* Cairo.

Kanawati, Naguib. 1980–89. *The Rock Tombs of El-Hawawish: the Cemetery of Akhmīm. The Cemetery of Akhmīm, 1.* Sydney: Macquarie Ancient History Association. 1–9.

Kanawati, Naguib, and Reece Scannell. 1988. *A Mountain Speaks: The First Australian Excavation in Egypt.* Sydney: Maquarie University.

Kees, Hermann von. 1914. "Das Felsheiligtum des Min bei Achmim." *Recueil de travaux relatifs à la* philologie et à l'archéologie égyptiennes et assyriennes. Fascicules 1–2:51–56.

Kees, Hermann von. 1949. "Panopolis, Panopolites." PW 18,3:649–53.

Kuhlmann, Klaus P. 1979. "Der Felstempel des Eje bei Achmim." MDIK 35:165–88.

Kuhlmann, Klaus P. 1981. "Ptolemais—Queen of Nectanebo I." MDIK 37: 267–79.

Kuhlmann, Klaus P. 1982. "Archäologische Forschungen im Raum von Achmim." MDIK 38:347–54.

Kuhlmann, Klaus P. 1983. Materialien zur Archäologie und Geschichte des Raumes von Achmim. Mainz: Philipp von Zabern.

Kuhnel, Ernst. 1960. "The Rug Tiraz of Akhmīm." The Textile Museum Workshop Notes. Paper no. 22.

Lacau, Pierre. 1904–6. Sarcophages antérieurs au nouvel Empire. 2d. Cairo: IFAO.

Lacau, Pierre. 1911. "Textes coptes en dialecte akhminique et sahidique." BIFAO 8:43–109.

Lefort, L. Theophile. 1939. "Les premiers monastères Pachómiens: exploration topographique." Le Muséon 52:379–407.

L'Hôte, Nestor. 1840. Lettres écrites d'Égypte en 1838 et 1839. Avec des remarquies de M. Letronne. Paris: Didot fréres.

Lenzen, Victor F. 1960. The Triumph of Dionysos on Textiles of Late Antique Egypt. Berkeley/Los Angeles: University of California Press.

Leo Africanus. 1896–98. Description de L'Afrique, Tierce partie du monde escrite par Jean Leon African, premièrement en langue arabesque.... ed. Charles Schefer. Recueil de voyages et de documents pour servir à l'histoire de la géographie 15. Paris: E. Leroux.

Lepsius, Richard. 1849. Denkmäler aus Ägypten und Ethiopien. I Berlin:Nicolaische Buchhandlung.

Lepsius, Richard. 1852. Letters from Egypt, Ethiopia, and a Penninsula of Sinai. London: H.G. Bohn.

Lesquier, Jean. 1918. L'armée romaine d'Égypte d'August à Dioclétien. Mémoires publiés par les membres de l'Institut Français d'Archéologie Orientale du Caire 41. Cairo: IFAO.

Letronne, Jean Antoine. 1842. Recueil des Inscriptions grecques et latines de l'Égypte 1:103–10. Paris: Imprimerie royal.

Lloyd, A.B. 1969. "Perseus and Chemmis (Herodotus II 91)." JHS 89: 79–86.

Livrea, Enrico. 1989. Parafrasi del Vangelo di S. Giovanni. Naples: M.D'Auria.

Maccoul, Leslie S.B. 1985. "Three Cultures under Arab Rule: the Fate of Coptic." Bulletin de la Société d'Archéologie Copte 27: 61–70.

Mahmoud ali Mohammed and Peter Grossman. 1991. "On the Recently Excavated Monastic buildings in Dayr Anba Shinuda: Archaeological Report." Bulletin de la Société d'Archéologie Copte. 30: 53–63.

al-Maqrizi, Ahmed Ibn 'Ali. 1901. Description topographique et historique de l'Égypte. Translated by U. Bouriant. Mémoires publiés par les membres de la mission archéologique française au Caire 80. Paris: E. Leroux.

Martin, Maurice. 1972. "Notes inédites du P. Jullien sur trois monastères chrétiens d'Égypte: Dêr Abou Fâna. Le couvent des 'sept-montagnes.' 'Dêr Amba Bisâda.'" BIFAO 71:119–28.

Martin, Victor. 1962. "Releve topographique des immeubles d'une metropole." Recherches de Papyrologie 2:37–73.

Maspero, Gaston Camille Charles. 1892. "Fragments de manuscrits Coptes-Thébains." Mémories publiés par les membres de la mission archéologique française 16.

Maspero, Gaston Camille Charles. 1893. Études de mythologie et d'archéologie égyptienne. Bibliothèque égyptologique 1. Paris: E. Leroux.

McGing, Brian C. 1990. "Lease of a Linen-weaving Workshop at Panopolis." ZPE 82: 115–121.

McNally, Sheila. 1991. "Churches of Akhmīm," "Dayr al-Adhra," "Dayr Anba Pachom," "Dayr Anba Bisada," "Dayr Mari Jirjis," "Dayr Mar Tumas," "Dayr al-Shuhada." Coptic Encyclopedia. 1: 79–80; 3: 713–14; 3: 730–31; 3: 733; 3: 832–33; 3: 835–36; 3: 865–66.

Meinardus, Otto F.A. 1965. Christian Egypt Ancient and Modern. Cairo: Cahiers d'Histoîre Égyptienne.

Morenz, S. 1963. "Lautiliches und Sachliches in der Gleichung Min-Perseus." Revue d'Egyptologie 15:125–27.

Munier, H. 1940. "Les monuments coptes d'après les explorations du Père Michel Jullien." Bulletin de la Société d'Archéologie Copte 6:141–68.

Nestorius. 1905. Nestoriana: die Fragmente des Nestorius, gesammelt, untersucht und herausgegeben von Friederich Loofs. Halle: Niemeyer.

Orlandi, Tito. 1972. "Un project milanais concernant les manuscripts coptes du Monastère Blanc." Le Museon 85:403–13.

Orlandi, Tito 1986. "Coptic Literature." *The Roots of Egyptian Christianty*. ed. Birger Albert Pearson and James E. Goehring.42-50..

Palladius. 1965. *Palladius: The Lausiac History [Historia Lausiaca]*. Translated by Robert T. Meyer. Westminster, Md.: Newman Press.

Petrie, W.M. Flinders. 1932. *Seventy Years in Archaeology*. New York: Henry Holt and Company.

Pococke, Richard. 1743. *A Description of the East, and Some Other Countries*, 76–81. London, Printed for the author.

Porter, Bertha and Rosalind L. B. Moss. 1937. *Topographical Bibliography of Ancient Egyptian Hieroglyphic Texts, Reliefs, and Paintings*, vol. 3. Oxford: Clarendon Press.

Rémondon, Roger. 1952. "L'Égypte et la suprême résistance au christianisme (Ve–VIIe siècles)." *BIFAO* 51:63–78.

Roberts, Colin Henderson. 1979. *Manuscript, Society and Belief in Early Christian Egypt*. London: Oxford University Press.

Robinson, James M. 1986. "The discovery and Marketing of Coptic Manuscripts: the Nag Hammadi Codices and the Bodmer Papyri." *The Roots of Egyptian Christianty*. ed. Birger Albert Pearson and James E. Goehring.2-25.

Rostovtzev, Mikhail Ivanovich. 1914. *Antique Decorative Art in South Russia* (in Russian). St. Petersburg: Imperial Archaeological Commission.

Rostovtzev, Mikhail Ivanovich. 1919. "Ancient Decorative Wall-Paintings." *JHS* 39:144–63.

Rousseau, Philip. 1985. *Pachomius: The Making of a Community in Fourth-Century Egypt*. Berkeley-Los Angeles-London: University of California Press.

Rubensohn, O. 1906. "Archaeologische Funde im Jahre 1905: Aegypten." *AA* 1906:129–30.

Saint-Genis, M. 1821. "Notice sur les restes de l'ancienne ville de Chemmis ou Panopolis, aujourd'hui Akhmym, et sur les environs." *Description de l'Égypte; ou, Recueil des observations et des recherches qui ont été faites en Égypte pendant l'expédition de l'armée française*. 2d ed. 4: 43–65. Paris: C.L.F. Panckoucke.

Ṣalāḥ Ṣabr al-Maṣri, Yaḥyā. 1983. "Preliminary Report on the Excavations at Akhmīm of the Egyptian Antiquities-Organization." *Annales du Service des Antiquites de l'Égypte* 69:7–13.

Samuel al Syriany. 1990. *Guide to Ancient Coptic Churches and Monasteries in Upper Egypt*. [Egypt]: Institute of Coptic Studies.

Sauneron, Serge. 1952. "Le temple d'Akhmîm décrit par Ibn Jobair." *BIFAO* 51: 123–35.

Sauneron, Serge. 1962. "Persée Dieu de Khemmis (Herodote II, 91)." *Revue d'Égyptologie* 14:53–57.

Sauneron, Serge. 1983. *Villes et légendes d'Egypt*. 2d ed. Cairo: IFAO.

Schiaparelli, Ernesto. 1885. "Chemmis (Akhmīm) e la sua antica necropoli." *Études archéologiques, linguistiques et historiques dédiés a Mr. le Dr. C. Leemans*, 85–88. Leiden: E.J. Brill.

Sethe, Kurt. 1899. "Chemmis." *PW* 3, 2:2233–34.

Sherry, Lee Francis. 1991. "The hexameter "Paraphrase of St. John" attrributed to Nonnos of Panopolis: Prolegomenon and Translation." Ph.D. diss, Columbia University.

Skeat, T.C., ed. 1964. *Papyri from Panopolis in the Chester Beatty Library, Dublin*. Chester Beatty Monographs 10. Dublin: Hodges Figgis & Co. Ltd.

Sonnini de Manoncourt, Charles Nicolas Sigisbert. 1800. *Travels in Upper and Lower Egypt, Undertaken by Order of the Old Government of France*. London: J. Debrett.

Stegemann, Viktor. 1930. *Astrologie und Universalgeschichte: Studien und Interpretationen zu den Dionysiaka des Nonnos von Panopolis*. Leipzig/Berlin: B.G. Teubner.

Stephanus of Byzantium. 1958. *Ethnika*. Graz: Academic Press.

Timbie, Janet. 1986. "The State of Research on the Career of Shenoute of Atripe." *The Roots of Egyptian Christianty*. ed. Birger Albert Pearson and James E. Goehring. Philadelphia: fortress Press. 258-70.

Timm, Stefan. 1979. *Christliche Stätten in Ägypten*. Weisbaden: Reichert Verlag.

Timm, Stefan. 1984. *Das christlich-koptische Ägypten in arabischer Zeit: Eine Sammlung christlicher Stätten in Ägypten in arabischer Zeit*. Part 1, 3 vols. Wiesbaden: Reichart.

Turner, Eric Gardner. 1980. *Greek Papyri: An Introduction*. 2d ed. Oxford: Clarendon Press.

van Haelst, J. 1970. "Les sources papyrologiques concernant l'église in Égypte à l'époque de Constantin." In *Proceedings of the Twelfth International Congress of Papyrologists*, 497–503. Toronto: A.M. Hackert.

Vian, Francis. 1988. "Les cultes paiernes dans les Dionysiaques de Nonnos: Étude de vocabulaire." revue des Études anciennes. 90: 399-410.

Vielleux, Armand. 1968. *La Liturgie dans le cenobitisme pachômien au quatrième siècle.* Rome: Herder.

Wagner, Guy. 1982. "Dieux prières chrétiennes du Wadi Bir el-Aïn." *BIFAO* 82:349-54.

Welles, C. Bradford. 1946. "The garden of Ptolemagrius at Panopolis." *Transactions of the American Philological Association* 77:192-206.

Whittemore, Thomas. 1914. "The Sawâma Cemeteries." *JEA* 1:246-47.

Wilbour, Charles Edwin. 1936. *Travels in Egypt (December 1880 to May 1891).* ed. Jean Capart. Brooklyn: Brooklyn Museum.

Willis, William H. 1978. "Two Literary Papyri in an Archive from Panopolis." *Illinois Classical Studies* 3:140-51.

Willis, William H. 1979. "The Letter of Ammon of Panopolis to his Mother." *Actes du xve congrès international de papyrologie* 2:98-113.

Brussels: Fondations egyptologiques Reine Elisabeth.

Wipszycka, Ewa. 1965. *L'industrie textile dans l'Égypte romaine.* Warsaw: Zakład Narodowy Imienia Ossolińskich Wydawnictwoskiej Akademii Nauk.

Wipszycka, Ewa. 1971. Review of Itskhok Fisclevitch Fikhman, *Egipet na rubeje dvukh epokh. Journal of Juristic Papyrology* 11-12: 217-236.

Wipszycka, Ewa. 1986. "Les aspects economiques de la vie de la communaute des Kellia." *Le Site Monastique Copte des Kellia: Sources historiques et esploration archéologiques.* Geneva: 117-140.

Wipszycka, Ewa. 1988. "La christianisation de l'Égypte aux IVe-Vie siecles, aspects sociaux et ethniques." *Aegyptus* 58: 117-166.

Youtie, L.C., D. Hagedorn, H.C. Youtie. 1971a. "Urkunden aus Panopolis." *ZPE* 7:1-40.

Youtie, L.C., D. Hagedorn, H.C. Youtie. 1971b. "Urkunden aus Panopolis." *ZPE* 8:207-34.

Youtie, L.C., D. Hagedorn, H.C. Youtie. 1973. "Urkunden aus Panopolis." *ZPE* 10:101-70.

ADDENDA

Gelzer, Thomas. 1993. "Heidnisches und Christliches im Platonismus der Kaiserzeit und der Spätantike." *Begegnung von Heidentum und Christentum im spätantiken Ägypten. Riggisberger Berichte 1.* Riggisberg: Abegg Stiftung. 33-48.

van der Vliet, Jacques. 1993. "Spätantikes Heidentum in Ägypten im Spiegel der koptischen Literatur." *Begegnung von Heidentum und Christentum im spätantiken Ägypten. Riggisberger Berichte 1.* Riggisberg: Abegg Stiftung. 99-130.

Willers, Dietrich. 1993. "Zur Begegnung von Heidentum und Christentum im spätantiken Ägypten." *Begegnung von Heidentum und Christentum im spätantiken Ägypten. Riggisberger Berichte 1.* Riggisberg: Abegg Stiftung. 11-19.

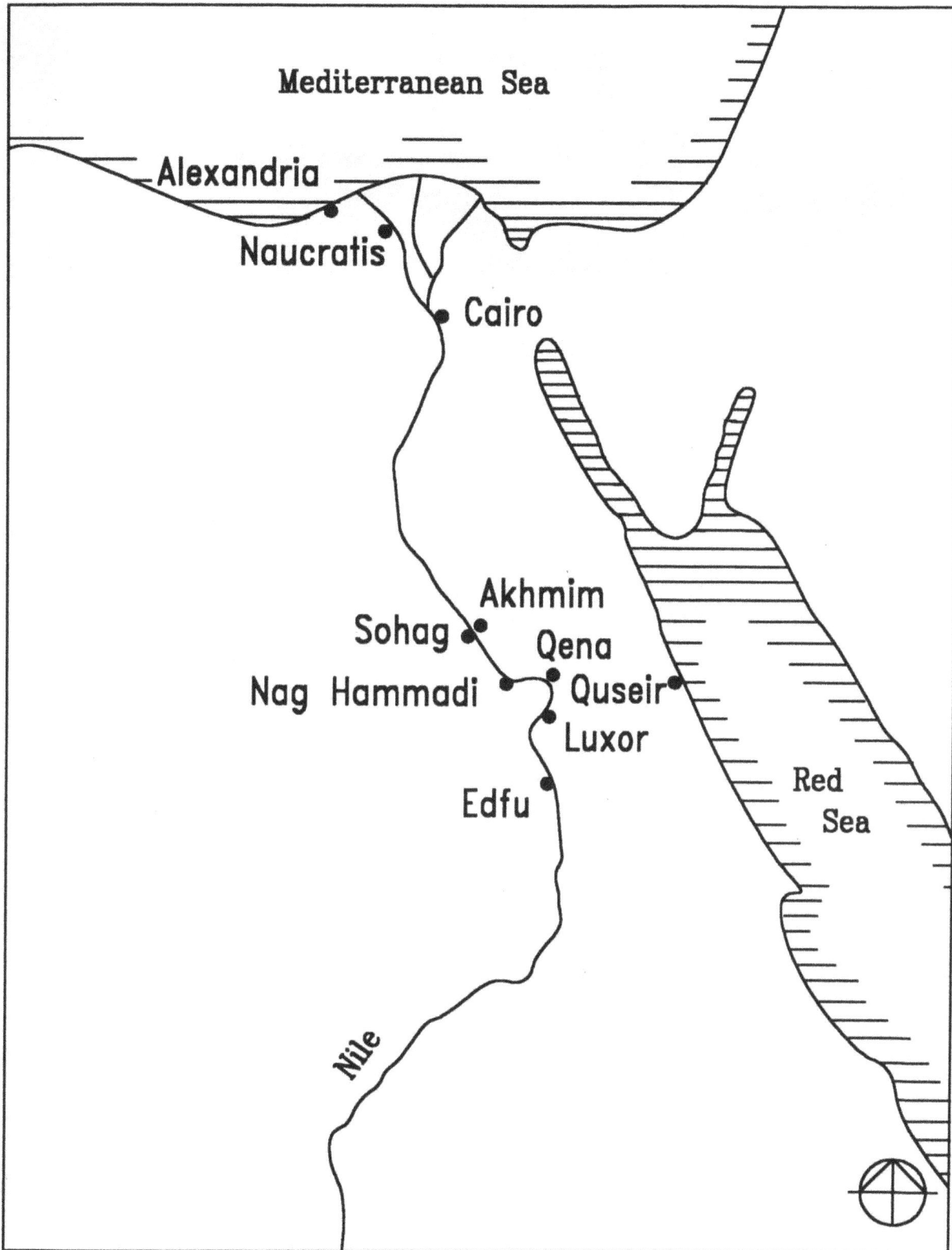

MAP 1: EGYPT, SHOWING POSITION OF AKHMIM

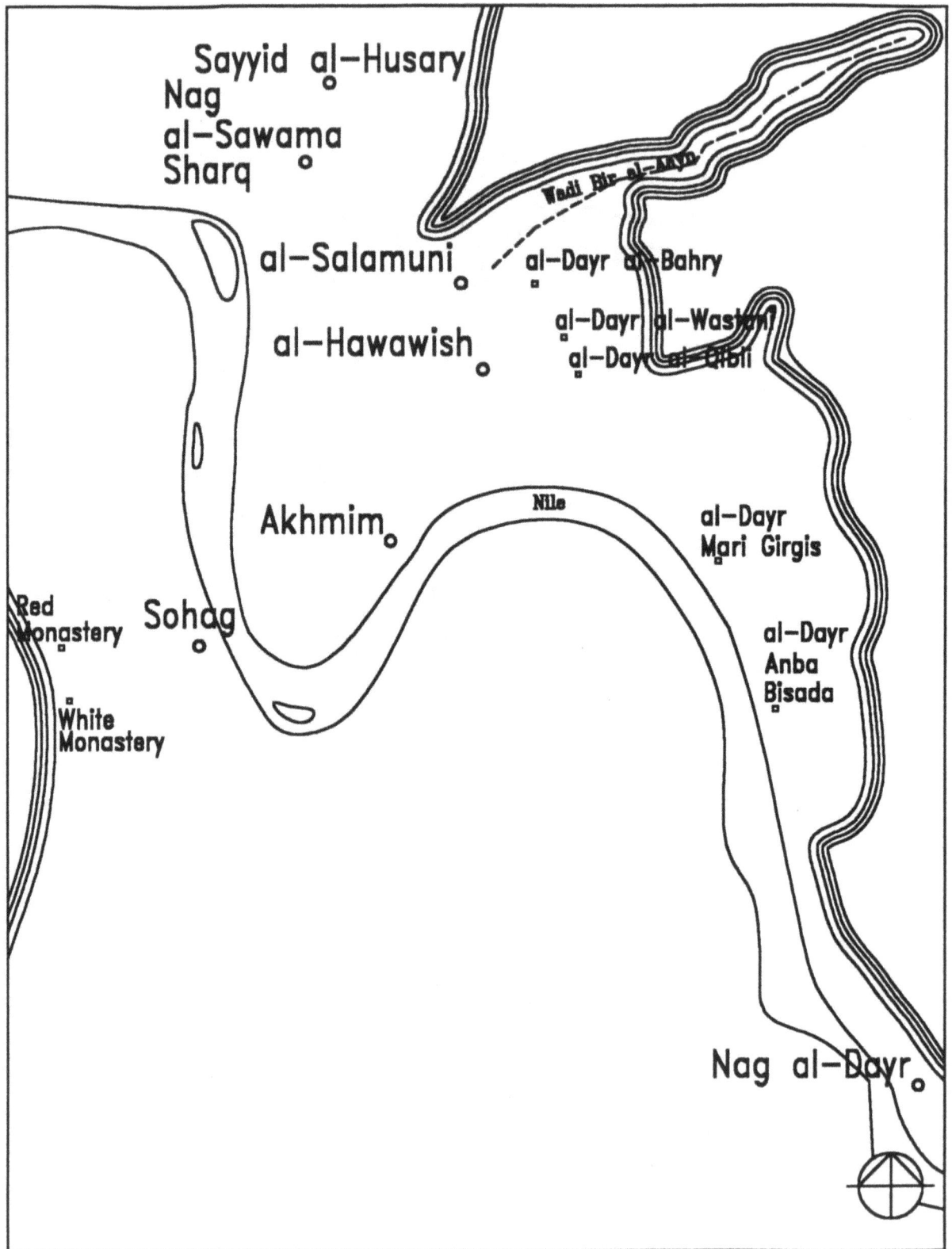

Sayyid al-Husary

Nag
al-Sawama
Sharq

al-Salamuni

Wadi Bir al-'Ayn

al-Dayr al-Bahry

al-Dayr al-Wastani
al-Dayr al-Qibli

al-Hawawish

Akhmim

Nile

al-Dayr
Mari Girgis

Red
Monastery

Sohag

White
Monastery

al-Dayr
Anba
Bisada

Nag al-Dayr

MAP 2: CITY OF AKHMIM AND ITS SURROUNDINGS

MAP 3: CITY OF AKHMIM WITH SITES PROPOSED FOR EXCAVATION
(see p. 21)

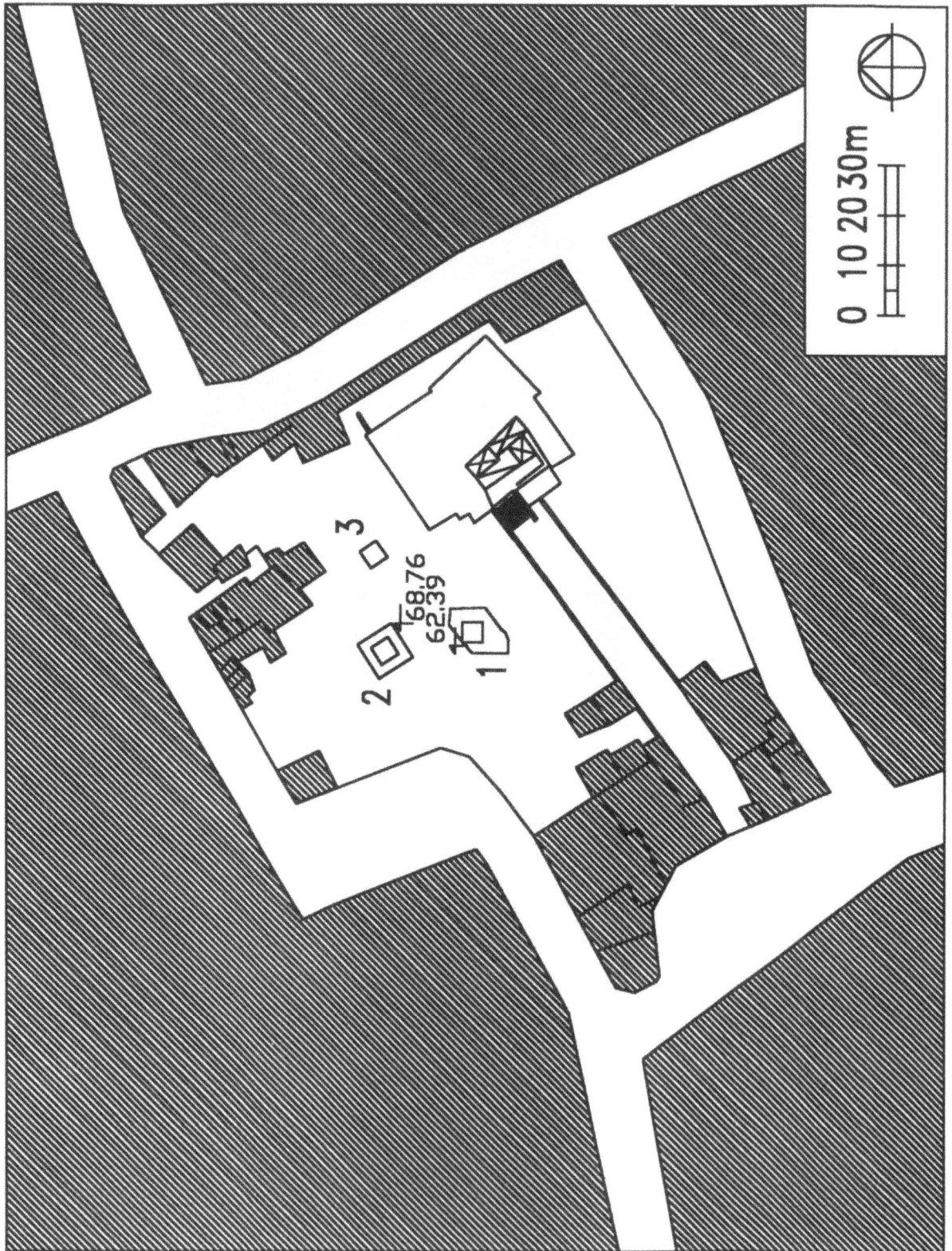

MAP 4: SECTOR ONE
The Churchyard of Abū Sayfayn, showing position of Squares One, Two and Three
(see pp. 21-22)

Chapter 2

HISTORY OF THE PROJECT

Project design

The University of Minnesota's study of urban development at Akhmīm has involved three sessions of work at the site and a series of research projects at the University, during which theses and articles were produced.

The site was chosen for two reasons: its importance in the late Roman period, and its continued existence to the present day. The original impetus for this project was a desire to study the transition from Roman to post-Roman culture in Egypt, to see what the archaeological record could tell us about the about processes of arabization and Islamization, about the relationship between continuity and change. We did not, however, intend to concentrate on one period, but rather to trace long term development. We wanted to establish comparable data from a succession of periods, so that we could assess relative degrees of change. Many excavations concentrate, for good reason, on sites that have had short lives. Much archaeological study of city life therefore looks at what are, in some sense, failed cities. We were intrigued by the possibilities of studying a successful one, a survivor.

Limited funding curtailed the work that we were able to carry out, so that we cannot draw any conclusions about the life of the city as a whole. We may be looking at the activities of only one or two families. The sequences of finds, particularly of pottery and glass, nonetheless provide compelling evidence for both continuity and change.

Much work on finds remains to be done, but it is clear that more work on site will be necessary to clarify relationships between excavated areas. We do not intend to revive any semblance of the original project plan, because many areas are no longer available for study. Considering the rapid growth that is covering so many sites, we consider ourselves fortunate to have had, and to retain access to one undisturbed area.

Work in Egypt

Since Akhmīm is still a crowded and busy city, we were fortunate to find open spaces where excavation was possible. We hoped that some, at least, of these spaces would produce a sequence of strata from the present to the Late Roman period.

The project obtained permission to excavate in five open spaces (1–5 on Map 3, p. 19). Two of these lie inside the town, and three on its northern edges: the churchyard of Abū Sayfayn (1), the market place (2), the churchyard of Sitt Dimiyāna (3), an open area on the north edge of the tell (4), and the area of temple foundations in the sports place outside the town (5). The project also had permission to collect surface finds from the surrounding area where there are monasteries and ancient tombs (see above pp. 2, 6, 9 and Map 2).

Limited funding and other practical considerations caused us to concentrate on the first of these spaces, in which a continuous sequence of strate did indeed exist, although they have not been completely uncovered and related to each other.

1978

Work began during an eight week period in the fall of 1978. The full-time excavation staff consisted of Sheila McNally, University of Minnesota; Jerome Schaeffer, graduate student, University of Arizona; and Michael Buerger, graduate student, University of Michigan. They were assisted by Sameh Adley, an architect for the Coptic Patriarchate, and Ralph Mitchell, graduate student, American University in Cairo. Six local students helped with the recording, and other individuals from Akhmīm and Suhāj gave assistance in draughting, surveying, and other activities. The workmen, recruited from Akhmīm, quickly became an enthusiastic and capable team under the expert supervision of Rais Anwar from Quft.

The main focus of excavation was an open area near the church of Abū Sayfayn called Sector I (see Map 4, p. 20). Adjacent to the church is an irregular walled space of approximately 3300 square meters. The Coptic community had used this space as a cemetery for the churchgoers until about the middle of the Nineteenth Century. In 1952 the Bishop of Akhmīm decided to build a house on the open space. He had a garden laid out, and a foundation hole for the house dug to a depth of about 6.50 meters below the surface. People who had been involved in the project informed us that the work was abandoned because a solid foundation could not be built. They said that the water level lay just below the bottom of the hole. At the beginning of the University of Minnesota's work, coffins still projected from the slope of the hole and large fragments of concrete remained at the bottom.

Accordingly, work began at two different levels, in the belief that work at the lower level would be short-lived.

Each unit was originally staked out as a small four-by-four meter square, since the intent was to collect an intensive sample by total recovery from small areas. Although each was eventually expanded, for different reasons, the original four-by-four meter square continued to serve as "Statistical Zones" within which all earth removed, except for the mixed top strata, was sifted, and all artifacts, bones, and seeds large enough to remain in the 5 millimeter mesh were saved. Soil samples were collected for later analysis, since flotation could not be carried out at the site.

Square One was laid out in the bottom of the excavation, 62.39 m above sea level at one corner. Square Two was laid out on the upper level, the ground level before the Bishop's building efforts. It was 68.76 m above sea level at one corner.

All earth except mixed top strata was sifted. All pottery and other artifacts as well as bones and seeds large enough to remain above the mesh were kept. Flotation could not be carried out on the site. Soil samples were brought to the United States and were treated in the Minnesota State Archaeology Laboratory through the courtesy of the State Archaeologist, Christy Caine.

For pottery processing, Jerome Schaeffer devised a simple typology (see below, p. 70). He defined the types by broad characteristics that relate to technology and function and can be compared across periods. The pottery from each basket within a locus was sorted according to this system, and the sherds of each type were weighed. The pottery was then divided into a group to be registered and a group to be discarded. The registered pottery from 1978 amounts to approximately 10,000 pieces. The fine wares, together with fragments of glass and some other finds, were taken to Cairo for division. One complete glazed bowl was retained by the Islamic Museum in Cairo. The museum also retained the coins recovered from Square One, while those recovered from Square Two were brought to the United States. They were cleaned at the American Numismatic Society by Michael Bates.

Excavation in the upper square disclosed a number of graves, and under them a series of trash deposits. Small extensions were made at the upper levels for stability rather than examination of any specific feature. The excavation reached a level four and a half meters below the surface (c. 64.26 m ASL), still almost two meters above the top of the lower square, Square One (top 62.39 m ASL).

Since townspeople said that the recent builders had reached sterile soil and ground water, the work at the bottom of the building hole, i.e., in Square One, began with the expectation of quickly establishing the lower limits for possible excavation. The excavators found, however, that below a thin layer of disturbance lay strata of the Early Medieval period, showing that virgin soil must be far below. The water table, determined by the well, is at 56.42 m above sea level. By the end of 1978, an architectural discovery led to a one-meter extension of the original square, and to the making of a shallow probe in the adjacent area.

During this year one small probe was made in the market place, Sector II (2 on Map 3). Cleaning around the temple foundations, Sector V (5 on Map 3), also began. The Antiquities Service stopped the cleaning operation because of uncertainty about the date of the foundations.

1981

The second season spanned a nine week period in the winter of 1981. Project director Sheila McNally was assisted by field supervisors Jeremy Schaeffer and Peter Donaldson; ceramicist and chief registrar Ivančica Schrunk; assistant registrar Margarethe de Neergard; textile expert Cherilyn Nelson; draughtsman George Parker; and John Humm, who was in charge of floral collection. George Parker and Peter Donaldson were also responsible for the site photography. Sameh Adley again assisted with research and draughting. Six high school students from Suhāj and Akhmīm helped process artifacts.

Excavation in 1981 again focussed on Sector I. In addition, probes were carried out in Sectors II and III.

A large part of the area envisaged as Sector IV was now under excavation by the Egyptian Antiquities Service. Between 1978 and 1981 the North area of the town had been excavated mechanically to allow an apartment house to be built there. The excavation uncovered a Rammesid temple, and was taken over by the Antiquities Service (see above p. 3). The mechanical excavation also had cut through substantial remains of apparently Late Roman buildings. An observer when they were first revealed suggested that they might include remains of a weaving establishment. By the time that the Minnesota project began work in 1981, only a small amount of construction above the Pharaonic levels remained. Those remains were subsequently removed to permit further exploration of the temple area.

In Sector III, the area adjacent to Sitt Dimiyāna, Sameh Adley undertook a probe to determine whether undisturbed strata were present in an open area where a school had been razed. He discovered undisturbed deposits, but funding did not allow further work in this area.

Jerome Schaeffer directed the excavation of two squares opened in the marketplace, Sector II. This is a large open area on the Northwest of the town where a periodic market occurs on Wednesdays, and where townspeople bring animals to graze on other days. The probe showed that the surface had been artificially created in recent times. The top layers yielded mixed Islamic material. A massive reshaping of this area had occurred, roughly dated by a 1938 coin of King Farouk.

Underneath these recent layers were pre-Roman strata. The pottery has not yet been studied in any detail, so the latest date cannot be determined. Pharaonic pottery was recovered, as well as one sherd of a Late Helladic III B kylix (field reading later confirmed by Elizabeth Fisher). Attempts to study the wall at the edge of the marketplace had to be abandoned for fear of undermining the house built above it.

Excavation at Abū Sayfayn in 1981 was directed by Peter Donaldson with the assistance of Cherilyn Nelson. In the area of Square One the horizontal extent of the excavation was almost tripled and then explored to a depth between two and two and a half meters. A new grid, used on all drawings published here, was established. The major walls discovered during 1978 proved to form part of a three to four room structure provisionally termed a house: a second similar structure had been built up against this one. A series of phases became apparent, although not all could be fully investigated.

On the upper surface level a third square, Square Three, was opened, but almost immediately closed because of local objection. Work began with the advise and consent of the Bishop and a group of church members, but it became clear that many people believed this square lay in an area where the bodies of their relatives had been re-interred when the building excavation was made. This was not the case, since the ground above the graves was undisturbed, and the fill around them contained the same Ottoman and late Mamluke materials found around the other graves, but the project decided to stop work, and instead subsequently enlarged the existing upper square, Square Two, which met with no disapproval.

Excavation in Square Two proceeded to a depth of two and a half meters, at which point the sides became dangerous, so the upper levels were cleared back first in a small area, then in a meter strip at each side, resulting in an eight by eight meter square. Excavation in the new areas could only be carried down through the area of the graves during this season.

Below the grave level in the original four meter area we continued to find trash deposits. In the lower levels architectural debris was found, but no structures. At the bottom of the excavation a row of amphorae was uncovered. The excavation ended at 62.30 m ASL, about the level of the beginning of Square One. Comparing the finds from the two squares raises some problems that can only be solved by exploring the connection betweent hem.

During this year, because of the massive quantity of finds, sifting was carried on only in the limits of the original squares, the so-called "Statistical Zones," and a few other significant loci. Pottery from the Statistical Zones was both weighed and counted. Those loci produced 3,530 kilos of pottery (147,094 sherds) to be typed, weighed, and counted; 485 kilos (14,645 sherds) were catalogued. Several thousand more sherds from unsifted levels were also catalogued. This task was carried out by Ivančica Schrunk with the assistance of Jerome Schaeffer. Six high school students from Suhāj and Akhmīm helped efficiently with the processing. Margarethe de Neergard processed over two thousand small finds. John Humm collected soil samples and floral material to be brought to the University of Minnesota.

Sameh Adley carried out a survey of ten churches in and around Akhmīm, assisted by George Parker. Cherilyn Nelson collected textiles from the ransacked cemetery near the monastery of Dayr al-Shuhadā (also known as Dayr al-Wastanī) and from the area of the rock cut tombs at al-Salamunī (Map 2).

1982

The final field work of the project was a two month period in the winter of 1982, when Sheila McNally and Peter Donaldson completed several projects.

In the main sector of excavation, Abū Sayfayn, in addition to cleaning and recording profiles and features, an attempt was made to connect the two areas of excavation, but that could not be accomplished with the resources available.

A further probe was undertaken in the market place (Sector II). It once again encountered deep layers of recent fill, and under them reached an area of mud brick construction, probably late Pharaonic in date. Since wide exploration of the architecture was not feasible in the much-used area, the investigation was closed. Photographic and graphic recording of the local

monasteries was completed, and comparative material from the local mosques was completed.

Work in the United States

Between 1978 and 1981 work began on a computerized system for recording. The then director of the University of Minnesota Computer Center, Peter Patton, was consultant to the project. Debra Katz supervised the original phases, and Vicky Walsh and Tom Rindflesch continued to work on the project. By 1984 the design of the data base was essentially complete and was described in an article by McNally and Walsh for the *Journal of Field Archaeology.*

As part of the Academic Computing Humanities Consulting Group, Tom Rindflesch assisted the project from 1980 until 1990, when the University terminated this service. Rindflesch created and implemented the preliminary design for converting the data base from the hierarchical data base System 2000 on the University's Cyber mainframe to the relational data base RBase on a Zenith microcomputer. John Arndt, the research assistant who has worked with this project for several years, completed the design and the conversion. Control Data Corporation gave some technical assistance.

Undergraduate and graduate research assistants who played a major part in cataloguing and in checking the data base included Timothy Ecklov, Ruth Tate, George Atkins, and Fanny Georgiouargyropoulou, Mary Russell, and Sarah Blick.

Ruth Tate did preliminary studies of the glass. Ivančica Schrunk has worked on the Red-slipped wares and on the painted and glazed Aswan wares, giving papers at the Meetings of the American Research Center in Egypt (1980, 1988), and the Archaeological Institute of America (1981, 1987). In the spring of 1989, Mieczyslav Rodziewicz began work on a catalogue of the Late Roman Red Ware. It is hoped that he can return to Minnesota to finish this work in the near future.

Cherilyn Nelson wrote a doctoral dissertation entitled "A Methodology for Examining Ancient Textiles and its Application to VI–XIX Century Textiles from Akhmīm, Egypt" at the University of Minnesota under the direction of Robert Johnson. She has published several papers on her research and continues to work on the textiles at Rutgers University.

From 1990 to 1992 a number of graduate and undergraduate research assistants at the University of Minnesota have joined in work for this publication. Barbara Short prepared pottery charts for publication. Pieter Brouke, Michael C. Nelson and Scott Karakas produced drawings. Margarethe Eckhardt analyzed the pottery fabrics with advice and assistance from others in the Geology Department, particularly Professor James Stout.

Work now in progress includes catalogues of the painted fine ware and the unpainted red slipped ware, and further statistical analysis. Other categories of finds, including the highly important glazed wares and glass, remain to be fully studied.

BIBLIOGRAPHY

McNally, Sheila. 1978/79. "Excavations at Akhmīm, Egypt: 1978." *Newsletter of the American Research Center in Egypt* 107:22–28.

McNally, Sheila. 1981/82. "Survival of a City: Excavations at Akhmīm." *Newsletter of the American Research Center in Egypt* 116:26–30.

McNally, Sheila and Vicky Walsh. 1984. "The Akhmīm Data Base: a Multi-Stage System for Computer-Assisted Analysis of Artifacts." *Journal of Field Archaeology* 11:47–59.

Nelson, Cherilyn and Robert F. Johnson. 1988. "Attribute Characterization Schemes for Ancient Textiles." *Ars Textrina* 9:11–14.

Chapter 3

SQUARE ONE: EXCAVATION

(For complete listing of loci with references to illustrations and further discussion, see the Index of Loci, pp. 28-32. The Index of Walls is on p. 33. The Matrices, pp. 34-35, show the sequences of all loci except walls, and the sequence of sifted loci. The top of the designator for each locus is placed at the correct level ASL. A chart showing how loci have been classified appears on p. 36. The Level Plans, pp. 37-41, present the positions and sequences of levels, schematically: They do not accurately indicate the top and bottom of individual levels.)

Excavation began in a four meter square at the bottom of the hole left by the Bishop's building efforts. Discovery of walls prompted an extension of the horizontal area. By the end of 1978, the square itself had been extended by a meter along its east side, and a small shallow probe outside its limits had revealed the existence of additional walls. In 1981 the horizontal area under excavation almost tripled when the square was enlarged to a hexagon to fully as possible uncover the architectural complex. (The initial square and its first extension are indicated on Level Plan 1: the 1981 extension can be seen on the Level Plans and on Map 4). A new grid was established at this time, which is used in all the drawings of the square published here. One corner of the original square was at 62.39 m above sea level, about 6.50 m below the surface of the churchyard. Time constraints caused the excavation to terminate at different levels in different areas. The lowest point of the excavation was 59.78 m ASL.

Immediately below the existing surface (sometimes at heights above the corner of the original square) remains of construction appeared, too small and separate for interpretation. Walls farther down in the excavation formed the remains of two buildings. The buildings are discussed in detail in the next chapter: Their walls appear on Level Plans 5-9, pp. 39-41, as well as on the more detailed Phase and State Plans, pp. 52-56. On the matrix, the remaining loci have been grouped as "top" or as within the rooms that they emerged. This grouping reflects the way in which the excavators set the locus boundaries. They marked out large and somewhat arbitrary areas ("top") until walls appeared, after which they created separate loci in the areas between walls (Room 1, Room 2, etc.). They assigned loci on the periphery to the North and East areas.

This grouping by area should not, therefore, be taken as indicating anything about the way in which the deposits themselves originally formed, i.e., whether they built up while the rooms were in use, or after their abandonment. In many cases that is difficult to determine. Here three divisions of loci on the basis of formation processes are suggested. Within each, further subdivisions may prove useful.

The first division consists of rubble from the recent building efforts, and a series of loci that the excavators thought might have been contaminated by that activity. Below those come the second divisions, debris levels and other features formed after the major architectural complex had gone out of use. Last come the walls of that complex, and the loci that seem to have built up while those walls were in use. These large groupings have been referred to as "contaminated," "debris," and "habitation." "Debris" certainly represents several different activities, and may include some habitation levels. "Habitation" can be further subdivded inside Room 2. These divisions are summarized on a chart following the matrices (p. 36).

There were no sealed levels, and clearly some mixing occurred while the habitation and debris levels were first forming. Broad changes can however be observed, particularly in the type and frequency of glazed wares, and these will be further refined when that ware is more thoroughly studied. Glazed wares are all but absent in the lowest habitation levels. Glazed wares first become well represented in the post-habitation debris. Almost all the glazed sherds from the Square are pre-Fatamid and Fatamid wares. The small scatter of Mamluke sherds probably all represent contamination. Only 8 stratified coins could be cleaned well enough for certain identification. All appeared in the lower debris and habitation levels (Level Plan 5 and below). They are Byzantine and Abbasid in date.

1. Surface and Contaminated Loci.

On Level Plan 1, Loci 1, 5, 55, 56, 57, and 59 represent loose, clearly disturbed surface material. Locus 58 protruded around a wall stub, Q, and may be less disturbed, but the excavator thought that all of these levels should be considered contaminated, unlike those below them, i.e., 2, 3, 6, 7, and 60 on this plan. These "contaminated" levels contain glazed wares mainly of the Fatamid period or earlier, as well as a few isolated Mamluke pieces representing contamination, which also appear much further down.

2. Debris (and features that came into existence after the abandonment of the buildings, and before the recent construction).

This category includes small architectural remains, probably three walls and a floor, as well as three pits and one dump. Of these, the two walls Loci 76 and 77; the floor Locus 75; a small pit Loci 2 and 7; a larger pit Loci 63, 73, 85, 95, 97; and a dump Locus 9 all appeared at similar, relatively high levels. At lower levels appeared another wall, Locus 89; and a pit Loci 142, 150, 154.

No clear connections can be established between any of these features, or between any of them and the surrounding deposits, which are often arbitrary divisions. Finds underscore this arbitrariness, since adjoining or superimposed loci often contain one or two joining sherds. In the discussion below, joins are only mentioned when they are numerous enough to indicate a close relationship among loci.

Two groups of loci, one over Room 2 (Grid IL/3-6) and the other over Room 5 (Grid IK/8-9), yielded enough joining potsherds to suggest that a large amount of debris was dumped at one time into each room. In other words, it suggests that these two rooms, at least, were filled deliberately to prepare for some activity above (perhaps a new building phase, a new habitation), for which only fragmentary evidence survives. The pots found in the two room-filling dumps differ, and more study will be necessary to determine whether both rooms were filled at the same time. At the moment it seems that the debris dumped into Room 2 may be later than that dumped into Room 5.

Level Plan 1: Loci 60 and 3 represent general debris accumulation. Pot sherds found in Locus 7 join with sherds found in Loci 8, 12, 13, 18 and 20 on Level Plans 2 and 3, suggesting that these loci represent either a single room-filling dump, or a series of loose deposits in an open area with opportunity for mixing. The pottery in the room-filling dump contains several so-called "Fayoumi" bowls, probably Fatamid in date. Locus 17 is the equivalent of these upper levels in the extension to the original square. Loci 2 and 6 are a large, irregular pit cut into 3 and 7.

Level Plan 2: All loci formed after the buildings were abandoned. For Loci 8 and 17, see above under Level Plan 1. Pottery found in the bottom of Locus 62 joins with sherds in Loci 90/91, and 104/108 (Level Plans 3 and 4, Section 4) suggesting that all five loci represent either a single room-filling dump, or a series of loose deposits in an open area, with opportunity for mixing. (These loci are above Room 6: one sherd in the bottom of Locus 62 joins a sherd in Locus 53, debris over Room 5, suggesting that both rooms may have been filled in at the same time.) The pottery includes two shallow bowls, and several smaller, deeper ones, all with early glazes.

A number of loci probably came into existence during a (postulated) second phase of habitation that occurred after the buildings were abandoned, and after much of the debris had accummulated or been deliberately dumped. These loci indicate another phase of use of this area without being sufficient to define that use. They include the continuation of pit 2, which went down to 61.83 m ASL; and Locus 9, a sterile deposit of burnt material near pit 2 (Grid JK/4-5). There was also a deep pit beginning at this level in the east corner of the excavated area (Grid JKL/2). The whole feature, a pit or trench the bottom of which cuts into Wall D (Locus 96), was assigned the locus number 115. Its contents were excavated with arbitrary level divisions called Loci 63, 73, 85, 95, and 97. The edges of this feature were not always clear, so some surrounding material may have been included in the loci. Finally, there were three fired brick features in Locus 64 (Grid MO/7-8, see State Plan 5, p. 56) One, locus 75, may be a floor related to Walls MM (Locus 76) and NN (Locus 77).

Level Plan 3: All loci formed after the buildings were abandoned. For Loci 12, 18 and 20 see above under Locus 2, Level Plan 1. For Loci 90 and 91, see under Locus 62 under Level Plan 2 above.

In the east corner, the pit continues as Locus 73 under 63.

Level Plan 4. All loci formed after the buildings were abandoned. Locus 13 and 20 belong to large-dump group described under Locus 7, Level Plan 1 above. Loci 91, 104 and 108 belong to the large-dump group described under Locus 62, Level Plan 2 above.

In the east corner, the pit continues as Locus 85.

Level Plan 5: Most loci on this plan should still be considered post-abandonment debris. The distinction between habitation levels and later fill is in many cases difficult. In this level, not only walls have appeared, but the first level certainly associated with them, formed during habitation, Locus 14. One locus on this Level Plan, Locus 114, in Room 1, contained Byzantine coin as well as one that was probably Omayyid. Locus 15, continuing from the preceding level, resembles Loci 12 and 13, which were part of the "large dump" in Room 2, and is probably, like them, post-abandonment debris, as is Locus 78, which contained an Abbasid coin.

The later pit continues into 95 at the East. It was cut down past a wall fragment,

Wall EE (Grid JK/2-3 on State Plan 5, p. 56), that is separated by debris from an earlier wall on the same line.

Level Plan 6. Loci on the periphery may still be post-abandonment debris, but more of the interior loci represent habitation (see below).

The pit in the east corner ends in Locus 95 at this level. "Pit" walls were not clear, so the extent is indicated schematically.

Level Plans 7-9. Loci on the peripheries may still be post-abandonment debris, but most are habitation levels.

3. Habitation Levels.

The first locus that was clearly created during the period when a room was in use is Locus 14 in Room 2. Like it, most of the others consist of fill brought in to create new floors, rather than debris building up during habitation, although some pots were found in situ.

Level Plan 5: Walls, designated by letters, emerged, delineating a series of rooms (1-4, see Phase Plans 2-3, pp. 52-53 below) at the Southeast of the site. Locus 14 in Room 2 (Grid IL/3-6) consisted of a series of thin layers of earth floors, or foundations for tiled floors. It was removed in 0.10 m layers that should be considered as at least three separate deposits[46]. A glazed bowl, probably Fatamid rather than earlier, lay upside down on one of the first packed-debris floor levels. Locus 87 (Grid IL/3) is similar to 14. In Room 3 a tile floor, Locus 21 under Locus 15 at 61.36 m ASL, is the first locus clearly related to the walls (Grid EH/5-6, State Plan 4 and Section 3).

Level Plan 6: In Room 1, Locus 114 continues down to 60.83 ASL, end of excavation in that area. No clear sign of a floor appeared. In Room 2, evidence of floors continues (see below p. 49). In Room 3 also evidence of floors continues, and Loci 100, 176 and 173 seem to be associated

---

[46]The excavator suggested separating baskets 1-7, 8-19, 20-24 as representing different floors. There is reason to suggest a break between 17 and 18, see under Level Plan 8.

with or form part of them (Section 3). Locus 100 runs under floor tiles (Locus 102), and adjoins a packed earth floor, Locus 79, in Grid FG/6. A pot was found on this floor, and two more were found set into Locus 100 immediately east of the spur wall, Wall R (Grid G/4, State Plan 3) This floor is probably one construction with Locus 102, a series of tiles, and Locus 21, tiles at a slightly higher level. Within Locus 100, three features, i.e., Loci 103, 110, and 111 (Walls FF, GG, HH, State Plan 3), may be remains of storage facilities. Wall FF may also be the remains of the outer boundary of the room, unless the room extended farther to the Southeast at this time.

In the North (Grid KO/7-10), mud brick Walls U (Locus 137), W (Locus 134), and T (Locus 136, a continuation of Wall A) were recognized. The area marked by these walls is referred to as the North Area, because we are not sure how to interpret it architecturally. Wall U divides Locus 135 from Locus 140: Both loci were carried down to 61.08 m ASL, the end of excavation in the North Area.

The first locus assigned to Room 5, Locus 124 (Grid HK/8-9) cannot be distinguished clearly from the post-abandonment debris levels above it, to which it probably belongs. It contained an Abbasid coin.

Level Plan 7: In Room 2, subfloors and floors continue as Loci 14, 151, and two patches of tiles, Loci 153 and 157, (Sections 1 and 2; 157 State Plan 1, JK/5). Locus 151 contained two Abbasid coins. In Room 3, under Locus 100 the continuation of Wall D into this area appeared at the same level as a group of small walls: I (184), J (188), M (185), L (186), P (170), and the cross Wall S (169), as well as a packed earth floor (192). In Room 4 (Grid BE/2-7) there are two rows of pots, AA (Locus 127) and BB (Locus 128), set into a clay floor, Locus 129. In Room 5, a neatly cut, nicely lined pit appeared in the corner (Grid JK/8-9). The pit (Loci 142, 150 and 154) was cut through Locus 138 while the walls were standing at least, if not while the room was in use. (The upper edges of this pit were not clear, and there is some mixing with adjacent loci.) Wall X appeared in Locus 121 and 125, dividing Room 5 from Room 6. (Fortuitously, the division

between extension of the square was immediately above this wall, so that levels over the spaces later recognized as Room 5 and Room 6 had been excavated separately. Probably, however, they form part of one post-habitation fill.)

Level Plan 8: Excavation continued only in Rooms 2, 3, 4, and 5. In Room 5, the pit continued as Loci 150 and 154. There was a large amount of glass in the pit, especially in Locus 150. The adjacent loci in Room 5 contained several pieces of whole or nearly whole pottery that have led Anne Salisbury, who is studying the material, to suggest that these loci are habitation levels. Simply for reasons of caution they continue to be classified as debris levels here. In Room 3, under Wall C, Wall N (187) appeared. Loci 159, 161, and 168 are in two of the small spaces between this wall and the small walls noted on Level Plan 7. Wall O (171) appeared in Locus 161. These loci completed excavation in this room. The lack of fine wares in these loci suggests that they may have accumulated while the spaces were in use for storage. In Room 2, excavation under the tiled floor Locus 157 continued only in a trench 1.50 m wide along the line of Wall B. The arbitrarily divided 0.10 m levels called Loci 155, 158, 164 contain pottery joining with sherds from the lowest baskets (18 through 24) of Locus 14, and from the locus immediately beneath, 166. These should probably be considered as one sizable leveling deposit for a floor, or, less probably, as a series of leveling deposits or plain earth floors made up of material drawn from the same debris.

Level Plan 9: Additional loci were excavated in the trench in Room 2. Locus 166 contains a Byzantine coin, the oldest stratified coin from the site, but the locus is probably part of a larger grouping containing part of 14, and 155, 158, 164 (see above under Level Plan 8). Small walls of storage bins appeared at the bottom of the trench (H, OO and possibly K on State Plan 2). Loci 174, 177, 180, and 195 contain less fine wares. The character of the wares may indicate an early date, a relative impoverishment, or simply the use of this space for storage.

SQUARE ONE: EXCAVATION

SQUARE ONE: INDEX OF LOCI

Almost all loci that consist of strata appear on one or more of the eight Level Plans. The exceptions are surface loci, mixed loci from cleaning, and one locus that appears on a State Plan.

Number	Interpretation	Area	Level Plan	State Plan	Section
1	contaminated	top	1	3, 4	
2	debris	top	1–3		4
3	debris	top	1		3
4	debris	top	2		3
5	contaminated	top	1		1–3
6	debris	top	1		4
7	debris	top	1		1–3
8	debris	Room 2	2		1–3
9	debris	Room 2	2		
10	habitation feature	Wall A	2–9	1, 2, 4	2, 3
10A	debris	Room 2	part of Locus 18		
11	debris	top	2	4	
12	debris	Room 2	3		1, 2
13	debris	Room 2	4		1, 2
14	habitation	Room 2	5–7		1, 2
15	debris	Room 3	3–5		3
16	habitation feature	Wall A (see 10 above)			
17	debris	top	1, 2		1, 2
18	debris	Room 2	2, 3		1, 2
19	mixed	top	(mixed)*		
20	debris	Room 2	3, 4		1, 2
21	habitation	Room 3	(floor)	4	3
22	habitation feature	Wall C	5–9	1, 3	1
23	(foundation material)	Room 2			
24	habitation feature	Wall B	2–9	1, 2	1
25	mixed	Room 2	(mixed)*		
___1981					
50	contaminated	top	(surface)		4
51	feature in debris	Wall Q	1–8	1, 2	5
52	contaminated	top	(surface)		
53	debris	top	2		4
54	debris	top	3		4
55	debris	top	1		4
56	contaminated	top	1		3, 4
57	contaminated	top	1		2
58	contaminated	top	1		
59	contaminated	top	1, 2		1, 2
60	debris	top	1, 2		3
61	debris	top	2		3
62	debris	top	2		4
63	feature in debris	East(pit)	2, 3		
64	debris	North	2		

* A list of mixed loci follows this Index.

Number	Interpretation	Area	Level Plan	State Plan	Section
65	debris	top	3		3
66	habitation feature	Wall A (see 10 above)			
67	habitation feature	Wall B (see 24 above)			
68	habitation feature	Room 2(facing of Wall A)			
69	debris	top	4		3
70	debris	Room 2	2, 3		1, 2
71	debris	top	4		3
72	debris	Room 2	3		1, 2
73	feature in debris	East (pit)	3		
74	debris	top	2		4
75	feature in debris	North	(floor)	5	
76	feature in debris	Wall MM		5	4
77	feature in debris	Wall NN		5	4
78	debris	Room 3	5		3
79	habitation feature	Room 3	(floor)	4	
80	habitation feature	Wall R	5–8	1	
81	debris	Room 1	2, 3		
82	debris	top	3		4
83	debris	Room 2	4		1, 2
84	habitation feature	Wall C (see 22 above)			
85	feature in debris	East (pit)	4		
86	debris	Room 1	2		
87	habitation	Room 2	5		1, 2
88	debris	top	3, 4		4
89	feature in debris	Wall EE		5	
90	debris	top	3		4
91	debris	top	3, 4		4
92	habitation feature	Room 2	(floor)	1	1, 2
93	debris	Room 2	6		1, 2
94	mixed	East	(mixed)*		
95	feature in debris	East (pit)	5, 6		
96	habitation feature	Wall D	6–9	1	2, 3
97	debris	East	6, 7		
98		Room 2, collectively			
99	mixed	Room 1	(mixed)*		
100	habitation	Room 3	6		3
101	debris	North	3, 4		
102	habitation feature	Room 3	(floor)	3, 4	
103	habitation feature	Wall FF		3	
104	debris	top	4, 5		4
105	debris	Room 1	4		
106	debris	East	6, 7		
107	debris	top	4, 6		4
108	debris	top	4		4
109	debris	Room 4	2		

* A list of mixed loci follows this Index.

SQUARE ONE: EXCAVATIONS

Number	Interpretation	Area	Level plan	State plan	Section
108	debris	Room 5	4		4
109	debris	Room 4	2		
110	habitation feature	Wall GG		3	3
111	habitation feature	Wall HH		3	
112	not used				
113	habitation feature	Wall RR		1	
114	debris	Room 1	5, 6		
115	East (pit): contains 63, 73, 85, 95, 97				
116	debris	Room 4	3		
117	habitation feature	Wall G	3–8	1	
118	debris	North	5		
119	debris	East	3–5		
120	debris	Room 4	3, 4		
121	debris	Room 5	5, 6		4
122	mixed	top	(mixed)*		
123	debris	Room 4	5		
124	debris	Room 5	6		4
125	debris	Room 6	5		4
126	habitation feature	Wall X	7, 8	1	4
127	habitation	Room 4	7, 8 (AA)	1	
128	habitation	Room 4	7, 8 (BB)	1	
129	habitation feature	Room 4	(floor)	1	
130	habitation feature	Wall E	4–8	1, 4	
131	habitation feature	Wall F	3–8	1	
132	habitation feature	Wall Z		1	
133	habitation feature	Wall JJ		1	
134	habitation feature	Wall W	6–9	1	4
135	debris	North	6		4
136	habitation feature	Wall T	5–8	1	
137	habitation feature	Wall U	6–8	1	4
138	debris	Room 5	7		4
139	debris	Room 6	6		4
140	debris	North	6		4
141	feature in debris;pit, consists of Loci 142, 150, 154				
142	feature in debris	Room 5	7		4
143	mixed	Room 1	(mixed)*		
144	debris	East	3		
145	debris	Room 4	6		
146	habitation	Wall KK		1	
147	habitation	Wall II		1	
148	Room 3, collectively				
149	Room 4, collectively				
150	feature in debris	Room 5	8		4
151	habitation	Room 2	7		1, 2
152	habitation	Wall A (see 10 above)			

---

* A list of mixed loci follows this Index.

Number	Interpretation	Area	Level plan	State plan	Section
153	habitation	Room 2	(floor)		1
154	feature in debris	Room 5	8		4
155	habitation	Room 2	8		1, 2
156	debris	Room 5	8		4
157	habitation	Room 2	(floor)	1	2
158	habitation	Room 2	8		1, 2
159	habitation	Room 3	7, 8		3
160	habitation	Wall K	8, 9	2	1
161	habitation	Room 3	7, 8		
162	habitation	Wall CC		1	
163	habitation	Wall Y	6–8	1	4
164	habitation	Room 2	8		1, 2
165	habitation	Room 2	(pot/contents)	5	
166	habitation	Room 2	9		1, 2
167	contaminated	top	(backfill)		
168	habitation	Room 3	8		3
169	habitation	Wall S	7, 8	1	
170	habitation	Wall P	7, 8	1	3
171	habitation	Wall O	7, 8	1	
172	habitation	Room 2	(mixed)*		
173	habitation	Room 3	6		3
174	habitation	Room 2	9		1, 2
175	debris		Room 6	7	4
176	habitation	Room 3	6		3
177	habitation	Room 2	9		1, 2
178	habitation	loose bricks	(see Locus 160, Wall K)		
179	debris		Room 6	8	4
180	habitation	Room 2	9		1, 2
181	habitation	Room 2	(equals 177)		
182	habitation	Room 2	(mixed)*		
183	habitation	Wall H	8, 9	2	
184	habitation	Wall I	7, 8	1	
185	habitation	Wall M	7, 8	1	3
186	habitation	Wall L	7, 8	1	
187	habitation	Wall N	7, 8	1	
188	habitation	Wall J	7, 8	1	
189	habitation	Room 2	(equals 180)		
190	habitation	Wall V	9		2
191	habitation	Room 5	8		4
192	habitation	Room 3	floor	1	3
193	habitation	Room 5	8		4
194	habitation	whole	(mixed)*		
195	habitation	Room 2	9		1, 2

---

* A list of mixed loci follows this Index.

SQUARE ONE: EXCAVATION

MIXED LOCI
(from cleaning)

Number	Area	Material from Loci
19	top	5, 7, 12, 13, 14, 15
25	Room 2	14, 18, 20
94	East	70, 71, 83
99	Room 1	81 and 86
122	top	60, 61, 65, 69, 71
143	Room 1	81, 105. 114
172	Room 2	158, 164, 166
182	Room 2	166, 174, 177
194	whole	final cleaning

INDEX OF WALLS

Wall	Locus	Grid	Level Plan	State Plan	Section
Wall A	10, 16, 66	EM/7–6	2–9	1, 2, 4	2, 3
Wall B	24, 67	L/3–6	2–9	1, 2	1
Wall C	22, 84	HI/3–6	5–9	1, 4	1
Wall D	96	EL/2–3	6–9	1	2, 3
Wall E	130	EF/2–5	4–8	1, 4	
Wall F	131	BC/1–4	3–8	1	
Wall G	117	DE/1–2	3–8	1	
Wall H	183	KL/4–6	8, 9	2	
Wall I	184	FG/6	7, 8	1	
Wall J	188	FH/6	7, 8	1	
Wall K	160	KL/4	8, 9	2	1
Wall L	186	FG/5	7, 8	1	
Wall M	185	GH/5	7, 8	1	3
Wall N	187	HI/3–6	7, 8	1	
Wall O	171	FG/3	7, 8	1	
Wall P	170	GH/4	7, 8	1	3
Wall Q	51	NO/6–7	1–8	1, 5	
Wall R	80	FG/4–5	5–8	1	
Wall S	169	G/3–6	7, 8	1	
Wall T	136	MO/7	5–8	1	
Wall U	137	MN/7–9	6–8	1	4
Wall V	190	JK/6	9	2	2
Wall W	134	KL/8–10	6–8	1	4
Wall X	126	HI/8–9	7, 8	1	4
Wall Y	163	DE/7–8	6–8	1	4
Wall Z	132	CE/6	7, 8	1	
Wall AA	(pots)	BE/3–4	7, 8	1	
Wall BB	(pots)	E/2–3	7, 8	1	
Wall CC	162	EH/6–7		1	
Wall EE	89	J/2		5	
Wall FF	103	H/2		3	
Wall GG	110	GH/3–4		3	3
Wall HH	111	FG/3		3	
Wall II	147	BC/2–3	1		
Wall JJ	133	GL/7–8		1	
Wall KK	146	FG/7–8		1	
Wall MM	76	MN/8–9		5	
Wall NN	77	M/7–8		5	4
Wall OO	(1982)	J/8	8, 9	2	4
Wall RR	113	JL/1–2	1		

33

SQUARE ONE: EXCAVATION

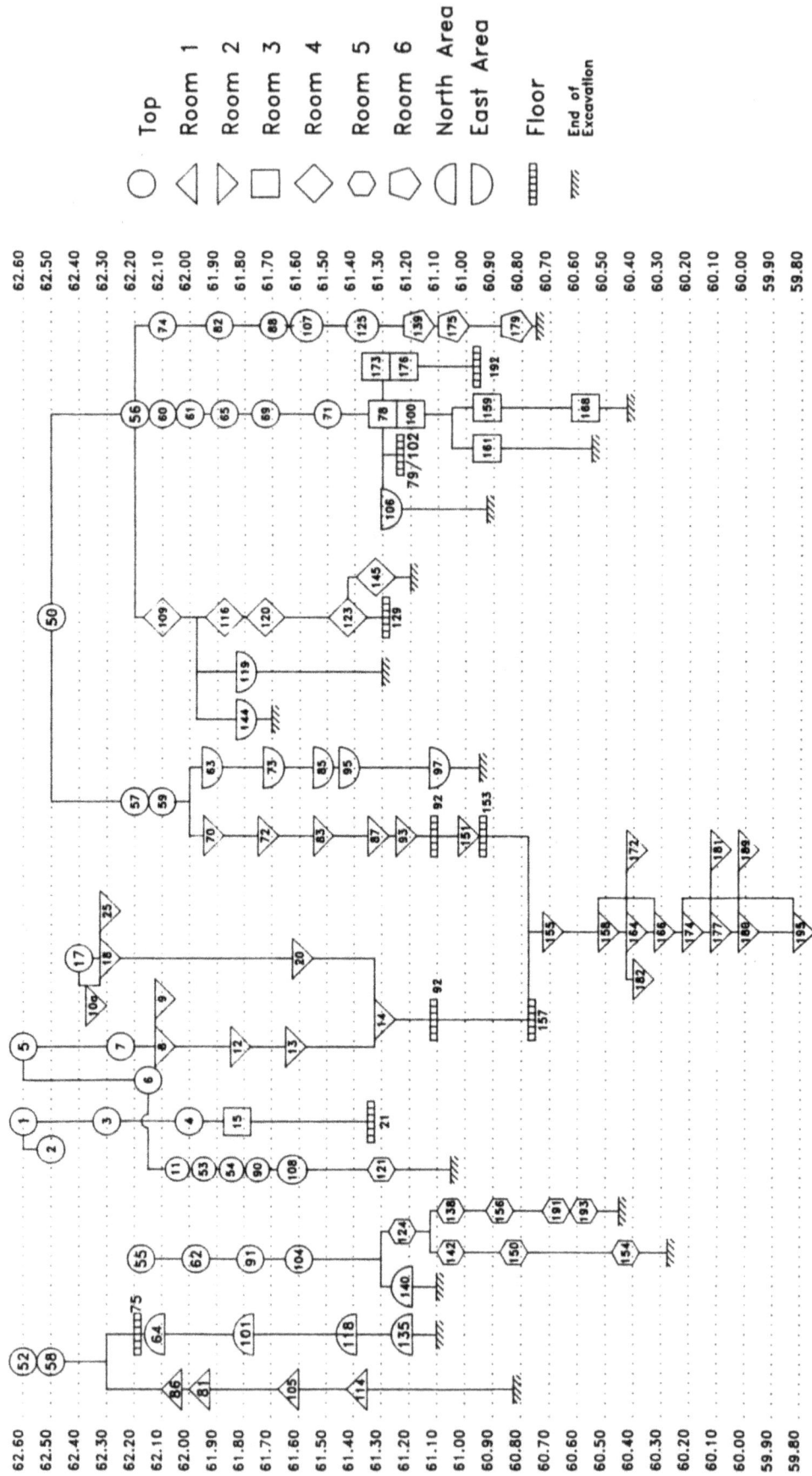

SQUARE ONE MATRIX

Top ◯

Room 2 ▷

Room 3 □

Room 5 ⬡

Floor ▥

End of Excavation ▨

62.60 62.50 62.40 62.30 62.20 62.10 62.00 61.90 61.80 61.70 61.60 61.50 61.40 61.30 61.20 61.10 61.00 60.90 60.80 60.70 60.60 60.50 60.40 60.30 60.20 60.10 60.00 59.90 59.80

78 159 161

152

92 151 153

25 25 172 181 189

17 18 20 155 158 164 166 174 177 180 95

109 9 182 182

5 7 8 12 13 14 68 92 157

19

6

1 3 4 15 21

2

11 53 54 90 108 121

62.60 62.50 62.40 62.30 62.20 62.10 62.00 61.90 61.80 61.70 61.60 61.50 61.40 61.30 61.20 61.10 61.00 60.90 60.80 60.70 60.60 60.50 60.40 60.30 60.20 60.10 60.00 59.90 59.80

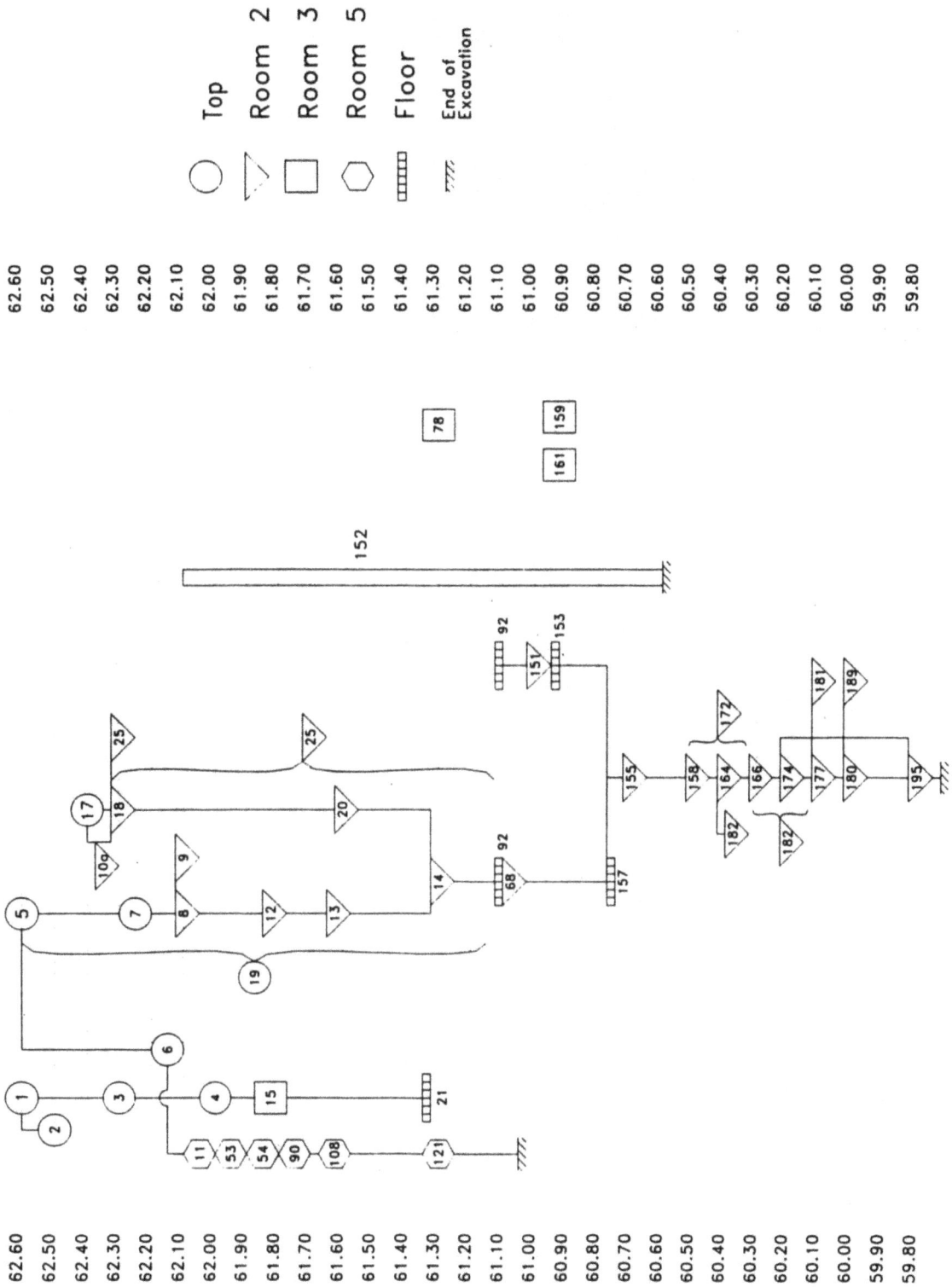

MATRIX OF SIFTED LOCI

SQUARE ONE: EXCAVATION

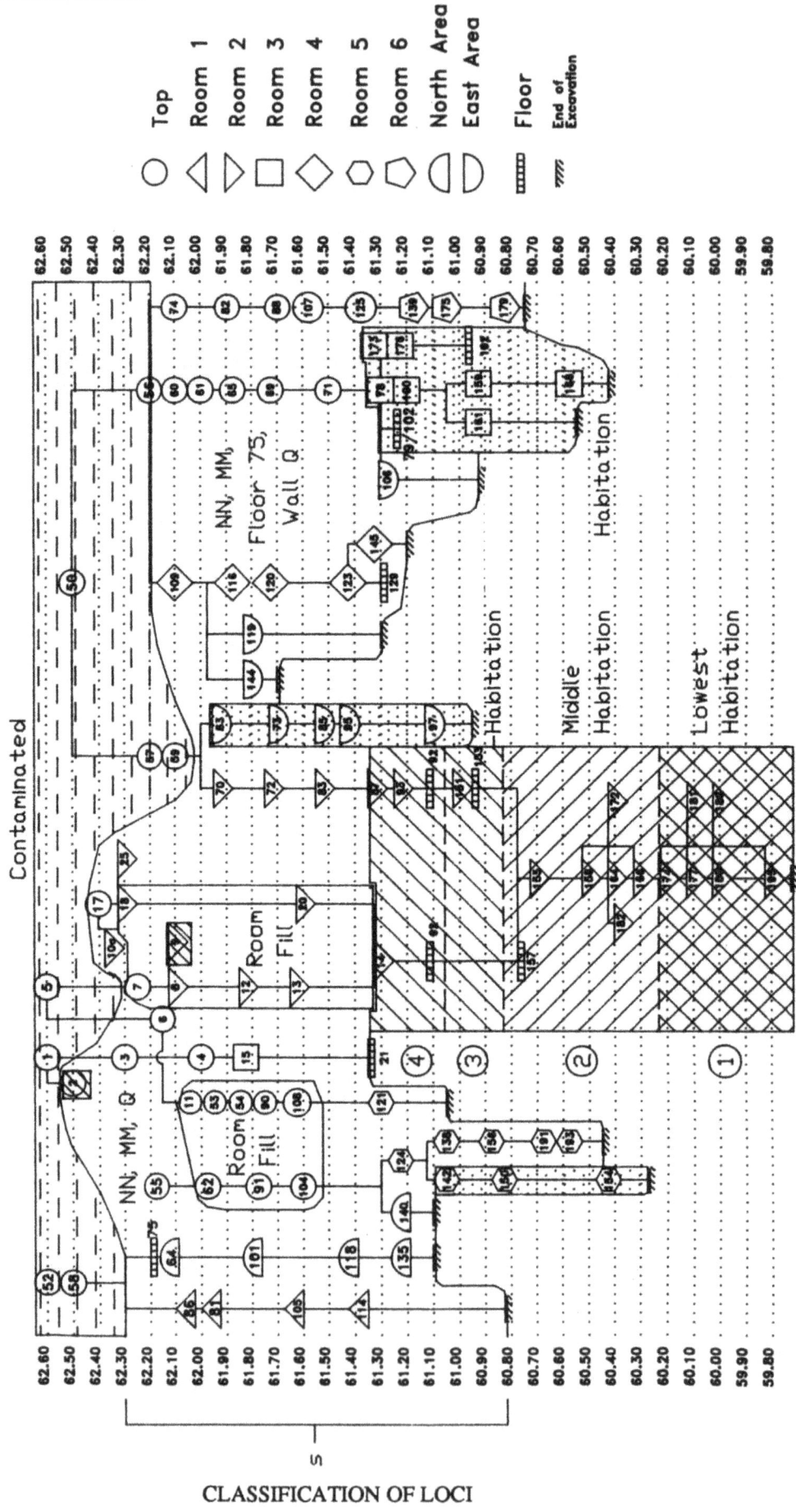

CLASSIFICATION OF LOCI

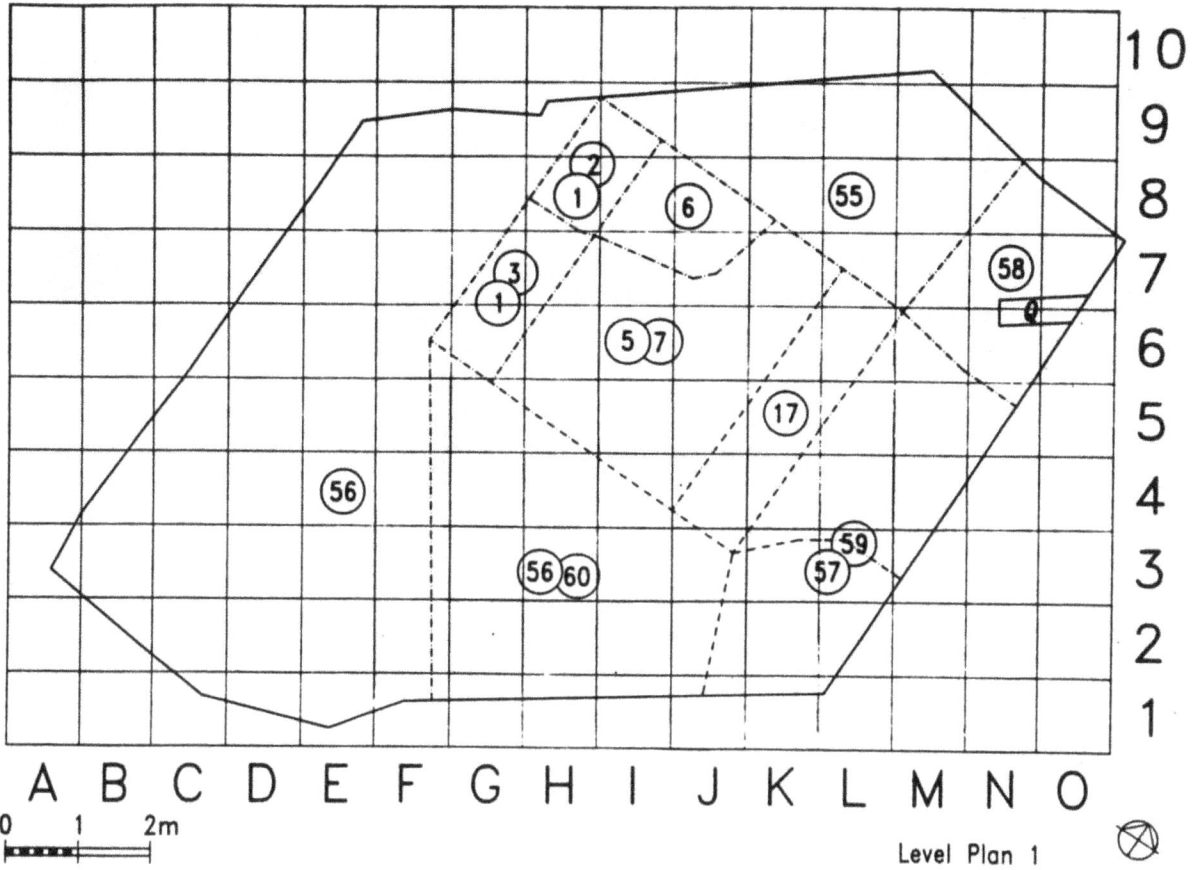

Level Plan 1

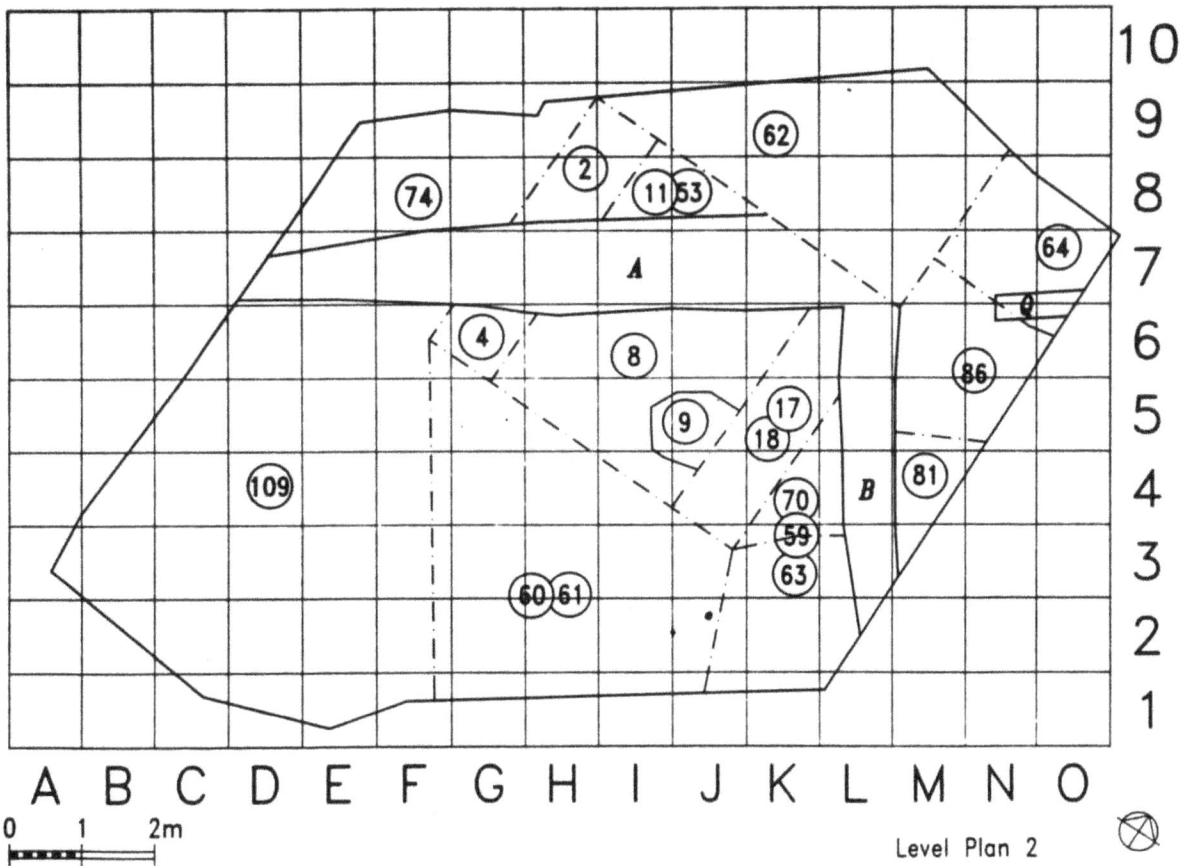

Level Plan 2

SQUARE ONE: EXCAVATION

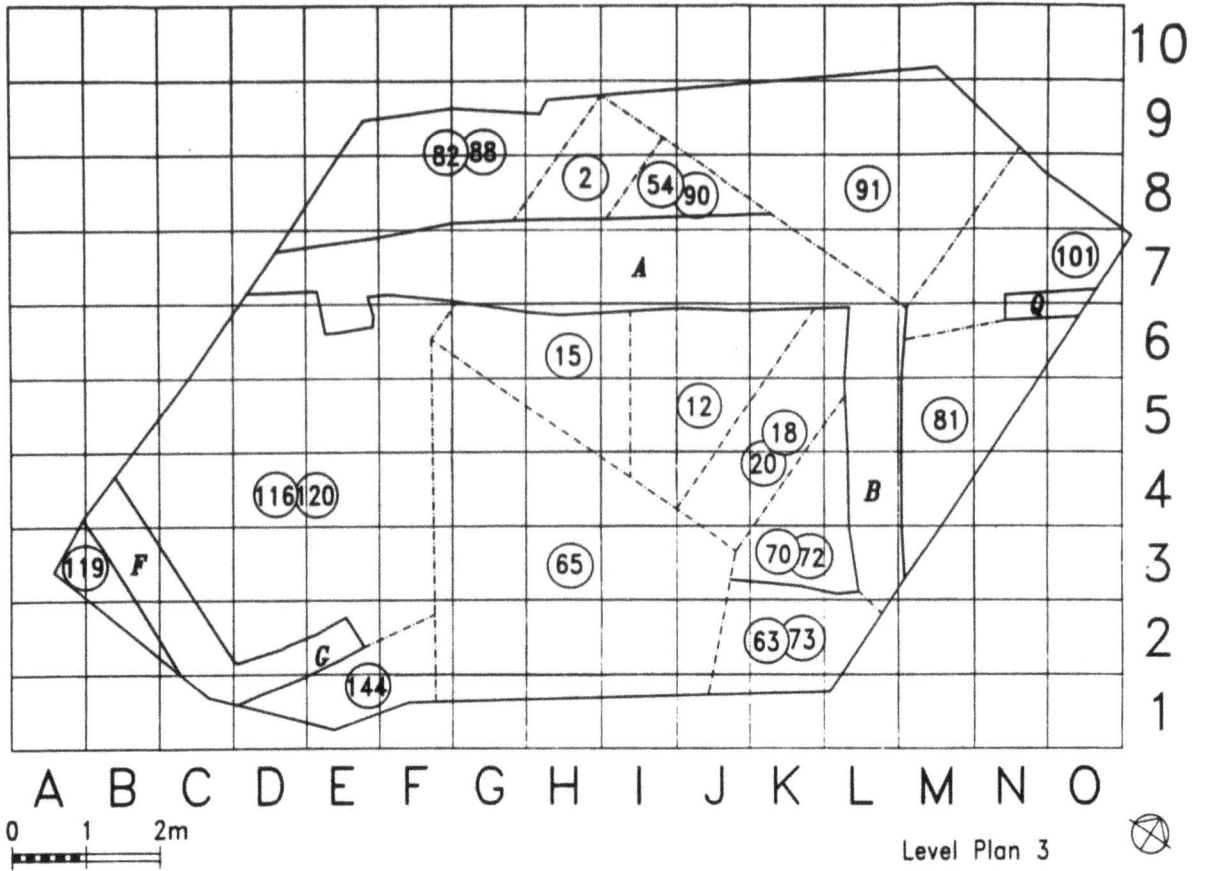

Level Plan 3

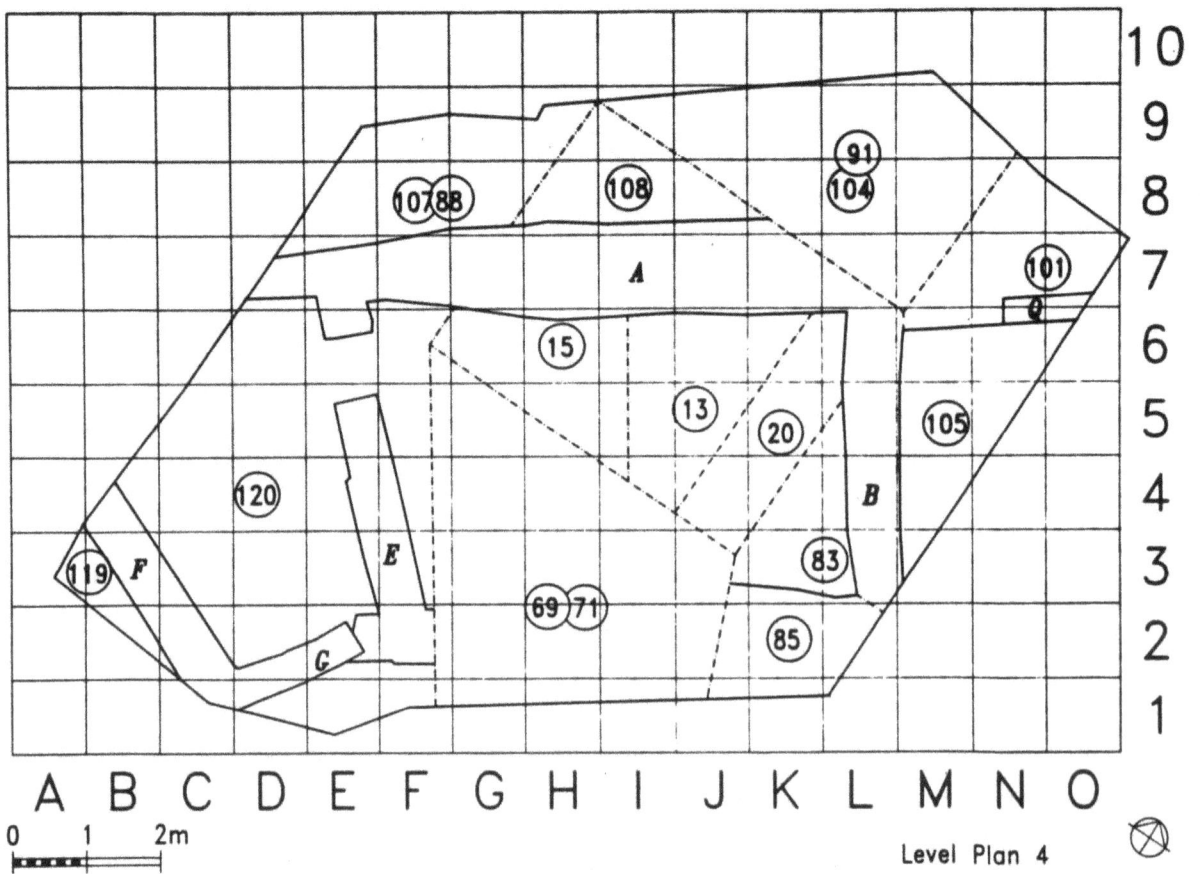

Level Plan 4

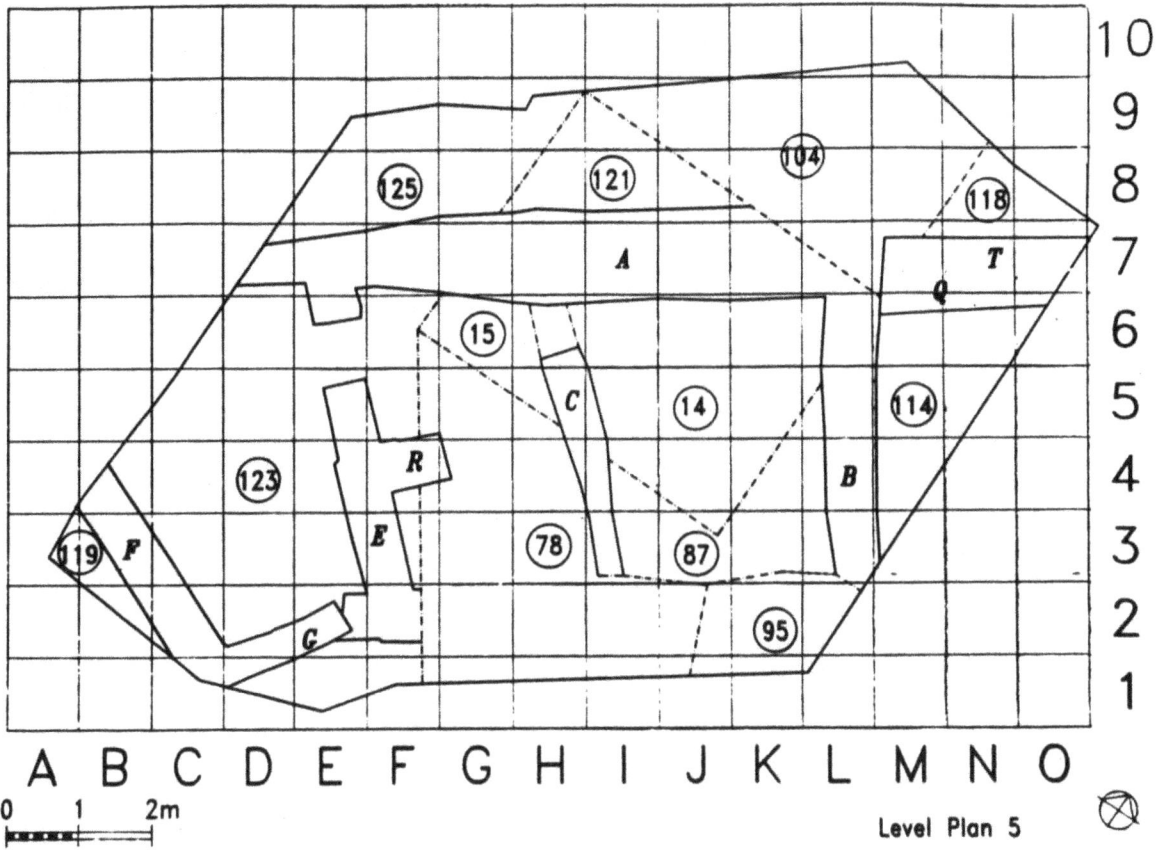

Level Plan 5

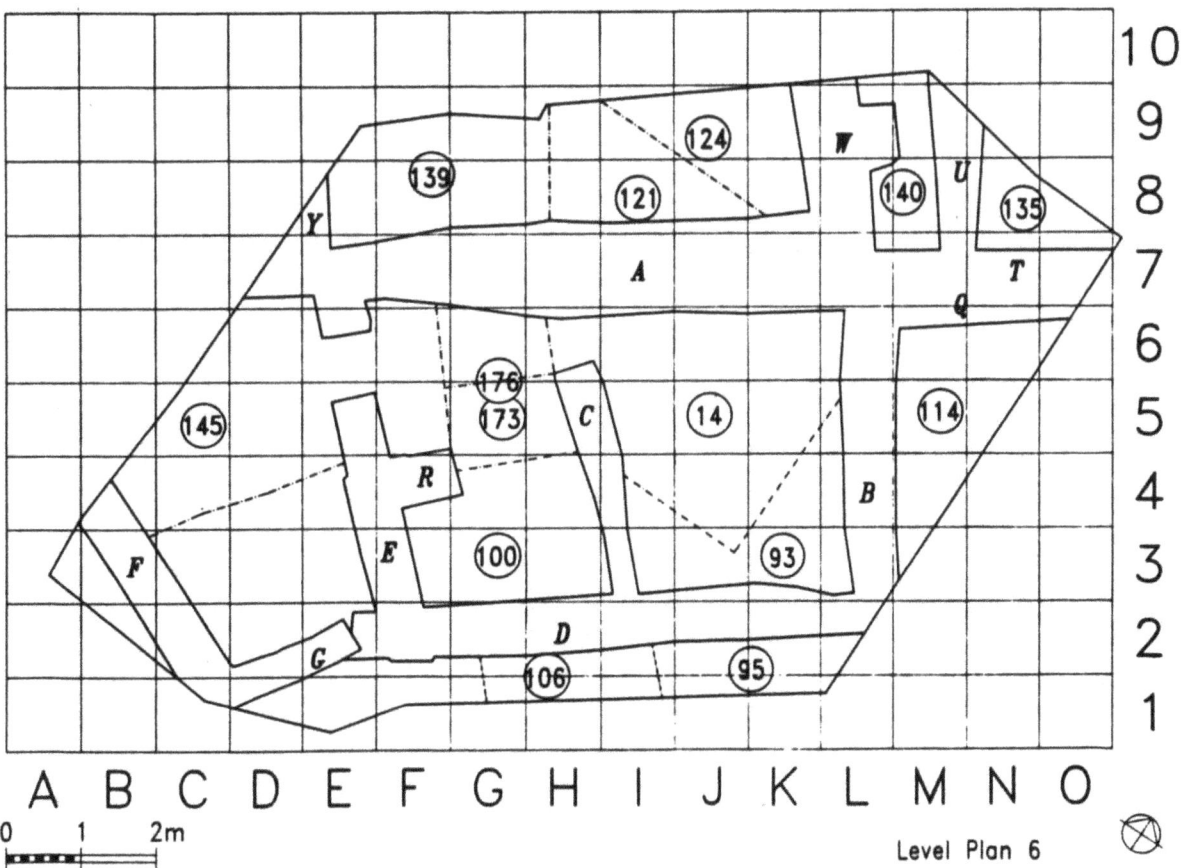

Level Plan 6

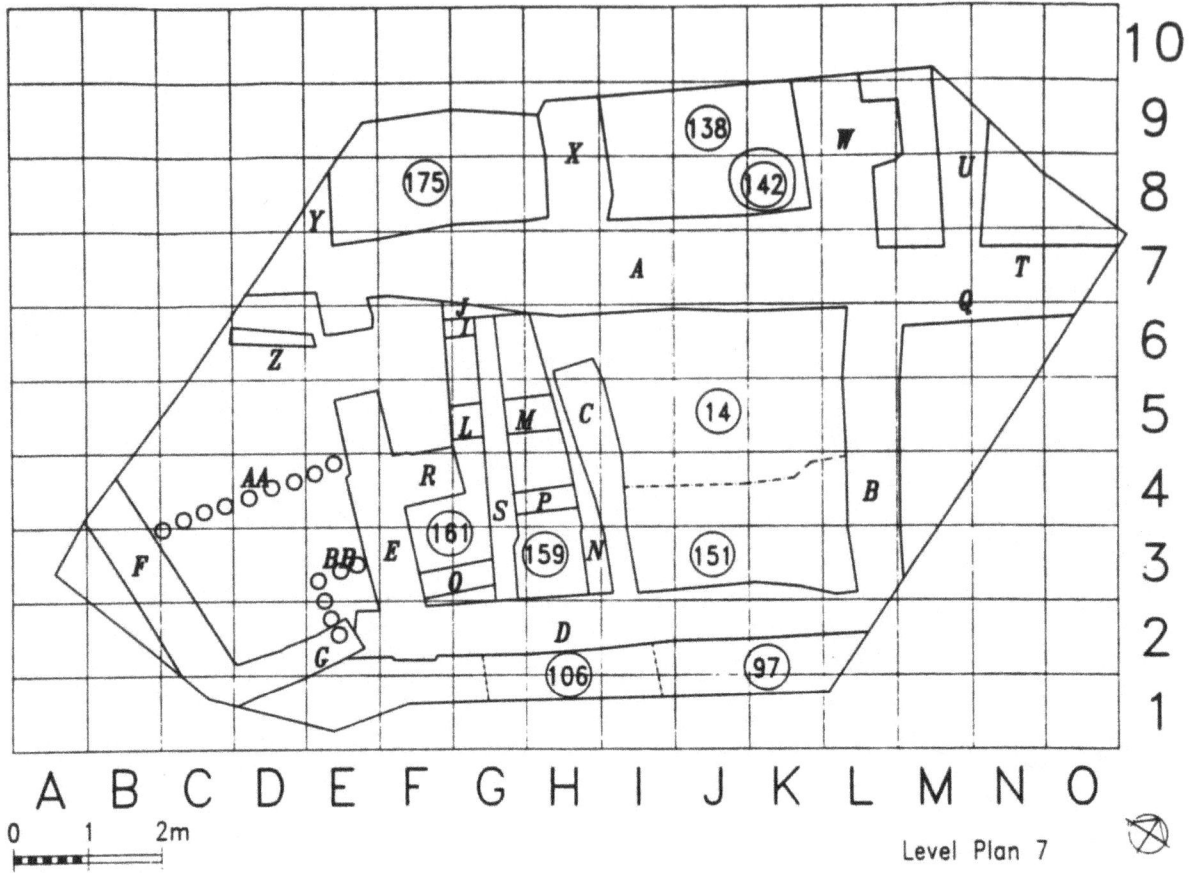

Level Plan 7

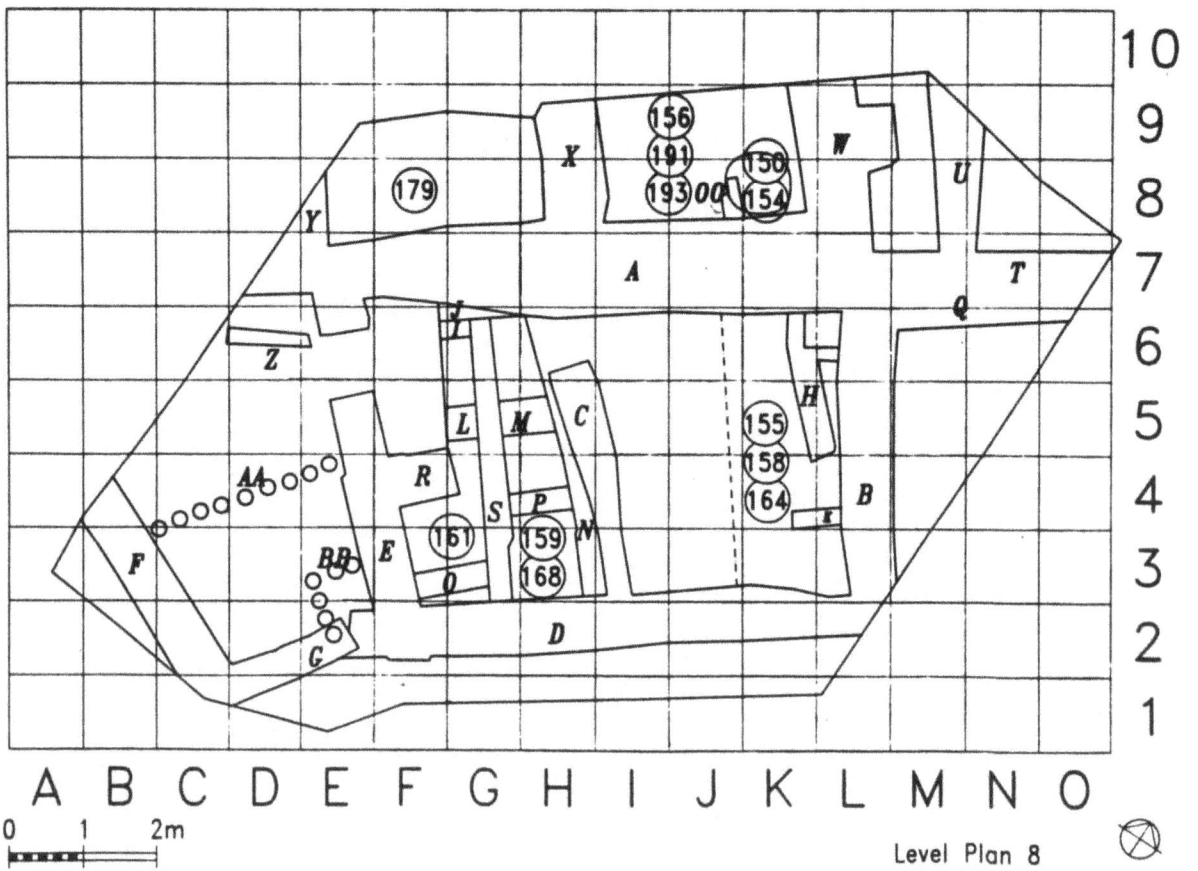

Level Plan 8

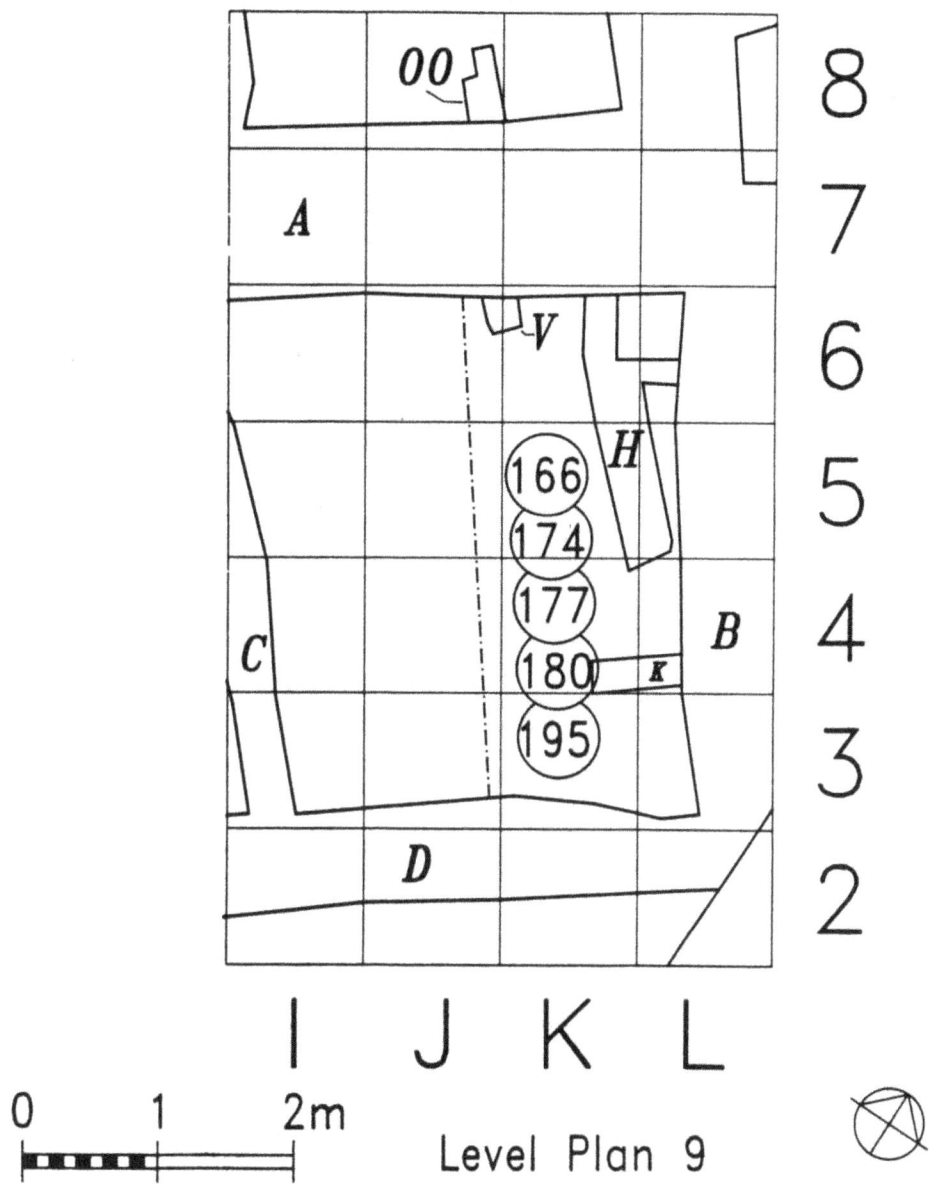

Level Plan 9

SQUARE ONE: EXCAVATION

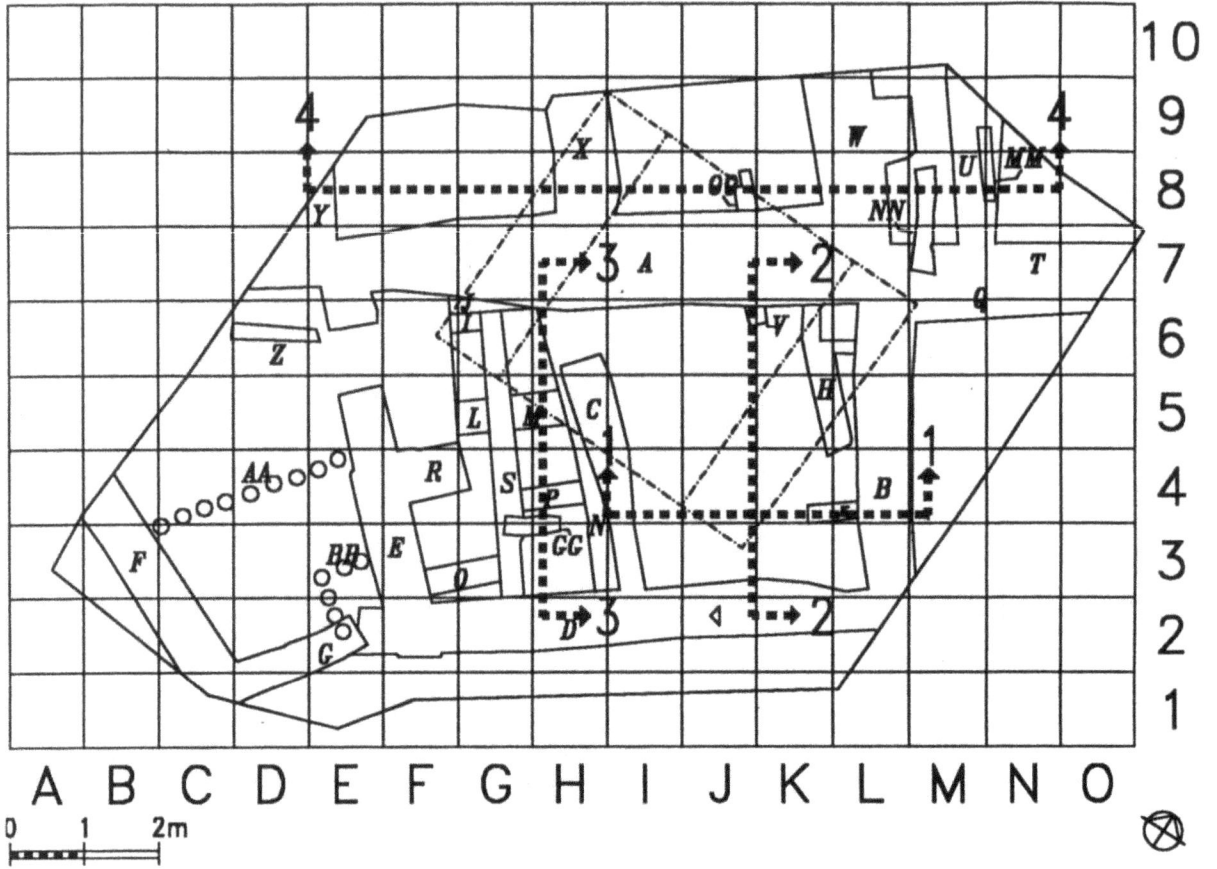

GUIDE TO SECTIONS

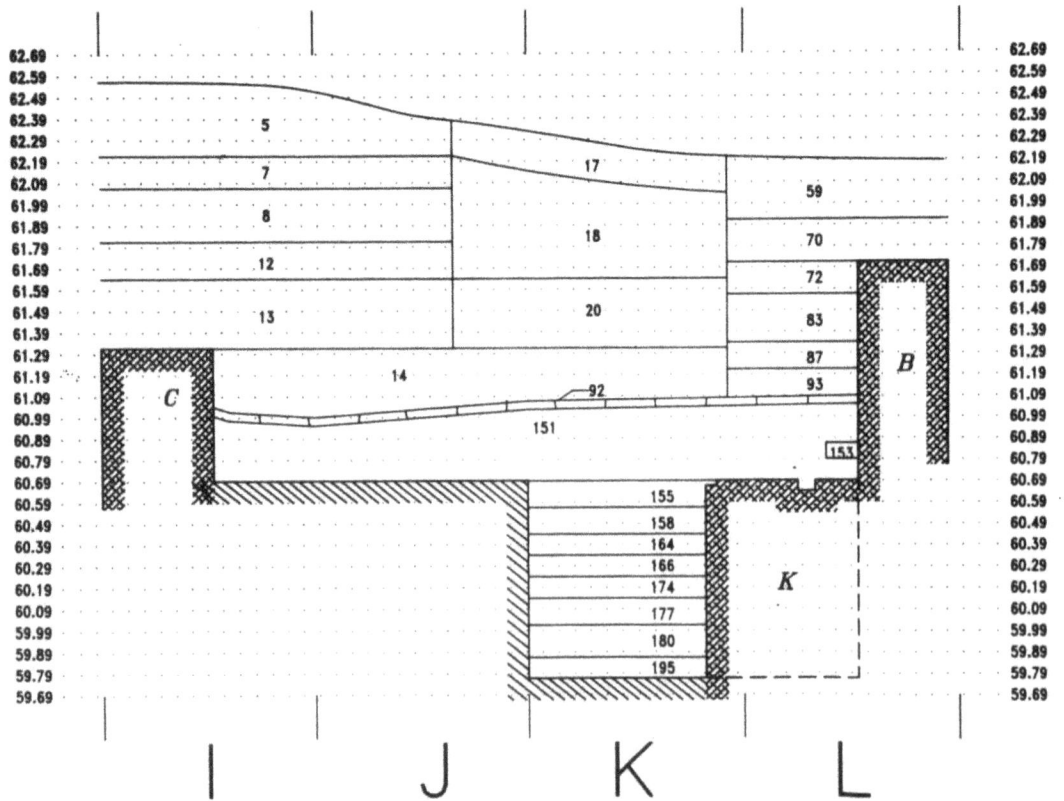

Section 1

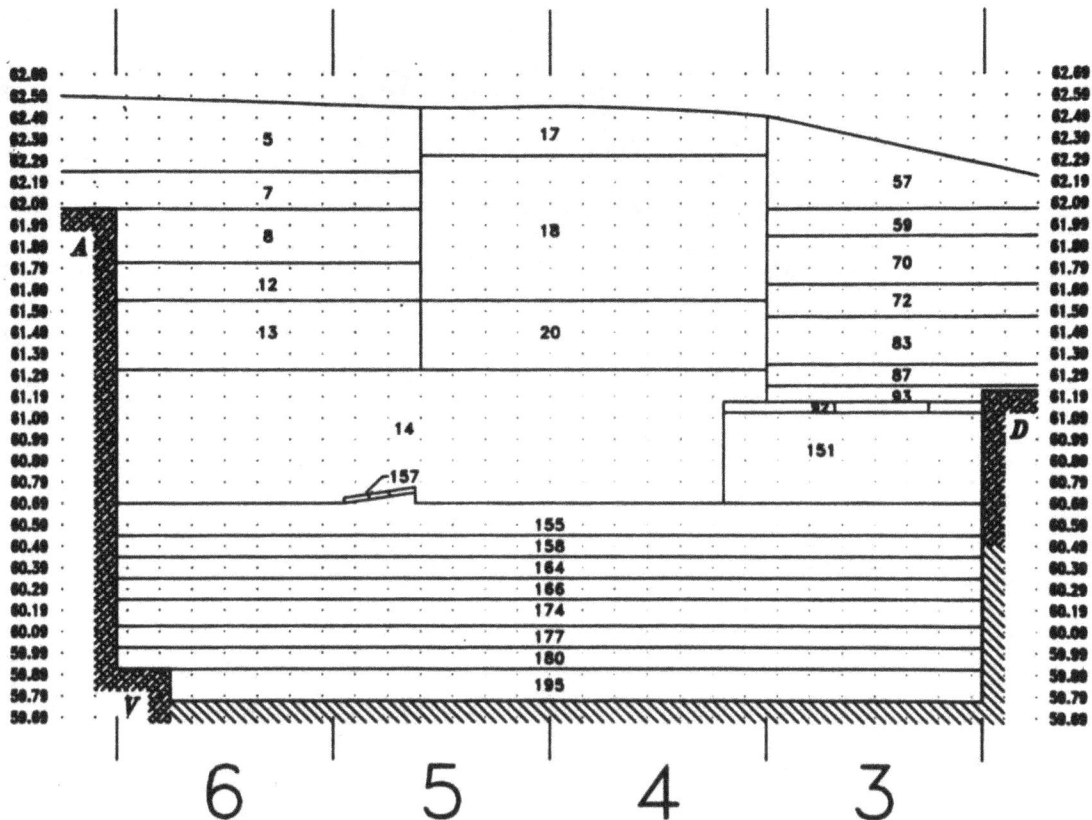

Section 2

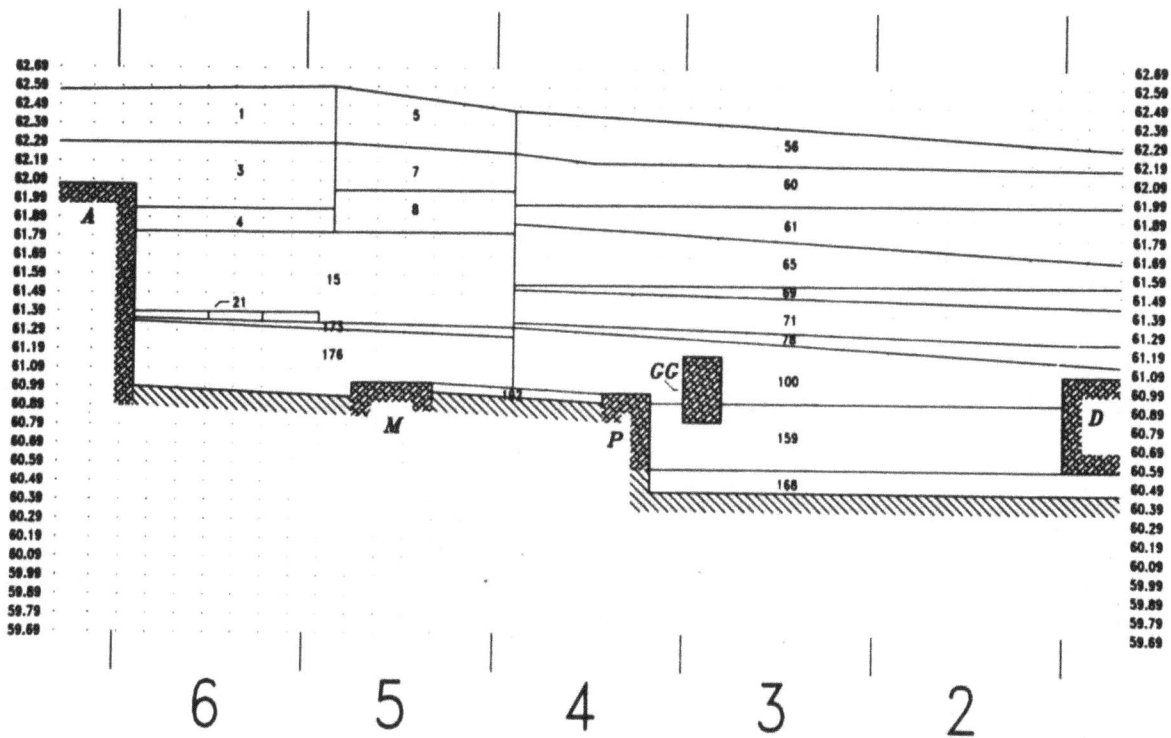

Section 3

SQUARE ONE: EXCAVATION

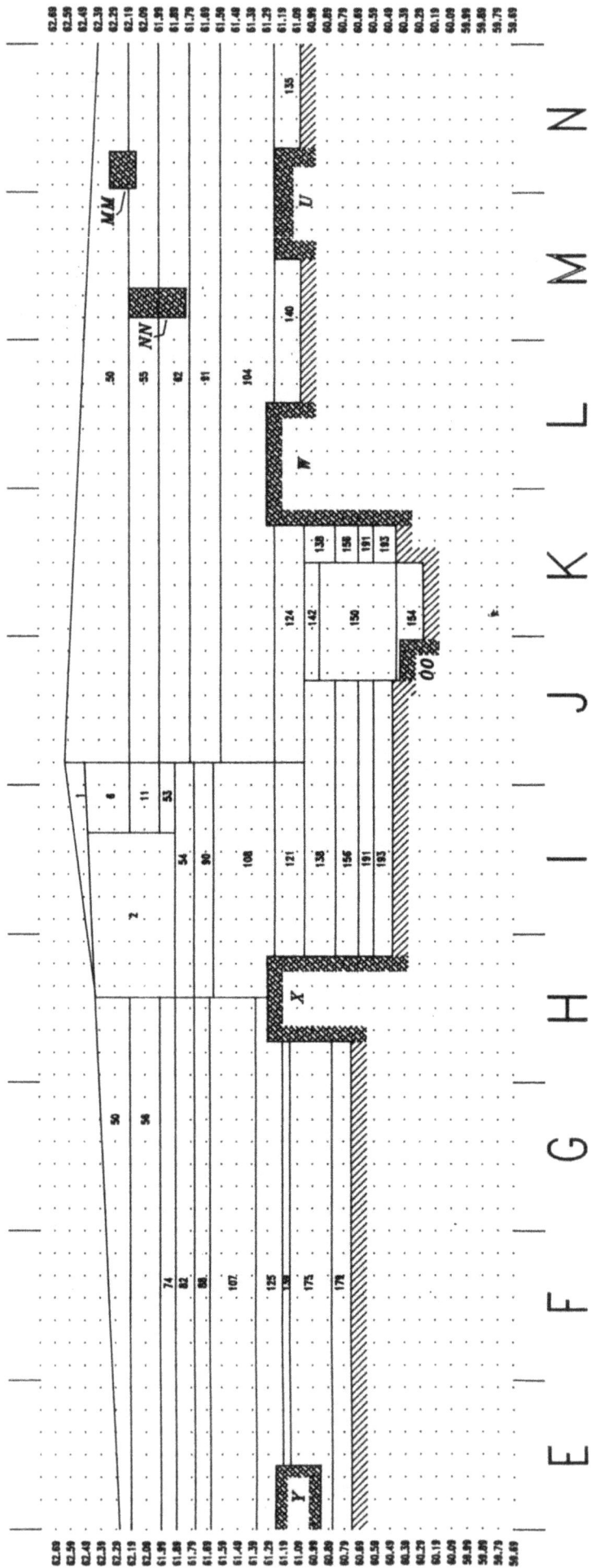

E F G H I J K L M N

Section 4

Chapter 4

SQUARE ONE: ARCHITECTURE

In 1981 Peter Donaldson divided the major architectural features of Sector One into four groups, illustrated here by his Phase Plans. This discussion follows his groupings, although it suggests some changes or uncertainties. Donaldson's Phase Plans do not purport to present an overall history of the site. Later phases of course include more features because the site was most widely excavated at the upper levels. Minor changes occurred continually. The division into "Phases" provides a convenient survey of processes that were continual, rather than sharply separated moments of construction.

The following discussion begins with a summary of the general characteristics of the buildings, sources for interpreting them, and their historical development. A detailed description of the building phases follows. For each phase, description of layout precedes description of individual features. Those descriptions trace the complex, gradual processes of change.

Most of the features described here appear on the appropriate Phase Plan or Plans (pp. 52-53), and on one or more State Plan (pp. 54-56). Level Plans include fewer architectural features, but general references to Level Plans are given for each phase. Fuller references for each locus appear in the Index of Loci (pp. 28-32), and for walls in the Index of Walls (p. 33).

General Characteristics

The remains of at least two buildings were uncovered. As far as excavated, each consists of a single row of rectangular to trapezoidal rooms running roughly southwest to northeast. The buildings stand side by side, so that a long outer wall of one abuts a long outer wall of the other. Each continues laterally outside the excavated area. The building at the Northwest has not been excavated to any great depth. Excavation has been carried deeper in the Southeastern building, and may have revealed its full depth.

The lowest construction traced in that area may belong to a third structure. At the lowest levels of excavation, those summarized in Phase One, we found evidence for a series of storage bins, associated with a few (from one to three) bearing walls. They may belong to a building with a configuration different from the ones found above.

In Phases Two through Four, five major walls, A, B, N/C, D, and E, created a row of three spaces (labeled Rooms 1, 2, and 3) in one building. A fourth room in the row appears in the Phase Three Plan. It may have existed earlier. Excavation in that area stopped at a higher level than in the area of Rooms 2 and 3, two adjacent rooms. By Phase Four, that room had apparently been demolished and alterations also occurred at the opposite end of the building, in the area of Rooms 1 and 2. The second

building was excavated only at this upper level. It can so far be said to consist of two rooms (5 and 6), which have been partially excavated. Traces of structures at either end of these rooms may or may not be continuations of the row.

The walls show great variety in techniques and quality of construction, but the construction of Wall A, described below under Phase Two, is typical for the more substantial walls.

Interpretation

These two rows of spaces belong to two different structures, most probably houses. They conform generally to what we know of Egyptian houses of the Late Antique and early Islamic periods. That knowledge however, indicates so much variety that it provides no certain criteria for identifying houses, still less for filling in gaps in excavated plans.

The major sites at which late Roman houses have been explored are Jēme (Medinet Habu), Elephantine, Karanis and Kom el-Dikka in Alexandria (Hölscher 1934, Grossmann 1980, Husselman 1979, Rodziewicz 1984). These four sites involve three different situations. The houses of Kom el-Dikka come from a well-to-do area of the thoroughly Hellenized city of Alexandria. Karanis was a city in the Fayoum, less sizable and less obviously Hellenized. Jēme and Elephantine on the contrary are both small settlements in the Luxor-Aswan area of Upper Egypt. The house types differ. Since Akhmīm, as a thriving city in Upper Egypt, presents still a fourth situation, its houses need not be expected to follow any of these models.

Husson's survey of terminology applied to Graeco-Roman houses summarizes much of the earlier scholarship based on both literary evidence and archaeology (Husson 1983). Her work indicates the wide range of possible arrangements in the houses of Late Antiquity.

The salient characteristics of the buildings at Akhmīm are (1) a pair of external walls constructed side by side; (2) an open area beside one external wall; (3) small rooms in a row; (4) storage areas inside rooms; and (5) construction using unfired brick on baked brick with intermittent stones.

(1) House walls side by side are the rule in Egyptian cities of this time. The most extensive plans showing many adjacent houses come from Karanis (Husselman 1979).

(2) The open area along the southeast Wall, Wall D, is harder to understand. It could be a street, a vacant lot, or a courtyard. Houses could have their narrow or their long sides fronting a street. Husson discusses the occurrence of vacant lots, with particular reference to Borkowski's evidence from Panopolis (1983, 296-299). If the space belongs to a large courtyard, rooms would once have been

on all sides of it, and the row of rooms we uncovered would be only a small part of the original house. Courtyards are invariable parts of houses, but they can be at the end of a row of rooms or in the middle, and there can be more than one (Husson 1983 47-48; cf. Husselman 1979, 49-54, also Nowicka 1969, 119-121).

(3) At the Northwest there are two adjacent rooms, possibly with two more on either side making a complete sequence of four. At the Southeast there are certainly three, and at one period four rooms in a row. Houses often contain rows of two to three rooms. In the villages of Jēme and Elephantine whole houses consist of such rows. At Karanis, also, most houses are only two to three rooms deep, but they differ from the village houses in that they are normally more than one room broad. Two at least, C45 and C42, have four rooms in a row. Both also exhibit the slanting walls found in Room 4 at Akhmīm. They are much earlier than the Akhmīm building, probably First Century A.C. (Husselman 1979, 11). At Alexandria, House B is four rooms long (Rodziewicz 1984, 128).

One space in the southeastern row might be a courtyard. Because of the arrangement of amphorae and the

nature of the flooring, the excavator suggested that Room 4 in the Southeastern building might be an open courtyard. Husson's research shows that houses could have more than one courtyard, so it is not impossible that this was a courtyard and that there was also a large central court as mentioned above.

Husson remarks that measurements given in documents suggest rectangular buildings with regular outlines, but that archaeological evidence indicates greater irregularity (1983, 172). At Karanis the latest, i.e., Fourth to Fifth Century Roman houses were more irregular in layout than earlier ones (Husselman 1979, 26). At Akhmim, the two outer walls of Rooms 3 and 2 run roughly parallel to each other, but show unevenness caused by slippage and rebuilding. Cross wall B runs almost perpendicular to the outer walls, but cross walls E and C, roughly parallel to each other, are not parallel to Wall B. Walls F and G create still greater deviation, but probably not a significant one.

The room sizes here are small, but not unusually so:

Comparison of room sizes and wall thicknesses: [47]

	room area in m^2	wall thickness
Akhmīm	11.5, 10.0	0.7 to 0.6
Elephantine[48]	11.7, 13.3. (Largest 17.6, smallest 9.2)	0.5 to 0.8
Karanis[49]	6.1, 13.4, 7.0, 3.1	0.7 to 0.6
Abu Menas[50]c (medieval)	7.7 to 19.4 (courtyards 68.5, 54.1)	0.6 to 0.7
Mārî Ġirǧis[51] (modern)	largest 17.2, smallest 3.4 most 6 to 10	0.25

[47]These measurements have been calculated approximately from published drawings. At Akhmīm measurements are given only for Rooms 2 and 3, the only ones where all four walls are present. The rooms of House B at Alexandria are 13 to 14 meters square (Rodziewicz 1984, 128). Nowicka emphasizes the range in room size in Greco-Roman houses, and lists dimensions (1969, 115).

[48]Grossmann 1980: all rooms on fig. 5 p. 50.

[49]Husselman c.1979: ground floor of house C 50/C51, Plan 31.

[50]Grossmann and Košciuk 1991: fig. 3, p. 75 .

[51]Henein 1988: ground floor of house fig. 8, p. 21.

Husson stresses the flexibility of room use. She questions that there were many specialized rooms. She specifically rules out interior kitchens, saying that their presence in monastic dwellings differs from domestic custom (Husson 1983, 161-2). Normally she suggests that people cooked, slept, and worked in the same spaces. Ash had been deposited in the habitation levels of Room 3, and isolated cooking pots were set into floors there and in Room 2.[52] No extensive hearths or ovens were found, perhaps because the whole building has not been excavated, or because rebuilding destroyed them.

There is no indication of an outer entrance. Husson believes that a house would typically have only one, which might be on either the long or the narrow side. She bases her argument partly on evidence from the Panopolis register that Borkowski had interpreted differently.[53]

Two features that are common in other excavated houses of Egypt are missing here. One is wall niches for storage. Probably the surviving walls do not rise high enough above the higher floor levels in the rooms for niches to survive. The second missing feature is a staircase. The walls are certainly thick enough to support upper storeys (see comparative chart below) and according to all comparative evidence at least one additional floor would have existed. The lack of stairs may indicate that the whole range of rooms in the houses has not been traced. Stairs could be in a front room, or in a central room. The spur wall in Room 3 is of the type used to support stairs, so it is possible that a stair might have stood there and been demolished.

(4) These rooms include two kinds of storage spaces: bins, and rows of pottery. The bins can be paralleled at Karanis in courtyards, and interior rooms (Husselman 1979, 49-53, 67-73). Husselman mentions vaulted underground rooms for storage, also found elsewhere. One room at Karanis was originally at ground level, but when the rising ground level caused it to become subterranean it was equipped with storage bins. We have no way of judging the relationship of the rooms with storage bins to a contemporary ground level. Husson has listed many words for storage, and emphasized the many different things that might be stored in houses, and the many possible arrangements (1983, passim).

(5) Alexandria, unlike the other sites, used stone extensively for domestic architecture. At all other sites, brick is used, and it is unbaked, as indicated by excavation and confirmed by Husson. What is unusual at Akhmīm is the amount of baked brick. It seems to be used as foundation for unbaked brick, even when walls are being renewed, so that the baked brick itself is placed on earlier courses of unbaked brick.

In the baked brick construction of the houses in Square One, two rows of stretchers alternate with single rows of headers (see p. 49; figs. p. 57).[54] Rodziewicz has pointed to similarities between this construction and that found in the final phase of the baths at Kom el-Dikka, dated to the first half of the Seventh Century (unpublished report, 1989). Alternating single courses of headers and stretchers can be found in the unbaked brick construction at Karanis, (e.g., the earlier Roman bins Husselman 1979 pl. 81.): Similar bonds occur in recently excavated outlying buildings of the White Monastery, and in one place at Fustat (White Monastery, personal observation, March 1992; Fustat, Gayraud 1986: fig. 7).

The unbaked brick at Akhmīm is usually laid in courses of stretchers (approximating Spencer's A5 and A8, Spencer 1979, pls. 3-4). In some courses, headers and stretchers may alternate. At Karanis and at Elephantine, courses of headers alternated with stretchers (Husselman 1979, 26; Grossmann 1980, 71).

Isolated blocks of stone are incorporated in walls in a seemingly random fashion. This casual placement of stone blocks in the brick courses can be paralleled elsewhere.

History

The major developments are, first, the long period of continual reworking the same buildings, sometimes slight, sometimes greater, and second, the complete obliteration of the buildings by debris dumping, probably as a prelude to reuse of the site (see above, p. 26).

Continual reworking can be seen also in houses of Akhmīm the present day. Husson alludes to it when she suggests that it may be impossible to determine how many storeys a house has because of the continual adding, or when she questions the attributions of specific rooms for specific purposes. Papyri seldom refer to new houses, probably because houses remain in good condition only a short time. References to old houses occur frequently, as do references to dilapidated and ruined houses (Husson 1983, 249-250; see also Goitein 1983, 21-24).

From the Genizeh documents it seems that in post-conquest times "buildings were planned so that they could be expanded, or that a smaller house could be erected adjacent to a larger one" (Goitein 1983, 77), Goitein thinks these alterations were for the use of extended families or rental, both of which appear as important considerations in the Roman documents cited by Husson (1983, passim).

We have little information about the extent of time a house could be inhabited. Some houses at Karanis survived through several phases of the city's life, while

---

[52] Ivančica Schrunk has noted high concentrations of cooking and storage wares in Locus 81 in Room 1, and Locus 12 in Room 2. These concentrations are not cited here as indications of room use, because these loci have been considered to belong to the post-habitation filling in of the rooms.

[53] He noted that multiple doors existed, but she takes the rare mentions to indicate they were exceptions that had to be noted Husson 1983, 100-103.

---

[54] The bricks vary slightly in size. The relationship between headers and stretchers varies, partly because they were not laid in a clear pattern and partly because of their varying sizes, but the bond approximates Spencer's C3 (1979, pl. 11).

others lasted only a generation or so. Documents from the Genizeh speak of houses over a century old, and imply still greater age (Goitein 1983, 97-100). These houses at Akhmīm seem to have been in use before the Arabic invasion, and to have been repaired in the early post-conquest period. The evidence of coins, and preliminary study of the glazed wares, suggests that they may have gone out of use before the Fatamid period. The loci that appear to have been dumped in to fill the abandoned structures are the first loci that contain statistically significant amounts of glazed wares (see below).

Husson cites references to houses that collapsed or were in ruins. Not much building debris was found in these rooms. Probably the houses were partly demolished. Then the area was filled in by deliberate dumping, probably during the Fatamid period (see above p.25: Study of the glazed ware will be necessary to provide better dates). Some construction took place above the dumping, but the fragmentary remains do not permit identification.

In both Roman and Islamic times, new houses were frequently built above those that had been ruined or demolished (Goitein 1983, 22; Husson 1983, 198).

The reason for the demolition and rebuilding on this site may have desire for newer housing, or for a different use of the space (not for housing). Although the pottery evidence mentioned above suggests that the demolition occurred at the same time that new types of tablewares were becoming common, the motive for the demolition was probably not a desire to rebuild to suit a different style of living introduced by arabization.

Arabization did not require a new house type. As far as one can judge from the Genizeh documents, the post-conquest houses of early Cairo were very similar to late Roman houses. Goitein points to the use of Greek terms in early Islamic times, and considers that a new house type only developed "in the thirteenth century or later" (1983, 48-49). Pottery evidence places the latest levels in Square One before that date. Apparently houses in post-conquest Cairo had kitchens, which may have been a change from Roman custom (see above). Otherwise, Goitein, like Husson, stresses flexibility in room use. Flexibility increased after the conquest when the use of furniture declined. The only new ingredient of a house plan until the thirteenth century was a large reception hall. The triclinium seems to have been the standard in Roman houses of any pretensions, so a reception hall would have involved only a slight change in function rather than plan.

Detailed Description
Phase One (includes all features on Level Plan 9 and a few on Level Plan 8).

The walls shown on the plan labeled Phase One represent the lowest structures uncovered on the site. None of this construction was excavated completely. Its assignment to one phase rests on similarities first in construction and probable function and, second, in the contents of associated loci. Most of the "walls" assigned to this phase are two to three bricks wide: thin, nonbearing construction. The loci between and immediately above them stand out from higher loci because of the minimal

presence of glazed or Aswan painted pottery. This peculiarity may relate to the function or to the date of the spaces.

The size of most Phase One walls, and of the spaces they define, indicates that they created divisions within rooms, probably for storage. The construction resembles that of storage bins at Karanis (Husselman 1979, 49–51, Pls. 80–81), where bins could occur singly or in combination in rooms or, more commonly, in courtyards. Literary sources indicate the wide variety of materials that could be sored in variousplaces in houses (Husson 1983, passim).

These walls appear under the later Rooms 2, 3, and 5 in the two areas where excavation was carried to the deepest levels, namely Grids IC/2–6 and Grids JL/3–8. Walls H, V, and OO are in the former area (State Plan 2), walls I, M, S, P, O, Z and N in the second (State Plan 1).

Walls H, V, and OO are fired brick, two to three bricks wide. The excavator thought that they antedated the building of Walls A and B, and that OO was the continuation of V, so that they had to belong to a space with a different shape. Another scholar thinks that on the contrary, H and V were under an early floor of Room 2. An early wall under Wall B, and the associated Wall K, represents later developments in this area that could be assigned to either Phase One or Two.

All the remains assigned to Phase One in the second area, Grid DH/1–6, are higher than Walls V, H, and OO, but resemble them in construction and in the associated pottery. The second group of walls can be divided into three subgroups: first Wall O, isolated; then Walls I, L, M, S, and P, clearly related, possibly also related to Wall Z (132, Grid DE/6); finally Walls FF, GG, and HH (on State Plan 3, not the Phase One Plan), still more rudimentary, intervening before the massive reorganization of Phase Two.

Wall O (171) in Grid FG/3 is the deepest. It is an isolated line of mud brick headers. At a higher level two long parallel walls, N and S, form a network with four short walls, I and L, which run parallel to each other in Grids FG/5 and 6, and M and P, which run parallel to each other in Grids GH/4–5. A slanting floor, 192, lay between P, S, and M. and marked the limit of excavation in that space. Wall Z may represent a continuation of Wall I.

Debris in the "bins" created by these walls, i.e., three loci, 159, 161, and 168, had no glazed or Aswan painted wares, both of which become plentiful in the level (Loci 100, 173, and 176) above these walls.

Wall N has not been fully revealed, but it is apparently wider than the others and may have been a bearing wall. Another bearing Wall, Wall D, may also have already existed at right angles to Wall N.

Structures omitted on Phase Plan One but shown on State Plan 3 indicate some activity intermediary between the dismantling of the storage bins and the construction of the major system of large walls. Their demolition seems to have occurred as glazed ware became plentiful.

Phase Two (includes some features on Level Plan 8).

Most of the major system of walls defining one building was in existence by the beginning of this phase. In addition to N, surviving from Phase One, this system consists of Walls A and associated construction, B, D, and E (State Plan 1). They define three rooms (1, 2, 3). A fourth room may have existed (see Wall II below). There are two doorways in the northwestern side Room 3, linking it to the possible fourth room, and to Room 2. There were indications of several stages of flooring, particularly of a tile floor in Room 2. Smaller walls include a spur wall in Room 3, possibly once supporting a stair.

The stretch of Wall A in HL, bordering Room 2 and excavated as Loci 10 and 66, is the best preserved and most fully excavated (elevation p. 57). It probably represents a relatively unified process of construction. Its general pattern reappears, less well preserved, in other walls of this area: a sturdy but irregular foundation of fired brick supports upper courses of mud brick that incorporate pieces of fired brick and stone. Sometimes those pieces seem to have been inserted at random, sometimes as facing or repairs. The fired brick construction consists of two courses of stretchers alternating with one course of headers, a pattern recurring in other walls of the site.

The first remains of a floor are Locus 153, consisting of a white surface over tiles. They probably form part of the same floor as 157, a patch of tiles at 60.76 to 60.68 m ASL (Grid JK/5).

The fourth side of Room 2 is formed by Wall D (96, Grid FL/2–3), which continues to form one side of Room 3. It abuts fired brick courses of Wall B and continues on past Wall E. In Room 2, brick and stone course face the mud brick wall. The facing is mostly limestone blocks with bricks above, and the facing is set into mud brick. West of junction with Wall N there are two courses (one stretcher over one header) facing the mud brick on the interior of Room 3.

On the opposite side of Room 3, Wall J (188, Grid FH/6–7) continues the alignment of Wall A. Two courses of brick were exposed, the lower one entirely fired brick, the upper course partly fired and partly mud brick. The wall is under Wall CC (162) of Phase Three, and over S (169) and I (184) of Phase one.

Wall E (130, Grid EF/2–5) runs between Walls J and D. It was clipped by a temporary balk. It consists of mud brick faced with fired brick at the northwest end. There was a doorway in the north end, the form of which becomes clearer in the succeeding phase. The southeast face exposed at its junction with Wall D has one course of fired brick headers at the bottom.

From Wall E a short spur extends into Room 3: Wall R (80, Grid FG/4–5). Five courses of mud brick began at 61.52 m ASL, the upper course being fired brick on the northwest edge. After drying, lower courses could be seen, possibly extending to the same depth as Wall E.

A final feature attributed to this phase lies farther west: Wall II (147, Grid BC/1–3). Consisting of mud brick faced with fired brick, it ran under Wall F and into the balk. The alignment was similar to, but not, as might appear from State Plan 1, the same as that of later Wall F. The short length that was exposed did not suffice to indicate whether it had the same function as that later wall, namely to bound a fourth room in the row.

Wall T (136, Grid MO/7) seems to be the continuation of Wall A, although displaced slightly to one side. It appeared under Wall Q (Phase Four), forming the division between Room 1 and the North Area, and continuing down to 60.80 m ASL, the end of excavation in that area.

Phase Three (includes some features on Level Plan 8).

In this phase some rebuilding occurred around Room 3, and Room 4 was added (or reshaped, see Wall II above). On the edges of Room 3, Wall C replaced Wall N, and Wall CC (162) was built on top of Wall J. The door between Rooms 2 and 3 was rebuilt, with steps going down into Room 2. A door opposite it connected Room 3 with Room 4. New floors were laid in Rooms 2 and 3.

Walls G and F created Room 4, with a rough flooring and with rows of pots set into its floor.

Between Rooms 2 and 3 a new wall was built over Wall N on a slightly different alignment. The top preserved course of Wall C was at 61.14–15 m ASL. The wall (84, Grid HI/3–6) runs from Wall D to a doorway beside Wall A. At the door, steps led down from Room 3 into Room 2. At the doorway fired bricks formed the full width of the wall, but elsewhere fired bricks and mud formed an intermittent facing for a mud brick core. The construction of this wall presumably went together with the construction of floor 92 in Room 2. The wall later partly collapsed into the area of Room 2 from which floor 92 had been robbed.

Wall CC (162, Grid EH/6–7) is the southern line of bricks over Wall J, a line incorporating a column fragment. (The northern wall segment, KK, is a rebuilding in Phase Four.) Wall CC forms a corner with Wall E in which there was a doorway, but is not aligned with the edge of floor 79/102. The wall incorporates small limestone blocks. It continues westward alongside Y (163, Grid DE/7–8).

The heavy plastering of Walls A and B in Room 2 may belong to this phase. It consists of mortar over the wall surfaces, the mud brick courses, then a dark brown layer, a thin white layer, a slight sandy layer, and another white layer. These layers probably represent two phases of plastering, both of which continued without interruption around the corner of the two walls. At a lower level, only a simpler covering of one to two layers of dark brown mud plaster survives.

Several floors may belong to this period. In Room 2, floor 92 survives along the east side. Thirteen rows of tiles fill the space between Walls B, C, and D. At present, the longest row consists of five tiles (0.39 x 0.24 m). In the corner of Walls B and D the floor was at 61.09, slanting down to 61.05 m ASL toward the center.

In Room 3 scattered remains of one or more floors existed on the West (State Plan 4, p. 56). In 1978 a floor of very friable tiles was discovered beside Wall C at 61.36 m ASL. This floor was at the level of the doorway and top of the steps leading down into Room 2. In 1980, more tiles were discovered (Locus 102), adjoining an area of packed earth (Locus 79), probably where tiles had been robbed. The tiles measure 0.39 x 0.24 m. These traces of floor now exist only between the two doorways.

Two walls were built adding a fourth space at an angle to the other rooms. Walls G and F are bonded construction, roughly built of fired bricks incorporating limestone blocks. Wall G (117) was found at 61.93 m ASL. About eight courses survive. Wall F (131, Grid BC/1–4) is the return of Wall G forming the end of the room. It runs above the approximate line of an earlier mud brick wall with a partial fired brick facing, Wall II (147, Phase Two). A bench-like structure of limestone blocks was built into the base of this wall, inside room 4 and out over floor 129.

This floor, a rough discontinuous surface of fired brick, extends over the southeastern part of the room or courtyard, an area cut by two rows of pots. One of these rows, AA (127), consists of 13 pot bases, some of them containing other bases, so broken intentionally in antiquity, possibly to make storage containers and ladles for their contents.[55] The bases form a slightly curved line from Wall F in Grid C/3–4 to Wall E in F/4. Pieces of broken fired brick are packed around each pot. Two bricks, one above the other, may be the remains of a line of bricks running along the pots. A second row, BB (128, Grid EF/2–3), consists of six pot bases forming a right angle in the corner of the room. Wall G overhangs one of these pot bases by about 0.70 m, suggesting that it was built after they were in place, but this effect may be due to slippage. Walls, pots, and flooring seem to constitute one unified building activity. They also mark the limits of excavation in Room 4.

East of Wall D a feature called Wall RR (113, Grid JL/1–2) appeared at 61.08 m ASL. It is a line of red bricks with random brick rubble behind. Too little was exposed to show its function, and it is being assigned to this phase only because it is on the same approximate level as the floor in Room 3.

Phase Four (includes most of the features in Level Plan 6, and all those in Level Plans 5 to 1).

Rooms 1, 2 and 3 bounded by Walls A, B, C, D, and E all continue. Walls F and G were not preserved at

---

[55]The long rows of open vessels (in this case, closed vessels that have been cut to make them open) are reminiscent of the dyer's establishment excavated by Petrie at Athribis (Wypszecka 1965 fig. 3 p. 147). Wypszecka considers the question of whether dyeing could be carried out on a small scale in houses (1965, 150), and it is tempting to think that might have been the case here. However, while another of the furnishings, a bench, was present, but no trace was found of a well, a cistern, or an area for heating water, all of which would be necessary.

this height. (D survives to this height only in a few places.) A continuation of Wall A replaced Wall CC. The doorways between Room 3 and the adjacent spaces (Room 2 on one side, the space where Room 4 had been on the other side), were raised to a higher level.

A second building consisting of Walls JJ, X, W, and U (State Plan 1, p. 54) existed alongside the building traced in Phases Two and Three.

A number of other features discussed in this phase were small and isolated, making it hard to decide whether they represent remodelings of the two buildings, or replacements.

At 61.70 m ASL in Grid J/2 there was a two course wall, Wall EE, on the line of Wall D but separated from it by Loci 70, 72, 83, and 87.

A new stretch of Wall A was built in FH/6–7 over wall CC. It consisted primarily of mud brick courses, at least in part built continuously with the upper courses of Wall A in Grid HL. An apparent short return on the line of Wall C, reshaping the doorway there, was probably debris. West of the doorway this wall was removed as Locus 152 to expose the walls beneath. Wall KK (160, Grid FG/8) is probably a separate phase in the construction of Wall A. Five courses of fired brick and five small limestone blocks begin at 61.58 and continue to 61.18 m ASL. The lower courses are aligned with the facing bricks of Wall JJ, and may face a westward continuation of that wall, with the upper courses added as a later repair.[6]

Two other changes to the first building should probably be placed in this phase, although the excavator placed them in Phase Three. They are the "blockings" of the doorways linking Room 3 to the spaces on either side. These fillings are less likely to be intended to close the access route than to raise the thresholds to a new height, and therefore belong to the later period. The blocking of the doorway in Wall E contained a Corinthian capital of Late Coptic design. (If the construction does belong to Phase Three, this capital could be associated with the fragment of column shaft built into Wall CC as evidence of the same demolition.)

West of Wall A, Wall Y projects from the balk at 61.26–60.95 m ASL. There are four courses on the exposed face, alternately headers and stretchers. No relationship to Wall CC is obvious: the gray lenses of Locus 175 run up to the lower three courses (Wall CC, on the other hand, is above the gray clay).

Wall JJ (133, Grid IL/7–8) was recognized at 61.28 m. Built of mud brick with traces of fired brick facing at the West and where it joins Wall X, it runs parallel to and abutting Wall A and has returns. Wall X (126, Grid HI/8–9) between Rooms 5 and 6 was recognized at 61.03 but could be traced to 60.30 in the balk. It was built of mud brick with fired brick facings and had limestone incorporated in the core. Wall W (134, Grid KM/7–9), forming one end of Room 5, was recognized at 61.18 but seen at 61.68 in the balk, and not excavated in depth. The west side seems to have been buttressed. Wall U (137, Grid MN/7–9) under Locus 118 at 61.22 m ASL divides the North Area into two parts. It seems to be a mud brick return for the extension of Wall A into this area. It was not excavated in depth.

Three small features in the North Area seem unrelated to this wall, which they overlap (State Plan 5, p. 56). Possibly they relate to the latest stage of Wall A in depth. They may be the remains of two walls and a floor or debris. Wall MM (76, Grid MN/8–9) survived from 62.31–62.15 m ASL as two courses of fired brick and one stone. The Wall projects from the side of the trench. Wall NN (77, Grid M/7–8) consisted of four slightly curved courses of fired brick parallel to Wall MM (76) and between 62.19 and 62.15 m ASL. East of these two walls

was a line of five fired bricks at 62.28 m ASL and then an irregular spread of fired bricks with an irregular surface averaging 62.35 m ASL (75, Grid NO/7–8), possibly a floor or more probably debris.

Part at least of the Wall T extension of Wall A had been demolished by the time these features were built, but they seem to relate to the core of the wall, and to be contemporary with Wall Q, which may be remodeling of Wall A. Wall Q (51, Grid NO/6) was separated from Wall A by c. 0.30 m of fill except at the balk where a few bricks continued down to the top of Wall T. Wall Q first appeared in Locus 58 at about 62.00 m ASL.

BIBLIOGRAPHY

Gayraud, Roland-Pierre, Sopjia Björnesiö and Sylvie Denoix. 1986. "Iṣṭabl 'Antar (Fostat) 1985. Rapport de Fouilles. *Annales Islamologiques*. 22: 1-11.

Goitein, Solomon D. 1983. *A Mediterranean society: the Jewish Communities of the Arab World as Portrayed in the documents of the Cairo Geniza.* IV Berkeley: University of Californai Press. 47-82.

Grossmann, Peter. 1980. *Elephantine II. Kirche und spätantike Hausanlagen in Chnumtempelhof: Beschreibung und Typologische Untersuchung.* Mainz a R: Philipp von Zabern.

Grossmann, Peter and Jacek Kościuk. 1991. "Report on the Excavation at Abu Mina in Autumn 1989." *Bulletin de la Société d'Arche'ologie Copte* 333: 69-75.

Henein, Nessim Henry. 1988. *Mārī Girgis: Village de Haute-Egypte.* Cairo: IFAO.

Hölscher, U. 1934. *Excavations at Medinet Habu* I. Chicago: University Press.

Husselman, Elinor Millett. 1979. *Karanis: Excavations of the University of Michigan in Egypt, 1928–1935:* *Topography and architecture.* Ann Arbor: University of Michigan Press.

Husson, Genevieve. 1983. *Oikia: le vocabulaire de la maison privée en Égypte d'après les papyrus grecs.* Paris: Publications de la Sorbonne.

Luckhard, Fritz. 1914. *Das Privathaus im Ptolemäischen und Römischen Ägypten.* Giessen: Otto Kindt.

Nowicka, Maria. 1969. *La maison privée dans l'Égypte ptolémaïque.* Warsaw: Zakład Narodowy Imienia Ossoliñskich Wydawnictwoskiej Akademii Nauk.

Maehler, Herwig. 1983. "Häuser und ihre Bewohner im Fayûm in der Kaiserzeit." *Das Römische-Byzantinische Ägypten: Akten des internationaled Symposions 26–30. September 1978 in Trier* 119–37. Mainz: P von Zabern.

Rodziewicz, Mieczyslaw. 1984. *Alexandrie III. Les habitations romaines tardives d'Alexandria: à la lumière des fouilles polonaises à Kôm el-Dikka.* Warsaw: Centre d'Archéologie Méditerranéene de l'Académie Polonaise des Science.

Spencer, A.J. 1979. *Brick Architecture in Ancient Egypt.* Warminster: Aris and Phillips Ltd.

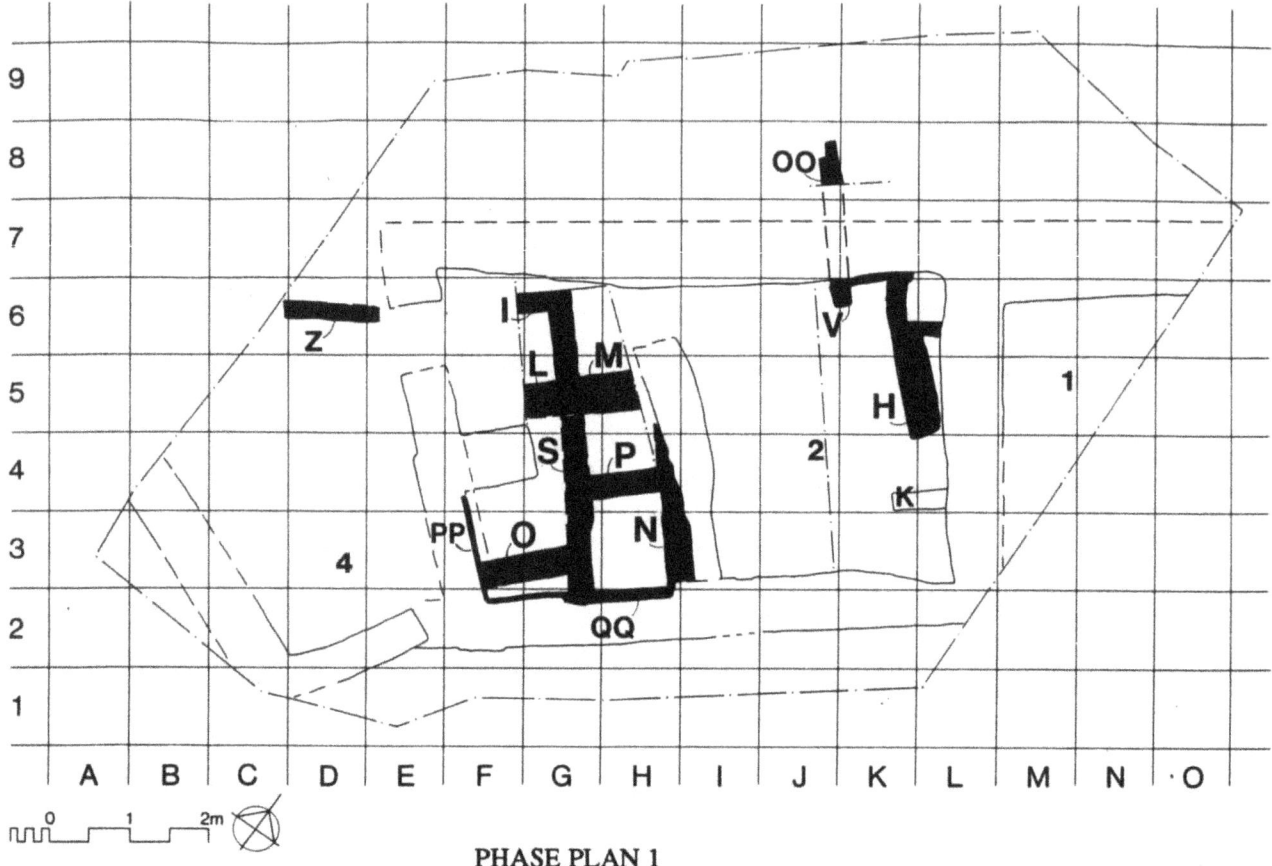

PHASE PLAN 1

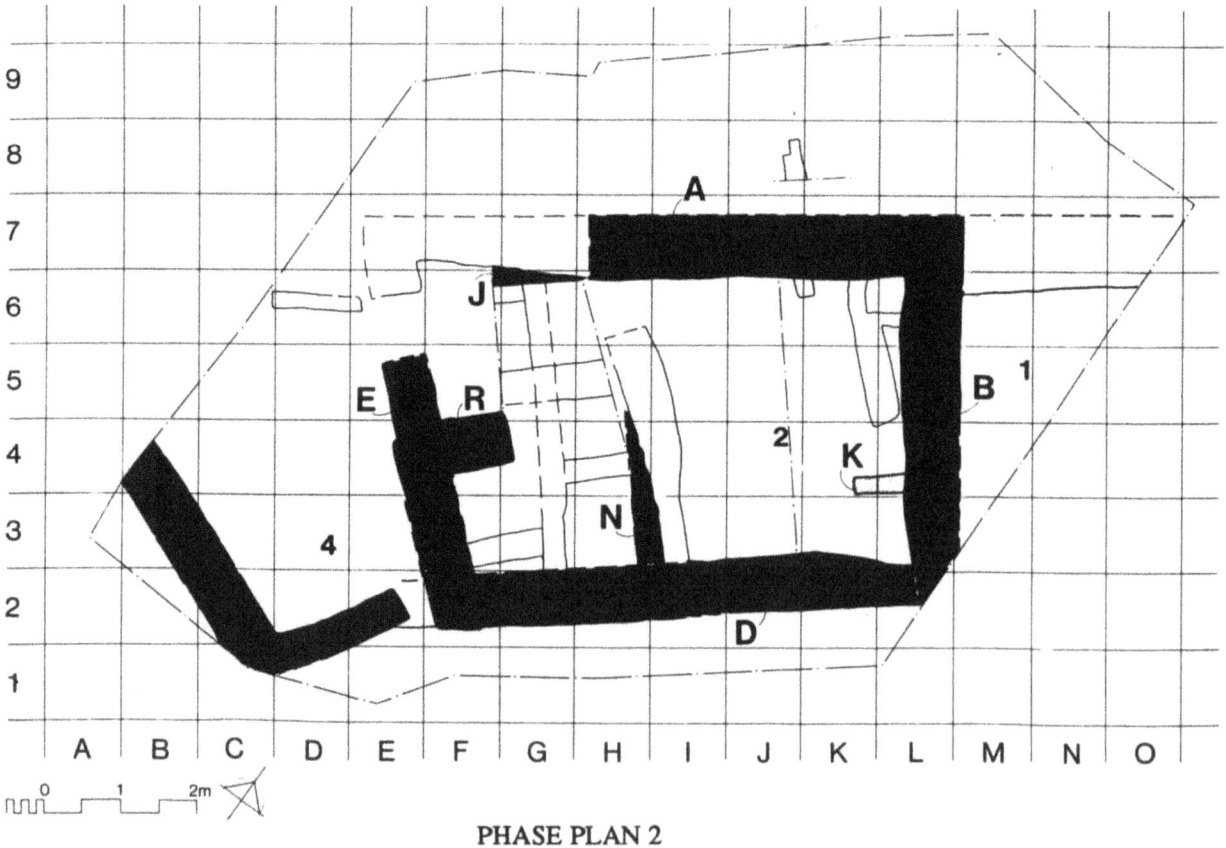

PHASE PLAN 2

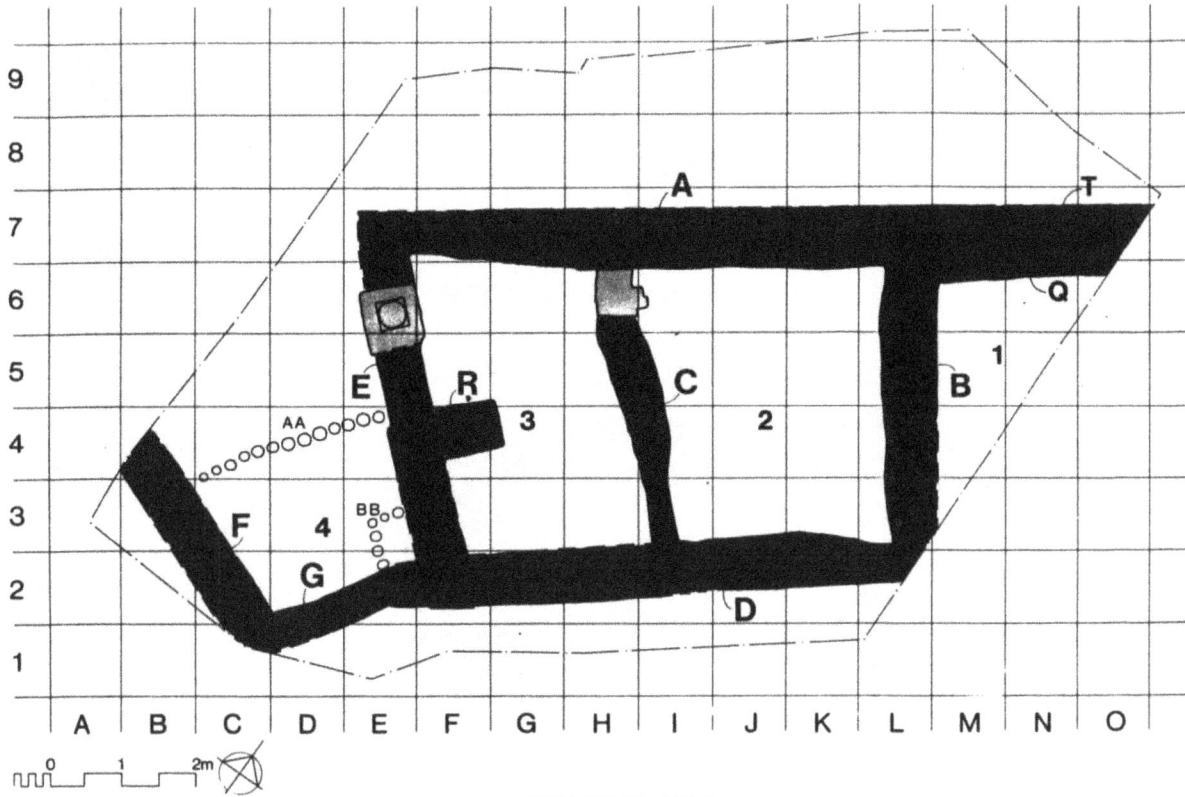

PHASE PLAN 3

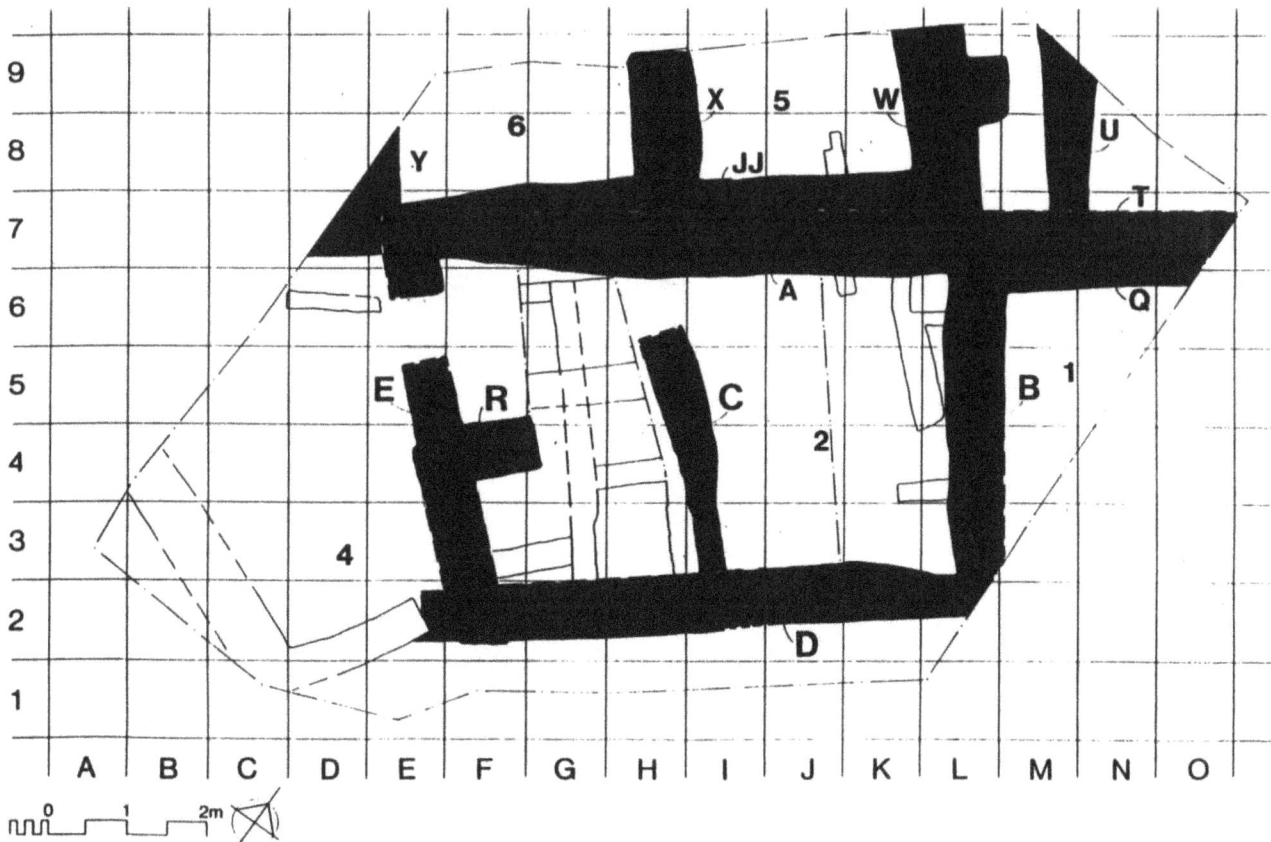

PHASE PLAN 4

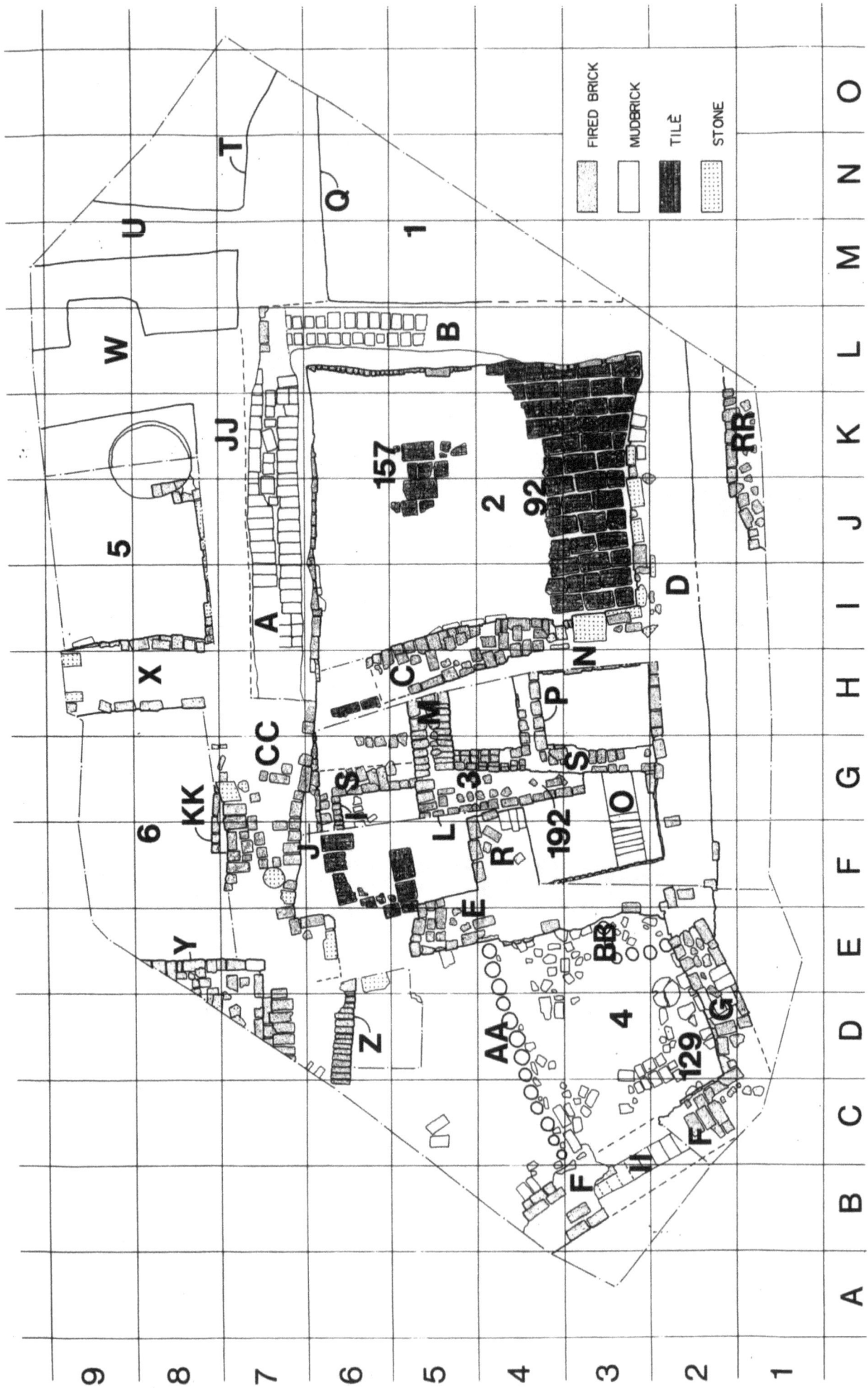

State Plan 1

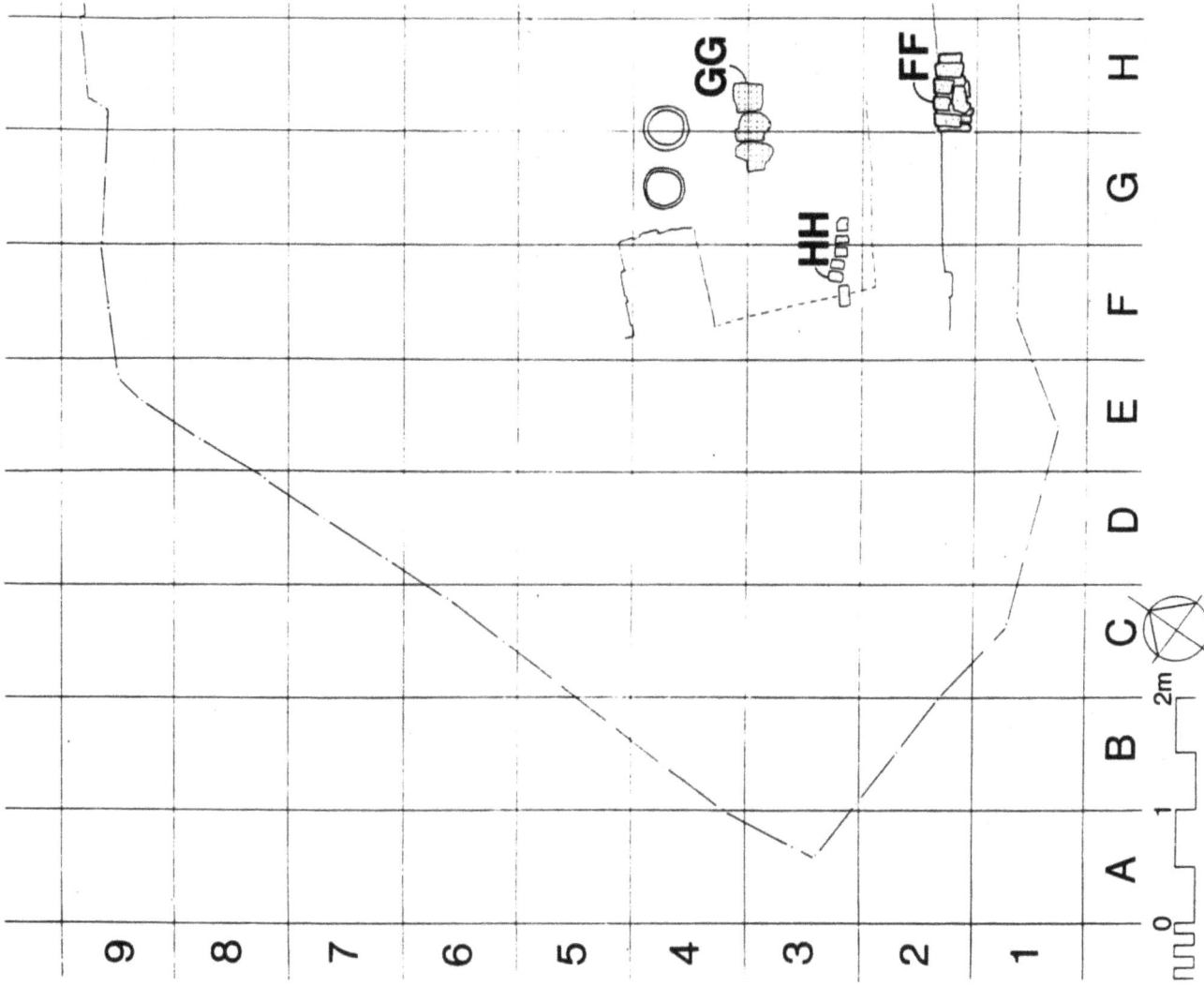

State Plan 3

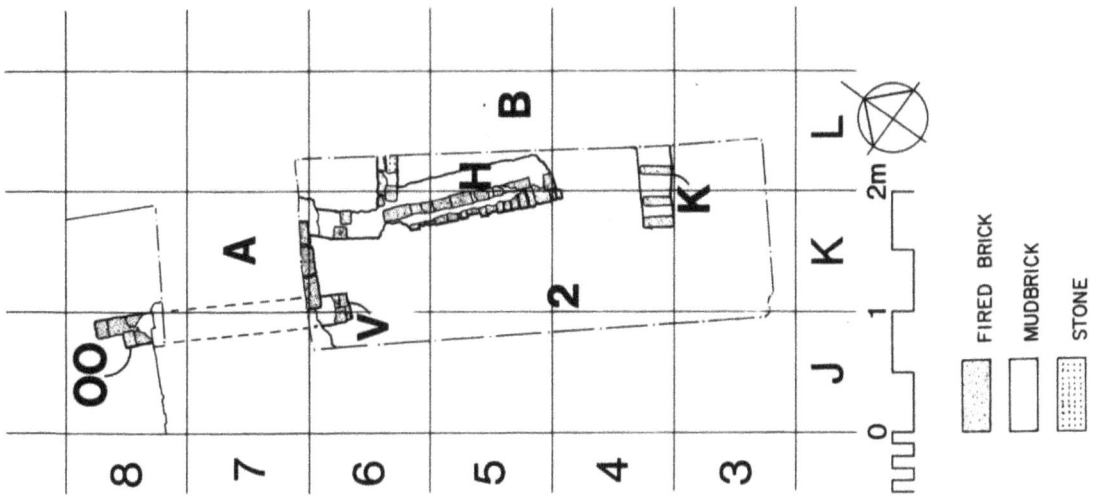

State Plan 2

FIRED BRICK
MUDBRICK
STONE

55

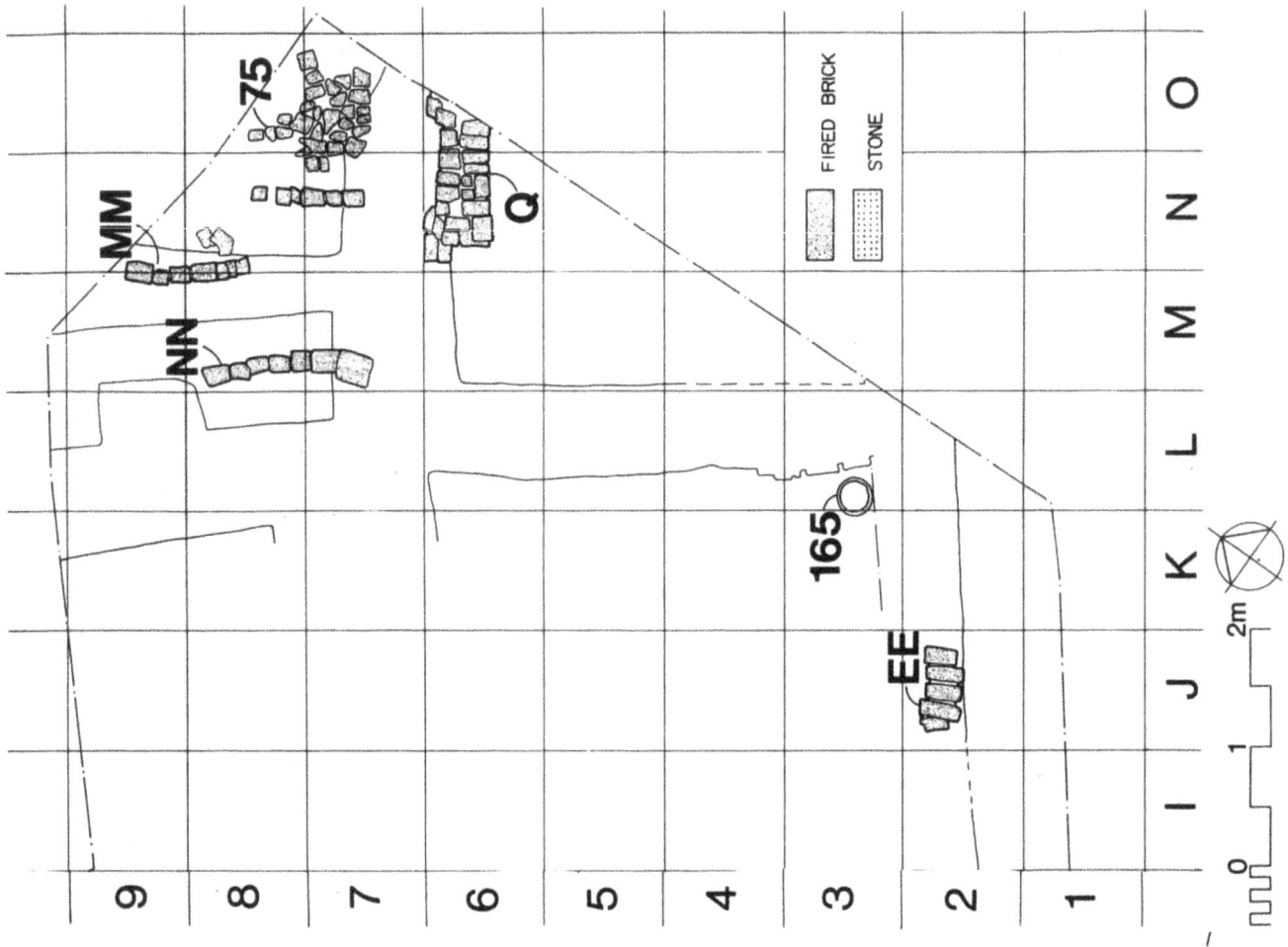

State Plan 5

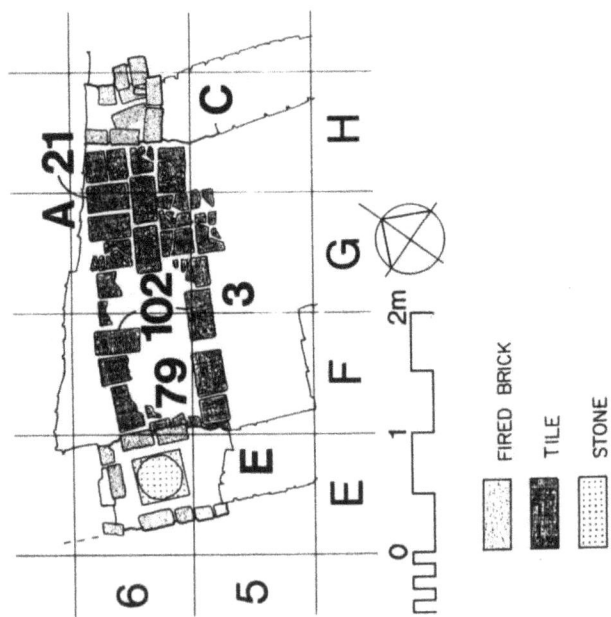

State Plan 4

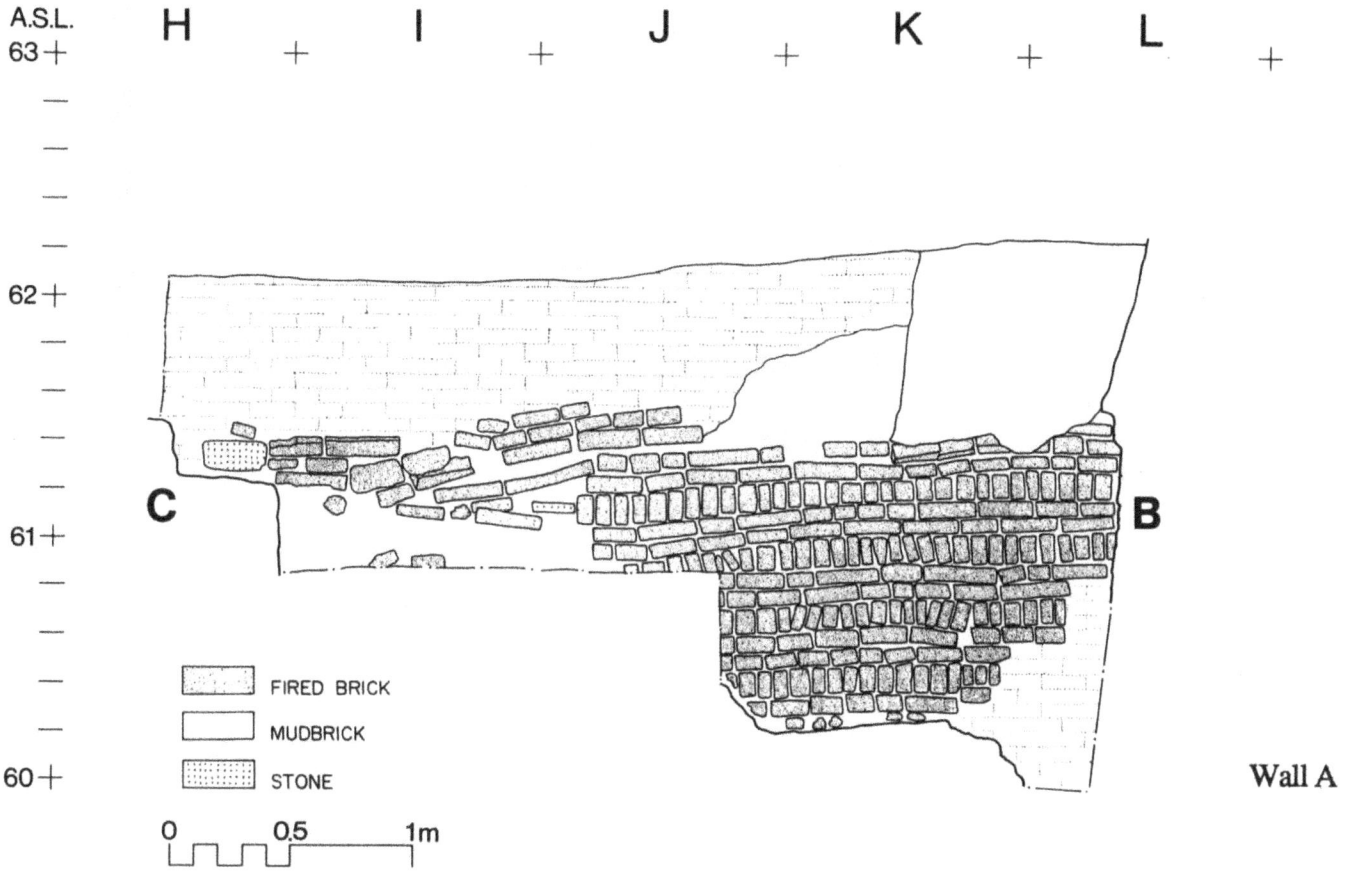

A.S.L.
63 +   H   +   I   +   J   +   K   +   L   +

62 +

C   B

61 +

FIRED BRICK

MUDBRICK

STONE

60 +

Wall A

0   0.5   1m

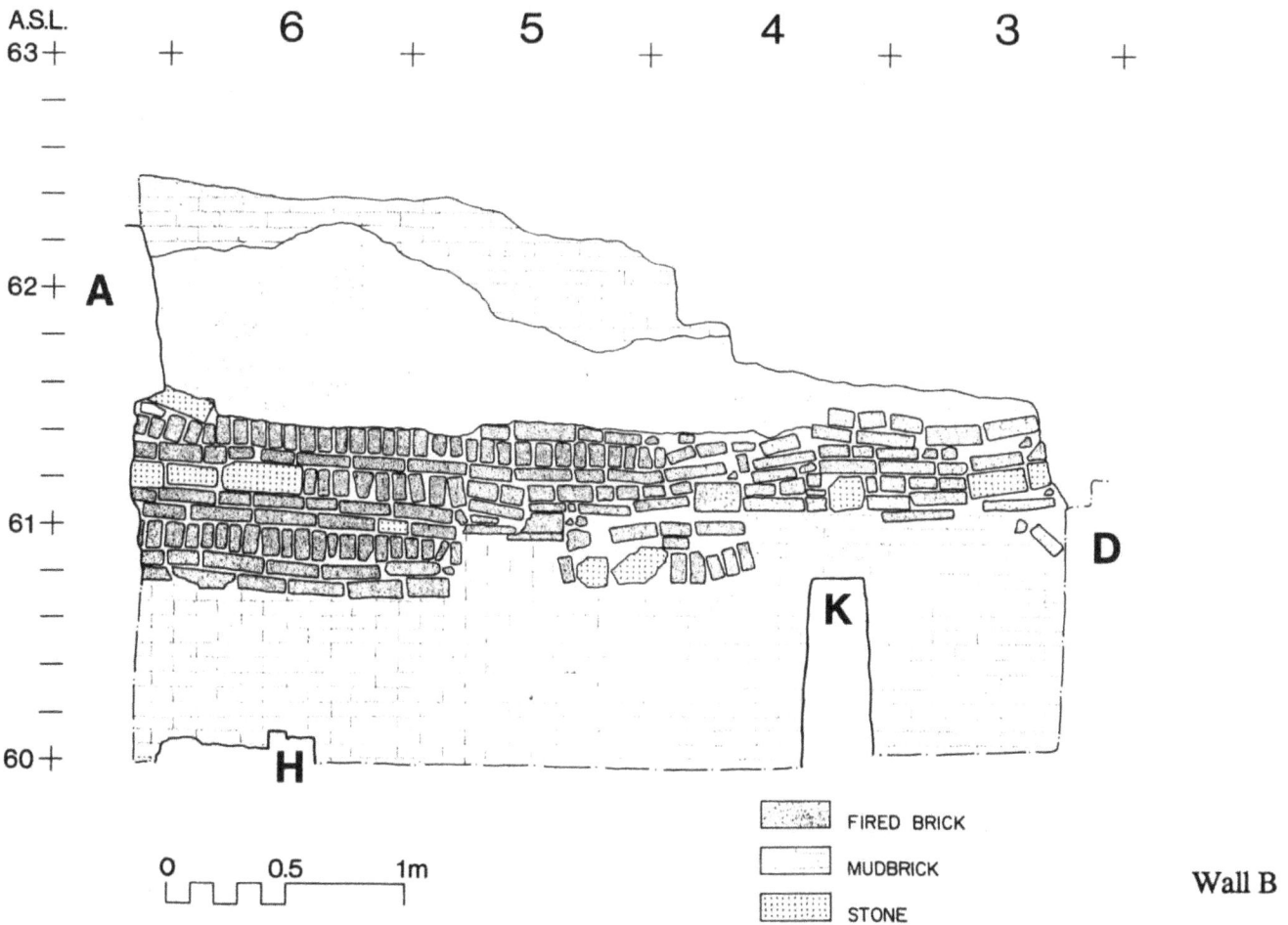

A.S.L.
63 +   +   6   +   5   +   4   +   3   +

62 + A

61 +   D

K

60 +   H

FIRED BRICK

MUDBRICK

STONE

Wall B

0   0.5   1m

57

Chapter 5

SQUARE TWO: EXCAVATION

(For complete listing of loci with references to illustrations and further discussion, see the Index of Loci, pp. 62-63. The Matrix, p. 34, shows the sequences of all loci except walls, graves and the conduit: Unlike the Matrix for Square One, it is not to scale. The chart on p.65, indicates the assignment of loci to phases of activity. The Level Plans, pp. 66-67, present the positions and sequences of levels, schematically: They do not accurately indicate the top and bottom of individual levels.)

Square Two was laid out on the upper level of the churchyard. Its history can be divided into five phases, differing greatly in probable duration. These are summarized on the Phase Chart, labeled as Recent Activities, Cemetery, Varied Usage, Large Scale Dumping, and Industry-Related. The uppermost loci reflect activities occurring within the last hundred years, while the area was an open space adjoining the church. Before that it has been used as a cemetery. Immediately below the cemetery are a number of small, irregular, and varied loci, suggesting that many different activities occurred in the area over a prolonged period of time. Lower down the loci are large and very similar in make-up. Building debris occurs in varying amounts. Some tip lines indicate that these loci were not all deposited as one dump stratum, but they were probably formed in relatively short period as a result of some clearance activities. Building debris appears in all, in varying amounts. Finally, a row of amphorae appeared beside a deposit of ash and slag. These and the material around them look like the byproduct of some nearby industry. The last level reached consists of firmly packed material, whether created as a base for the amphorae, or remaining from some earlier use of the site.

The excavation began at 67.76 m ASL (to 68.48 on an uneven surface), and reached 62.30 m ASL. Excavation in Square One began at approximately 62.39 ASL, so the two barely overlap. Excavation Square Two stopped above the level at which the buildings in Square One appeared (the top of Wall A in Square One appeared at 62.07 m ASL: some wall fragments in the North of the site were higher). In 1982 we cleaned the area, hoping to continue excavation and connect the two squares. Excavation could not be continued, so the relationship between debris accumulation and habitation remains unclear. [1]

Recent (Level Plan 1, part of Level Plan 2)

During approximately the last seventy-five to one hundred years, according to local informants, this area had been open space belonging to the church. In recent years it had contained a garden. Before that, leveling had been done,

possibly in several stages, and still earlier some manufacturing may have occurred over the abandoned cemetery.

At the beginning of excavation, the surface was uneven and loosely covered with debris from the Bishop's construction efforts (see above p. 21). This surface debris, from which a wide variety of glazed ware was collected, formed Locus 1. Beneath it ran a modern water conduit, Locus 2. Local Copts told us that this had served a garden laid out in 1952, the same year that the construction attempt was made. Beside the conduit hard packed dark soil, called Locus 3, containing some mud brick fragments seemed to have been deposited in several layers as flooring for the open space. Locus 6 and Locus 10, as well as Locus 13, a large pit from 6 down through 12, may have accumulated before or after the cemetery went out of use. Locus 11 (below) was a thin black layer with vitreous material that ran up to the broken remains of a cemetery wall (Locus 14, see below) and probably formed after the cemetery went out of existence and before this leveling.

Cemetery (Level Plan 2)

Remains of the cemetery included three mud brick walls. Walls A (Locus 5) and B (Locus 16) were built at right angles and bonded, then Wall C (Locus 17) was built as a continuation of Wall A. Bricks in Locus 14 on top of Wall C are probably remains of a higher portion of the wall. Walls A, B, and C create parts of two chambers that contained graves. Locus 4, in the angle of Walls A and B, contained 3 graves, including one coffin burial, Locus 9. Under Locus 4 a packed surface, Locus 7, floored that chamber. In the angle of Walls C and B, Locus 15 contained twelve burials, some of them cut down below the bottom of the walls into the next locus.

Three courses of brick, Locus 14, are all that remain of a fourth wall, Wall D, that may have created a smaller tomb chamber, or other subdivision at the top of one grave chamber. Extensions of the Square at the end of 1978 and in 1980 (see Level Plan 2, and Map 4 showing fullest extension) uncovered more graves in Loci 33 and 54, including coffin burials 35 and 36, and the partially destroyed coffin burial Locus 55. These may have been within the same chambers, the other twalls of which have been destroyed by the earlier construction.

Several levels built up against these walls. Locus 11 ran up against the top of Walls A and C, and probably formed after the rooms went out of use. On the other hand, Locus 12, typical sabah (compost of organic materials), built up in several segments north of Walls A and C. On the other side of Wall A no graves were found. Two Debris levels, 6 and the very small 10, accumulated outside and partly above the area with burials. A pit, Locus 13, began in Locus 6 and continued down into Locus 12. Since there

---

[1] A sherd catalogued as from Locus 61 joins a sherd from Locus 52 in Square Two, but it seems clear that the basket was mislabeled.

were not burials on this side, it is hard to say whether these loci are contemporary with the cemetery, or later.

The square was extended to eight by eight meters at the end of 1981 (see Map 4). Excavation was carried down only through the cemetary level. Loci began with 70 and ran through 106: most were assigned to burials and fragments of burials. Locus numbers 70, 73, 77, 81 sand 106 were assigned to the loose soil around the graves. Only two fragments of walls, Loci 82 and 105, came to light, insufficient to indicate whether they connected with the other walls, or formed independent structures.

The pottery around the coffins presumably antedates them, since the earth must have been excavated to be piled within the chambers. It contains Late Mamluke and Ottoman material.

Varied Activities (Level Plans 3, 4, and 5)

Immediately below the walls, loci running across the whole area (Level Plan 3), contain much vegetal material, as well as some debris from graves. Below them, are more complex accumulations, reflecting various activities (Level Plans 4 and 5, showing very much simplified outlines).

Locus 18 was under Wall A. Locus 19 was the continuation of 18 running under Walls B and C (Locus 16 and Locus 17). The portion of this stratum directly under Walls A, B, and C was excavated separately as Locus 20 [4]. All three loci, i.e., 18, 19 and 20, represent one activity. They contained much organic material--seeds, twigs, sheep dung, as well as debris that had filtered down or from the sides from the cemetery: coins, glass bracelets. (Graves in Locus 15 did go below the level of the walls.) In the 1980 extension of the upper part of this Sector, Locus 56 was equivalent to Locus 18, and Locus 57, equivalent to Locus 19. The unevenness of the original surface meant that there were no preserved levels above these.

Below Loci 19/20 were some large sabah deposits, as well as irregularly shaped lenses and pits, differing in color and density of materials, representing various dumping or demolition activities. Locus 21 contained seeds, twigs, sheep dung, animal bones as well as still some objects from the cemetery above: coins and bracelets. Locus 22 was a lens of fine, sandy soil. Loci 23, 25, 27, 28, 31 and 32 were fine dark sabah soil. Locus 24 was full of ash. Locus 26 was a mass of decomposed vegetal matter, like a pit but without clear pit walls. Locus 29 was the remains of a fired brick wall. (Locus number 30 was not used.)

The glazed wares seem to be mainly Mamluke in date. Several fifteenth century coins were found.

Dump (Large-scale dumping: Level Plan 6, top of Level Plan 7)

At about 65.10 m ASL , larger loci begin, most of them extending across the whole excavated area. The proportion of glazed and fine unglazed wares increases strikingly in these loci as compared with those above 34,

as did the amount of glass. Considerable amounts of building debris were found.

Locus 34 was a debris layer covering the whole area except north corner, where it was interrupted by Locus 39, lighter in color and with more organic matter. After clearing these two loci, we reduced the area of excavation to a 2 x 2 m. square at the Northeast, hoping to reach the level of Sector One, and to see if character of area changed. The final eighty centimeters excavated in 1978 all consisted of similar material, and resembled Locus 34. Loci 38 through 40 and Locus 42 are arbitrary 20 cm. levels, Locus 41 is a tip or lens in Locus 40. Locus 42 ended at 64.07 m ASL, the end of excavation in 1978.

In 1980 the first activity was to bring the rest of the original 4 meter square to the level of lowest excavation in 1978. Locus 50 is 0.20 m, roughly equivalent to 38 and 39 in depth, and similar in nature except that it contained more building debris, namely white flecks and brick fragments. These grow denser in the next locus, an arbitrary 0.20 m division, Locus 51, and continue in Locus 52. An amphora base was found in Loci 51 and 52, and its contents were called Locus 53. Locus 58 covered the whole 4 by 4 m area. It contained white and red brick building debris, and a large amount of pottery. Locus 59, underneath it, was similar.

All these loci consisted of yellowish, sandy soil with interleaved tip lines, hard to detect during excavation. Mamluke glazed wares were frequent in Loci 34 through 52, but almost disappeared in the lower loci.

Bottom (By-formation of industrial activity: Level Plans 7 and 8)

The lowest levels reached in this square contain a row of nine amphorae standing upside down, the earth that had been poured around them, a heap of industrial debris, and a compact level running underneath all these.

Locus 60 was darker brown than the loci above it. In it, the toes of seven amphorae appeared. Locus 61 and Locus 62, also dark brown, were the material that surrounded these seven, and two additional amphorae that first appeared in Locus 61.

The rims of all nine amphorae were missing. Some amphorae had "collars" around them made from body sherds of other amphorae. The amphorae were identified by M. Rodziewicz as Hermopolite amphorae from Ashmunein. Such vessels are usually thought to have been made between the Third and the Tenth Centuries (see Schrunk, this volume, p.79).

Beginning in Locus 61, to one side of the amphorae, and continuing down to the bottom of Locus 63 there was an oval mound of ashy soil, Locus 62, containing few potsherds, but a large amount of glass and slag, perhaps debris from glass making near by.

Locus 63 was a layer about 0.10 m thick, consisting almost entirely of potsherds, around the mouths of the (upside down) amphorae. This locus probably had to be in place when the amphorae were set up, or have been added immediately afterwards, so that they could stand.

SQUARE TWO: EXCAVATION

Locus 61 had lenses to the tips of the rubble deposit, Locus 62: it accumulated after that deposit. The amount of pottery in Locus 61 was greater than in the preceding levels, and became still denser in Locus 63. Very few glazed sherds appeared in these loci. There was an Abbasid coin in Locus 63.

The line of amphorae rested on Locus 64, which differed slightly in color from 62, was more compact, and contained less sherds. Excavation of this locus was carried down only in a two meter square. It reached 62.30 m ASL, the end of excavation in this Square. The locus contained a Byzantine coin from the Mint of Alexandria.

INDEX OF LOCI

Sector One, Square Two

Loci excavated in 1978 are numbered 1 to 42, loci excavated in 1980 are numbered 50 to 64. Locus numbers 100 through 104 were assigned to cleaning the four sides of the square in 1992. All excavated loci have been assigned to a phase indicated on the Phase chart (some assignments are tentative, see text) . Most also appear on one or more Level Plans and Sections.

Number	Phase	Level Plan	Section
1.	recent	1	1,2,3,4
2. water conduit	recent	1	1,2,3
3.	recent	1	1,3,4
4.	cemetery	2	1,2
5. Wall A	cemetery	2	1
6.	recent	2	1,2,3,4
7.	cemetery	2	1,2
8. Wall D	cemetery	-	3
9. coffin burial	cemetery	-	4
10.	recent	2	3
11.	recent	2	3,4
12.	cemetery	2	3,4
13. pit	cemetery	2	1,4
14. building debris probably of Wall A	cemetery	-	3
15.	cemetery	2	2,3
16. Wall B	cemetery		2
17. Wall C	cemetery		3
18.	varied activities	3	1,2,3,4
19.	varied activities	3	1,2,3,4
20.	varied activities	3	4
21.	varied activities	3	2,3
22.	varied activities	4	3,4
23	varied activities	4	2
24.	varied activities	4	2,3
25.	varied activities	4,5	1,2,3,4
26.	varied activities	4	1,4
27.	varied activities	4	4
28.	varied activities	-	-
29. wall remains	varied activities	-	-
30. not used			
31.	varied activities	5	1,2,3,4
32.	varied activities	5	1,2,4
33.	cemetery	3	-

SQUARE TWO: EXCAVATION

Number	Phase	Level Plan	Section
34	large scale dumping	5	1,2,3,4
35. coffin burial	cemetery	-	-
36. coffin burial	cemetery	-	-
37.	large scale dumping	5	1,4
38.	large scale dumping	6	1,4
39.	large scale dumping	6	1,4
40	large scale dumping	6	1,4
41.	large scale dumping	6	1,4
42.	large scale dumping	6	1,4
50.	large scale dumping	7	1.2,3,4
51.	large scale dumping	7	1,2,3,4
52.	large scale dumping	7	1,2,3,4
53. amphora base	large scale dumping	7	-
54.	cemetery	2	-
55. coffin burial	cemetery	-	-
56.	varied activities	3	-
57.	varied activities	3	-
58.	large scale dumping	-	1,2,3,4,
59.	large scale dumping	7	1,2,3,4
60.	large scale dumping	7	1,2,3,4
61	industrial activity	7	1,2,3,4
62.	industrial activity	7	-
63.	industrial activity	7	1,2,3,4
64.	industrial activity	8	4

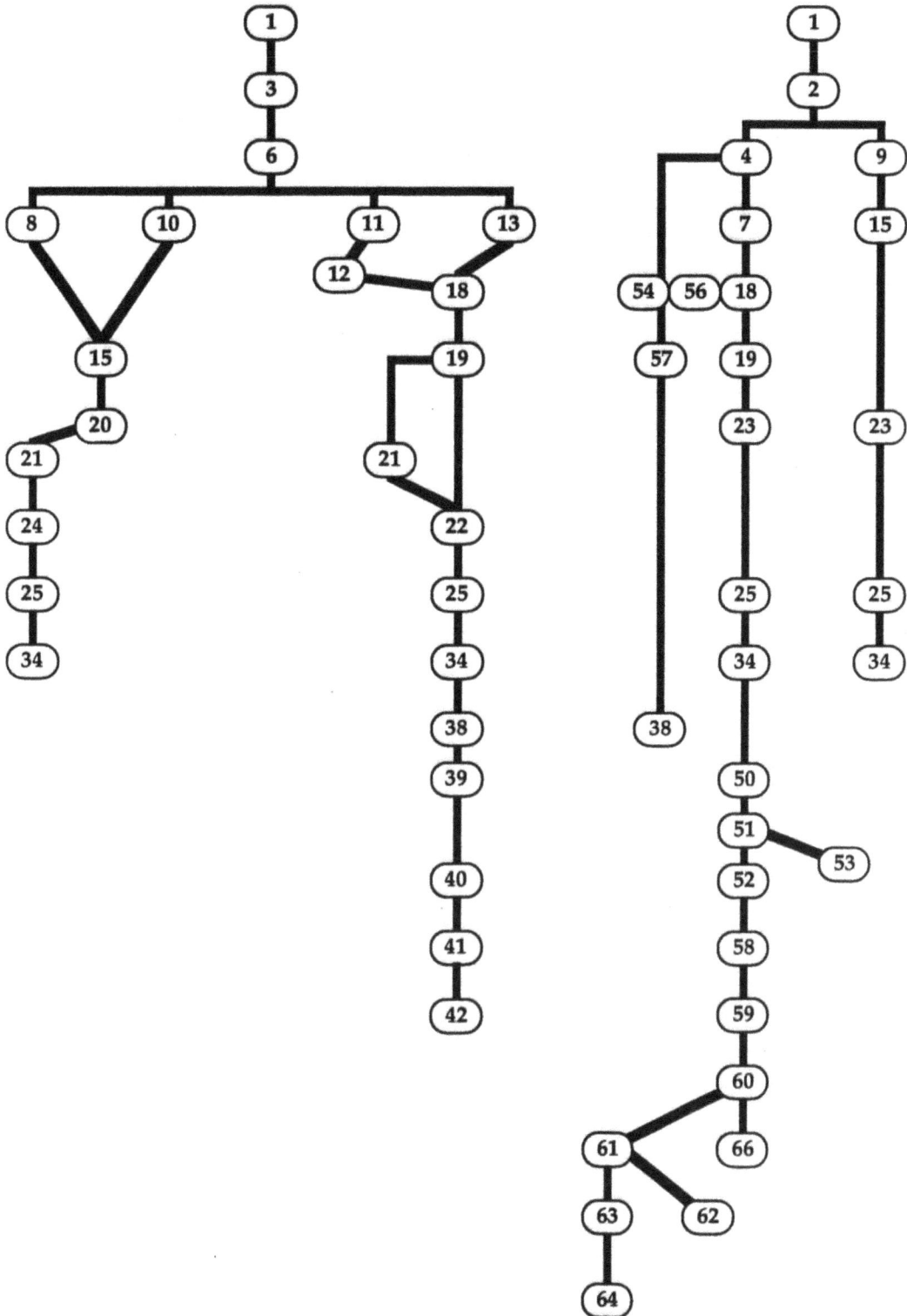

MATRIX

SQUARE TWO: EXCAVATION

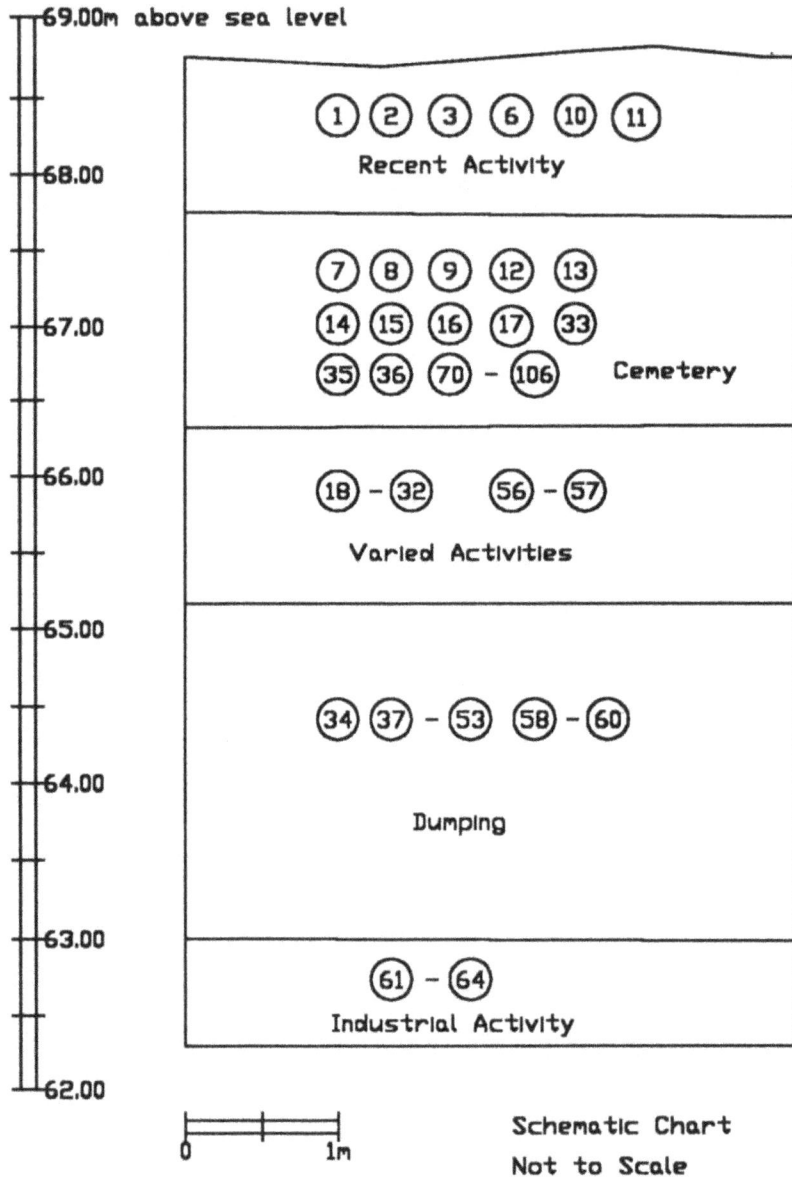

69.00m above sea level

① ② ③ ⑥ ⑩ ⑪
Recent Activity

68.00

⑦ ⑧ ⑨ ⑫ ⑬
⑭ ⑮ ⑯ ⑰ ㉝
67.00
㉟ ㊱ ⑦⓪ - ⑩⑥   Cemetery

66.00
⑱ - ㉜   ㊱ - ㊲
Varied Activities

65.00

㉞ ㊲ - ㊳ ㊳ - ㊳
34 37 - 53 58 - 60

64.00

Dumping

63.00
⑥① - ⑥④
Industrial Activity

62.00

0   1m

Schematic Chart
Not to Scale

CLASSIFICATION OF LEVELS

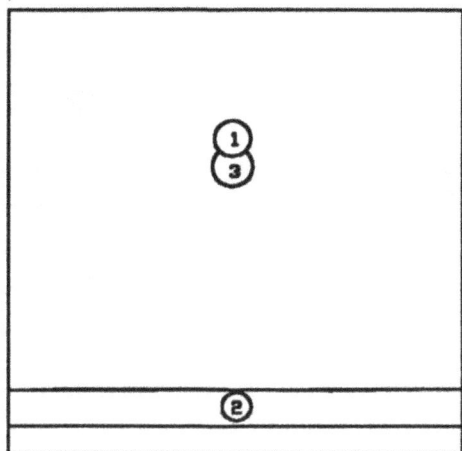

Level Plan 1

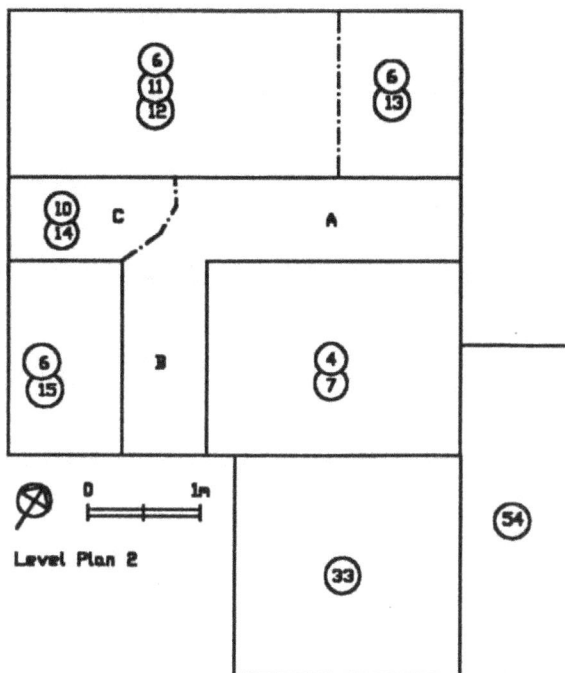

Level Plan 2

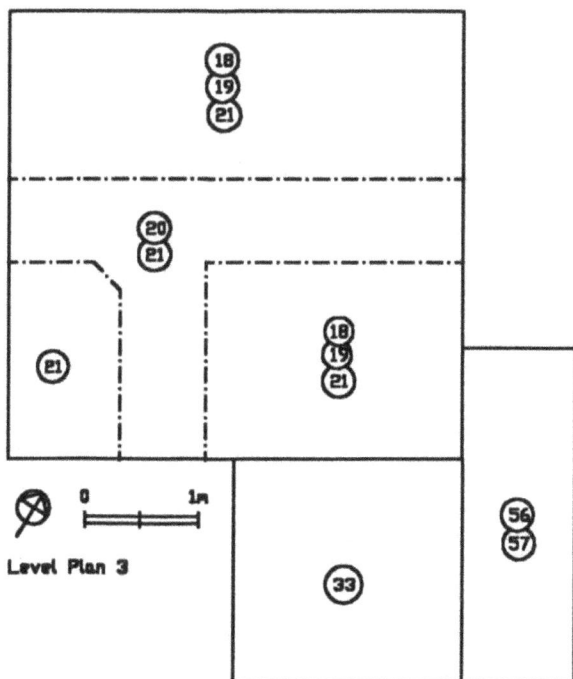

Level Plan 3

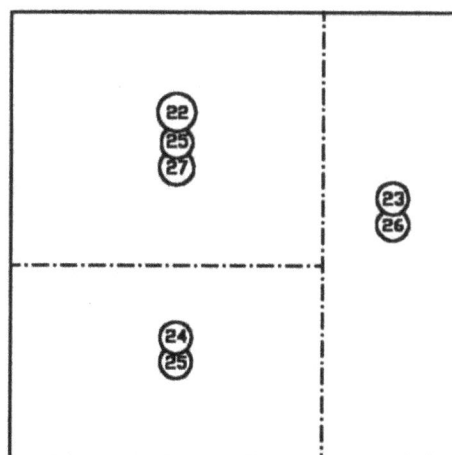

Level Plan 4

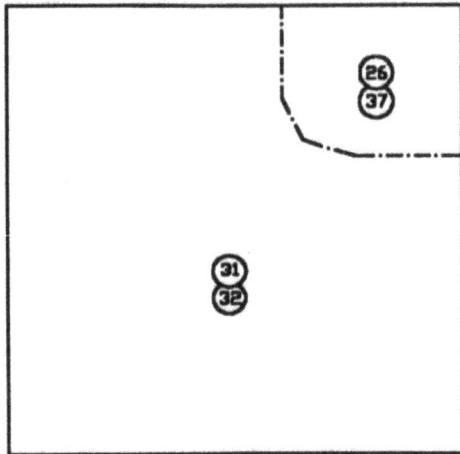

Level Plan 5

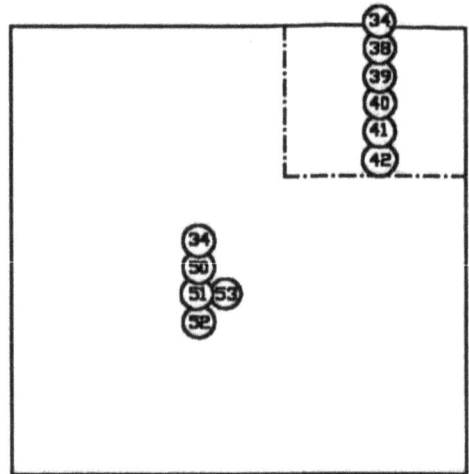

Level Plan 6

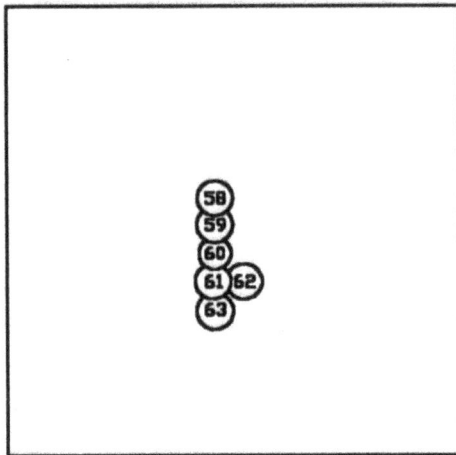

Level Plan 7

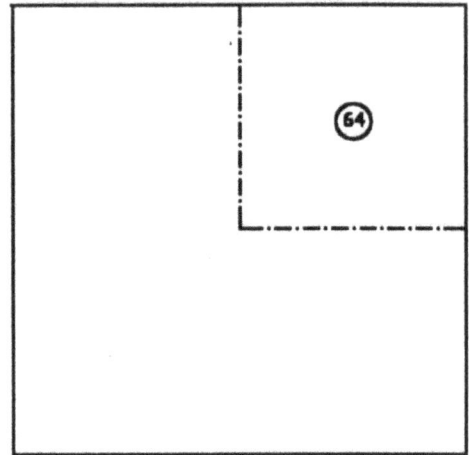

Level Plan 8

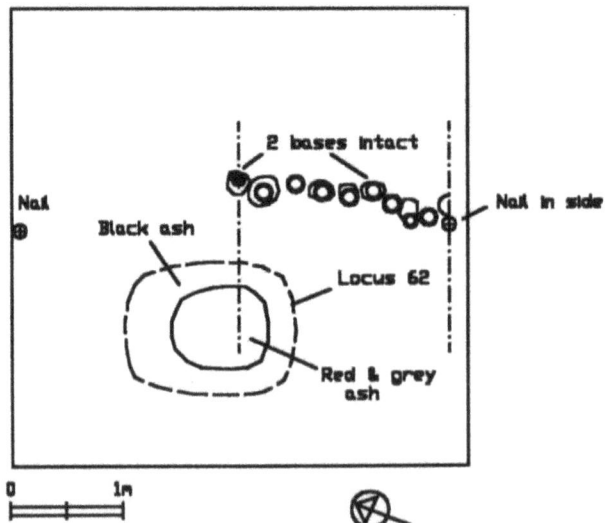

PLAN OF LOCUS 62 AND AMPHORAE IN
LOCUS 61 (62.70 m ASL)

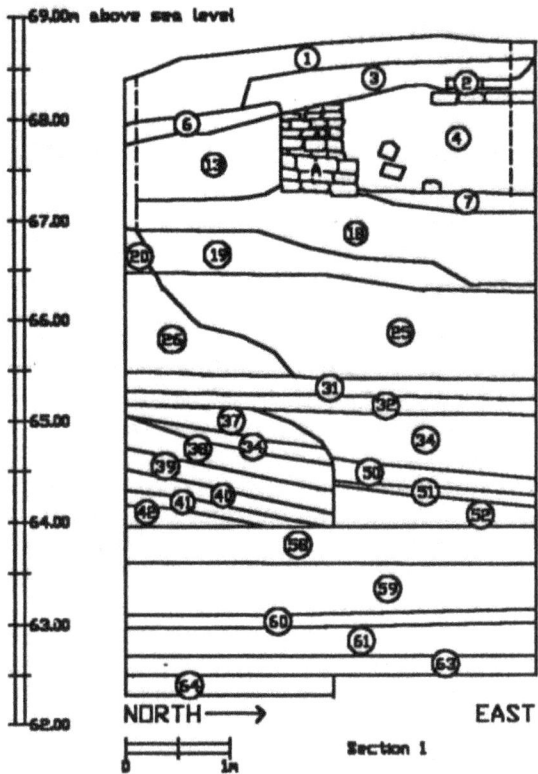

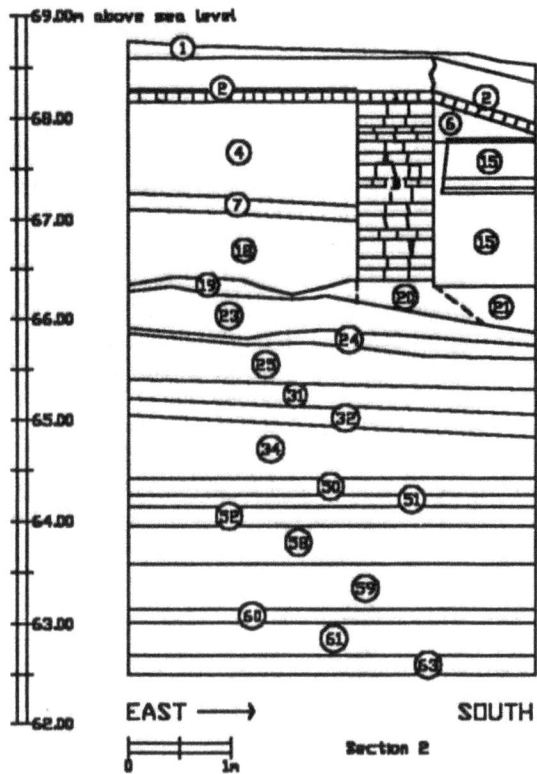

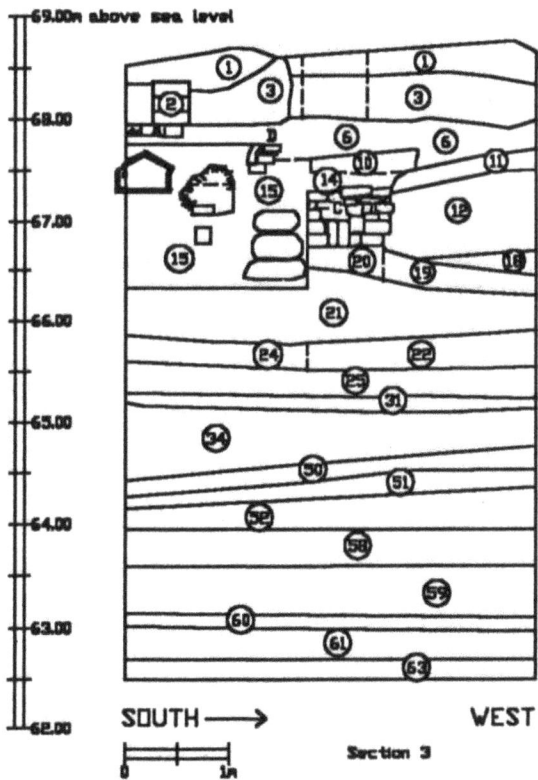

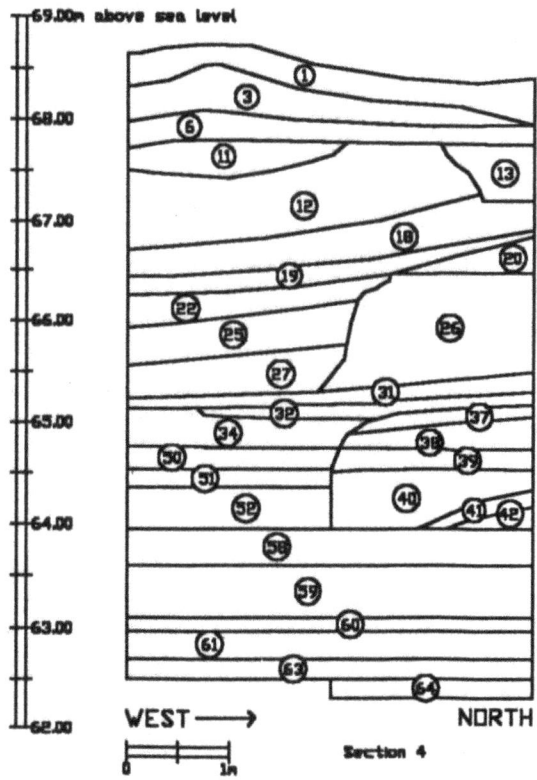

67

SQUARE TWO: CEMETERY

Because of the previous disruption, the Bishop and his community had no objection to excavation of some areas of the cemetery (see above, pp. 21, 25). They only required that the bodies be collected and placed place in coffins for burial in consecrated ground.

Before excavation could begin, numerous coffins protruding from the earth were collected. Most of the dead that were uncovered the first year, i.e., 10 adults and 4 children, had been placed in simple chambers of mud brick without floors. Some of them had been placed in shallow graves, slightly below the level of the walls. The rest were piled within the walls. The dead were buried facing east. The bodies were first placed in shallow graves inside the rooms, and then stacked with earth piled loosely around them.

In the extension of Square Two stubs of two more walls appeared, and in Square Three two mud brick walls for another burial chamber were found. In no case were all four walls preserved so that the total area of the chamber could be calculated. It is not clear if all burials were originally in chambers. Such chambers are not current today. Local informants said that they had been constructed as family mausolea.

The bricks measure 0.19-20 by 0.09 by 0.05-6 m. A header stretcher technique is used in which two courses of headers appear on the outside with two rows of stretchers on the interior, then one course is constructed of headers, where three rows of headers appear at the top. This shape of brick and type of bond are used in present day Akhmīm. They differ from the shapes and bonds found in the late Roman and early post-Conquest construction in Square One.

Most adults and some children were buried in coffins, including one with a gabled roof. The coffins were of two types, a wicker frame in which the wrapped body was placed, then covered with a cloth, and finally tied with a rope, and a wooden box covered with a cloth and secured in a similar manner with a rope. The wicker frame may be made from the central stem of the date palm trees. The ropes are of date palm fiber.

A few adults and most children (judging from body size) were simply wrapped in textiles bound with rope, without coffins. One woman lay on a plank, tied with a network of rope. A very small skeleton, apparently still born or a near term miscarriage, had been wrapped in a cloth and then placed in a tube made of vegetal fiber which we were told was an artificial beehive. Some grass had been put inside the tube, which was closed at both ends with mud brick.

Bodies were covered in several layers of cloth. There was usually a white shroud next to the body, a garment (i.e., caftan or dress) over the shroud, and then an off-white plain woven fabric tied by a cloth binding. The number of layers could differ. Additional pieces of cloth

were sometimes wadded up as packing around the body. One child, buried in a box coffin, had a cotton pillow under the head.

Several coffins, presumed to belong to women, contained jewelry, bottles for scent or kohl, and, in two cases, mirrors. Loose beads and other jewelry fragments may have fallen out of the coffins, or of the uncoffined burials. The most common jewelry consisted of glass bangle bracelets. Many remains of necklaces were also found: beads of glass, shell and metal, occasional coins and amulets. Bronze rings were also found. One woman had bronze bracelets on her wrists. Her grave was one of the richer ones, containing remnants of a necklace made of beads, an amulet, a silver coin and a bronze coin. On her coffin, above her head, a small mirror had been placed. Another woman had a mirror on a wooden slab next to her head, inside the coffin, and a kohl bottle in a cloth container. The woman buried tied to a plank had placed on her abdomen a wooden box containing a comb, a kohl bottle, a square object in a cloth container, and tassels.

Men did not usually have grave goods. One man, lying next to the woman with the mirror beside her head, wore a silk robe, and had silk wrapped around his head. The silk was charred, and there was ash under both of the burials, possibly from candles. One man had a scribe's equipment, a metal case for ink and pens. One infant had a circular metal object, possibly a coin, placed between the eyes. Infants often had finely made, sometimes embroidered, garments.

The simple grave goods could not be dated narrowly. Pottery in adjoining and underlying debris levels suggests a beginning for the cemetery in the late Mamluke or Ottoman period. A duration of burial there from the Seventeenth to the Nineteenth Century is not unlikely.

The adjoining church has two parts (see bibliography above p. 15, Samuel 1990, 74-75, McNally 1991, 80). The earliest part belongs to A type common in this area from about the beginning of the Seventeenth Century, but may have been built as late as the Nineteenth. It is not clear whether the cemetery grew up beside the church, or the church was built near the cemetery. No documentary evidence seemed to be available. Local informants believed there had been a church in this place since Early Christian times. No one remembered burials taking place here, but some thought that an immediately proceeding generation of their family had used the cemetery, perhaps in the late Nineteenth Century.

In Egypt it is not usual to have cemeteries beside churches inside towns, so it would be interesting to know more about the history of this site for that reason alone.

Directly under the graves that we excavated debris had been building up in open space for a longtime, perhaps since the Fatamid period. On the other hand, under the part of the cemetery destroyed before we came, i.e., in the area of Square One, there had been buildings, probably houses, at least until Fatamid times. Cleaning the sides of the hole dug for construction, and slightly extending the area of the Minnesota excavation would be necessary to determine how long habitation continued in the area, and perhaps to define more clearly the uses of the site after habitation stopped.

Chapter 7

LATE ROMAN AND ISLAMIC POTTERY

During the two seasons of excavation, in 1978 and 1981, more than 5,000 kilos of pottery or about 158,000 sherds were excavated in the two squares in the courtyard of Abū Sayfayn church. A total of 25,000 sherds were catalogued and kept, the rest was processed on the site and disposed of there. The immediate objective was a total recovery of ceramic finds for statistical and chronological purposes. A long term objective was a complete study of pottery production, distribution, and usage in Upper Egypt in the context of continuity and change between the late Roman and early Islamic periods.

This preliminary report presents a summary classification of all utility and most table wares both imported, i. e., made outside Egypt, and Egyptian-made, found in the two squares in 1978 and 1981. Painted and glazed wares are not discussed here. They will be the subject of a separate publication. A typology of the Egyptian-made fine slipped wares is presented in more detail in Chapter 8. The bibliography for both chapters follows Chapter 8.

Processing in the Field

The processing of the excavated pottery in the field had two major stages. The first stage was done on the site where all the excavated pottery from sifted and unsifted loci was processed. The second stage took place in the excavation house where only pottery to be catalogued was processed. The on-site processing involved only the excavators and ceramologists, Jerome Schaeffer in 1978 and 1981 and this author in 1981, assisted by Cherilyn Nelson in 1981. In the processing of the catalogued pottery five to six high school students from Sohag and Akhmīm also participated regularly.

All the washed and dried sherds were sorted on the site. The sherds from sifted loci (all loci in 1978 and the loci within the original 4 x 4 m squares in 1981) were first sorted into the types defined by the Field Typology. The count and weight of the sherds of each type were then taken and recorded in the Raw Pottery Book. Diagnostic sherds of each type were selected for cataloguing and their number was also recorded in the same book. Those selected were most of the rims, bases, handles, body sherds with distinctive decoration and all unique ceramic finds such as inscribed sherds and repaired or recycled pottery. Also, all suspected imported wares and all painted, glazed, and red slipped sherds (except some very small body sherds) were catalogued. The selected sherds were put in labeled cloth bags and carried to the excavation house for further processing. The remaining, uncatalogued, sherds also were placed in cloth bags. The bags were labeled and taken for storage at Akhmīm to be saved for future studies. The pottery from unsifted loci was sorted only for diagnostic, slipped, painted, or glazed sherds which were bagged and

taken to the house, while the rest was disposed of in the designated area on the site.

The cataloguing process in the excavation house began with sorting the selected sherds from the unsifted loci into types and labeling each group. The already sorted sherds from the sifted loci were also arranged into labeled type-groups on the tables. The high school students then wrote catalogue numbers in ink on each sherd. The catalogue number consisted of a Roman numeral (I or II) to indicate the excavation area and of several Arabic numerals separated by periods to indicate the square, locus, basket, and inventory number. The students then recorded these sherds in the Pottery Books (separate for each area and each square) indicating the catalogue number, type, and morphological part (rim, base, body, handle, neck). The catalogued sherds were photographed in type groups and placed back into the bags. At the end of the excavation season they were taken to the Islamic Museum in Cairo for inspection and division. The great majority was then shipped to the United States.

Field Typology

During the first season of excavations in 1978 Jerome Schaeffer designed a classification system to be used in the field. His objective was to divide excavated pottery into categories readily distinguishable for a speedy sorting and recording of large amounts of sherds. A total of thirteen types, designated A-M and P, were identified in 1978. More types were added in 1981, labeled with the letters Q, S, and Y. The letters N, O, and R were not used in this typology.

Speed and replicability determined the method of analysis. This field typology was therefore based on diagnostic traits that could be easily seen without the time consuming process of breaking open each sherd and examining it under a lens. The visual properties considered were:

1. Vessel Shape and Function:
   a) Brown amphorae = Type A
   b) Red slipped amphorae = Type Q
   c) Fire-blackened cooking pots = Type P
   d) Lamps or shipping containers ("grenades") = Type J
   e) Steatite bowls = Type L

2. Paste and wall thickness:
   a) Coarse with vegetal inclusions, thick walls = Types B and I
   b) Fine, micaceous, brown or reddish-brown, thin walls = Type C
   c) Fine, calcareous, light red, thin walls = Type D

d) Fine, buff, thick and thin walls = Type G

e) Light red with large quartz inclusions = Type F

3. Surface finish and decoration:

a) Red and white slipped fine wares = Type H

b) African Red Slip Wares = Type E (only in the early 1978 season, later H)

c) Painted fine and coarse wares = Type M

d) Whitewashed wares, thick walls = Type K

e) Whitewashed wares, thin walls = Type S

f) Glazed wares = Type Y (= Type M in 1978)

Although this typology was convenient and speedy, it inevitably led to inconsistencies and misclassification of a certain percentage of sherds. Primarily, it did not account for variations in fabrics of some types. For the types where the surface finish was a determinant, such as red slip (Type H), paint (Type M), and glaze (Type M in 1978 and Type Y in 1981), the fabric differences were deliberately ignored to gain speed in sorting. Since all sherds of red slipped, painted, and glazed wares were catalogued, it was possible to subdivide and classify the sherds in later studies.

I. IMPORTED WARES

The inhabitants of Akhmīm relied heavily on domestic, Egyptian-made wares, if the two excavated squares are any indication of a wider situation in the city. Sherds of imported, non-Egyptian wares of the late Roman and early Islamic periods were extremely rare in both squares. The nature of the excavation certainly accounts for the low numbers, since we have not reached below the levels of the sixth or early seventh century. Only sherds of African Red Slip Ware were uncovered so far at Akhmīm. However, Mediterranean red slip wares are generally sporadic on sites in Upper Egypt, while common in Lower Egypt. Imported amphorae of the same period, probably Syrian or Cypriot, are even less common. Levels with Islamic glazed wares have yielded two Nubian painted sherds and a few glazed sherds of Syrian, Chinese, and Spanish origin.

1. African Red Slip Ware

Five small fragments of four different shapes of bowls were found. Four come from central Tunisian workshops ("sigillata chiara C" in the European typology). Two rim sherds belong to each Hayes Form 50 and 53B. One rim and one body sherd belong to Hayes Form 82; the body sherd has rouletting decoration on the outside. One base sherd with rouletting on the floor belongs to Hayes Form 91, presumably from the Carthage workshops (= sigillata chiara D). The color of the paste is orange-red, in the range of 2.5YR 4/8 to 2.5YR 5/8. The slip is of the same color and glossy on both sides.

The range of the dates for production and distribution of these types in the fourth and fifth centuries is certainly earlier than that of the levels in which the

sherds were found. Four sherds came from debris levels above Rooms 2 and 5 in Square One (Loci 6, 7, 12, and 19), which also contained Fatamid glazed wares. The sherd of Form 91 was found at the bottom of the trash deposits (Locus 59) in Square Two, with very few glazed sherds.

2. East Mediterranean Amphorae (= Field Type F)

Three very small body sherds of what seemed to be Syrian or Cypriot amphorae were found in 1978. The paste is fine grained (particles not visible under a 10x lens) with large amounts of smooth quartz sand and small amounts of a white calcareous material. Inclusions are evenly sorted. The density is heavy and the fracture is even. The color of the paste is light red (5YR 6/6) and the surface is slightly darker (5YR 7/6). There are no carbon streaks. The surface is unslipped but smoothed with temper protruding through the surface. It is not possible to reconstruct the shape from the sherds found at Akhmīm, but the fabric has some parallels with the type called Late Amphora 1 found throughout Egypt in the sixth and seventh century contexts (for detailed discussion with references, see Ballet and Picon 1987, 21-26). This type seems to correspond to amphorae classified by Adams as Sub-family LS, Ware U3, common in Nubia from about 400 to 650 (1986, 580). The fragments from Akhmīm were residual, found in the top mixed level (Locus 3) of Square One with the material of the Fatamid date.

3. Nubian Painted Wares

Two certain Nubian painted sherds were found in Square One. The one from the surface debris (Locus 167) has a thick, bright, orange slip and design painted in black. The painted motifs are arranged in a vertical frieze. The sherd belongs to a vase of Adams' N Family of Nubian wares, specifically to type NV R22 (Adams 1986, 498, Fig. 282, shape F12). The date for this ware in Nubia ranges from A. D. 1000 to 1200. The second sherd comes from a probable floor level (Locus 100) in Room 3. An Abbassid coin was found in the debris level immediately above (Locus 78). The sherd belongs to a shallow bowl with a thick, white slip and a stylized floral motif painted in orange on the inside. The ware is NIV W6 in Adams' typology, common in Nubia between 850 and 1100 (1986, 493-94).

II. EGYPTIAN WARES

Terminology generally used for Egyptian pottery of Late Antiquity and of the early Islamic period is inconsistent. It encompasses both chronological and cultural determinants. A short explanation is due here to clarify the terms and their meaning in this study. The term "Late Roman" or "Byzantine" is often used for the pottery made in the period before the Arab conquest. In the present report the term "Late Roman" (rather than "Byzantine") is primarily used for red slip fine wares produced in the tradition of terra sigillata. The vessel shapes and surface finish are shared with such pottery produced in various centers in the Mediterranean from the fourth to the seventh century. Egyptian potters imitated for the most part vessel shapes of African, Phocaean, and Cypriot Red Slip Wares. Beside the standard red slip they also used orange and white slips. Present evidence from many sites in Egypt and Nubia indicates that Egyptian red slip wares were made and used long after the end of the Roman period in Egypt, i. e. well after the Arab conquest. The evidence from Akhmīm is particularly indicative.

Another common term for Egyptian pottery of the same period is "Coptic." This term should have primarily cultural connotations and seems to be best suited for fine and coarse painted wares. Some of the painted motifs, like the vine scroll, are however in the Graeco-Roman tradition. The term may also be used for red and white slipped vessel types which are outside the terra sigillata tradition. Such types seem to be for the most part made in Upper Egypt and Nubia. Some scholars have extended this term to glazed wares made in Upper Egypt and closely related in fabric and vessel shapes with red and white slipped wares of the same provenience (see below, Aswan wares).

The name "Islamic" is here used in a chronological meaning when speaking of the "Islamic period", the period after A. D. 639. The cultural meaning is contained in the term "Islamic pottery" when speaking of glazed wares produced inside or outside Egypt.

Egyptian-made utility wares presented here are classified into three groups according to the type of clay used in their manufacture. Further subdivision of the wares found at Akhmīm is based on vessel function and shape. Table wares from each group are further discussed in the next chapter. Scientific analyses and reserch in the field (Butzer 1974, Matson 1974, Tobia and Sayre 1974, Bourriau 1981, Ballet and Picon 1987, Ballet 1990, Mason and Keall 1990, Pierrat 1991) have identified three basic types of clay used in Egypt during the late Roman and early Islamic periods:

1. Alluvial clays (siliceous clays, Nile silt, Nile alluvium)

2. Marl clays (calcareous clays, carbonaceous clays)

3. Kaolinitic clays (refractory, probably mined clays)

These clays were used separately but also in mixtures of various proportions (Adams 1986, 561; Mason and Keall 1990). Some wares from Akhmīm classified under the group made of marl clays appear to have an admixture of the Nile silt (2a below). Workshops using all those clays were located in many parts of Egypt where such clays were available. Certain clays, especially those of high quality, like the kaolinitic clay of the Aswan area, could have been transported to distant workshops, as they are today (Tobia and Sayre 1974; Ballet and Picon, 1987, 43 and n. 74). For those reasons, clear connections between the particular type of clay and pottery workshops have been difficult and uncertain. Recent field research on locations of kiln sites and types of wares has produced valuable new evidence (Ballet et al. 1991). In these studies it became clear that certain types of vessels come from large workshops, which were multifunctional. They produced both table wares and utility vessels. Such workshops have been identified in Middle Egypt, notably at Antinoopolis and at Hermopolis Magna, where the alluvial clays were used. The largest group of multifunctional workshops used the kaolinitic clay and was located in the Aswan area. These two areas supplied most of the table and utility wares found at Akhmīm. The great majority of table wares however came from the Aswan workshops. The groups of wares made of marl and mixed clays seem more heterogeneous. They most likely came from either small, local workshops or from a large, regional workshop, which specialized in the production of vessels of a particular shape or function.

1. Alluvial Clays

These clays contain high amounts of silica and iron oxide and are rich in organic matter. When fired they turn to a red or brown color. They are obtained on the banks of the Nile and the cannals. Table and utilitarian wares made of the Nile silt were, and still are, made all along the Nile valley and in the Delta. W. Y. Adams (1986) classified these wares under his Family T, the Middle Egyptian Mud Wares. G. Pierrat distinguishes two types of the silt based pastes: a) with vegetal inclusions, and b) without vegetal inclusions (1991, 147-48). Several production centers have been identified in recent studies, but the extent of production and trade still remains unclear. Kiln sites have been found mostly in Middle Egypt at Antinoopolis, Hermopolis, and Zawyet el Maietin (Ballet et al. 1991). These centers could have supplied many places without local production or the same clay and manufacturing techniques could have been used at many places for local consumption. The former seems to be the case with widespread brown amhorae. The latter would apply to most of the utilitarian pottery. It is interesting to note that recent field research has indicated that workshops in the area of Edfou are the last ones up the Nile to have used exclusively the alluvial clays (Ballet et al. 1991, 140). The Nile silt wares found at Akhmīm could have come from these workshops, although pottery of the similar fabric is today made along the Nile bank at Akhmīm.

a. Ribbed Amphorae (= Field Type A; see fig. p. 76)

Fine grained paste (particles barely visible under a 10x lens) with small specs of mica scattered throughout the paste and small amounts of fine grain quartz sand. In many cases mica has floated to the surface during throwing and finishing , giving the surface a sparkling appearance. The paste is hard and dense and sherds are generally heavy. The fracture is slightly crumbly and uneven. The color of the surface is in the hue range of 5YR to 7.5YR. The paste is in the same hue range but with redder color near the surface, especially if a carbon streak is present. The surface is smooth but unslipped. Vessels have thick walls, usually between 0.75 and 1.0 cm thick.

Amphorae sherds found at Akhmīm and classified under the Field Type A need systematic typological and chronological study. Preliminary observations and analogies with the published material from elsewhere have established two distinctive categories:

1) The fabric classified under Type A in 1978 has red color of the paste with a black core color. This red fabric was found in Square Two and in upper levels of Square One. It was also observed in 1978 that this variant of Type A was not as easily distinguished from Type B in

Square Two as it was in Square One. Following the publications of P. Ballet (summary in Ballet 1990, 491), it seems likely that the sherds with these characteristics belong to red ovoid amphorae analogous to Egloff 187-190 from Kellia (Egloff 1977) and to Riley's Late Amphora 5/6 at Carthage (Riley 1975). The stratigraphic evidence, notably from Kellia and Fustat, indicates that such amphorae appeared around the middle of the seventh century and lasted until the tenth or later. However, research on the production center for such amphorae from Kellia has not produced any results (Ballet and Picon 1987, 39-40, for dates and provenience). Further study of the material from Akhmim, especially in relation to the recent research of production sites in the regions of Esna and Edfu (Ballet et al. 1991, 139-40) may be promising. Sherds found in the upper levels of Square Two may rather belong to Adams' Family E, Mamluke Heavy Utility Ware, U21.

2) The second category which comprises most of the sherds classified in 1981 under the Field Type A has consistant brown color of the paste and carbon streaks are rare. Nine nearly complete amhorae of this category were found *in situ* placed upside-down in the lowest excavated level (Locus 64) in Square Two. They belong to a common type of ribbed wine amphorae found throughout Egypt and Nubia and occasionally outside Egypt (summary in Ballet 1990, 490-91). Ballet equated this variant with Riley's Late Amphora 7 from Carthage (Riley 1975) and Egloff 173-177 from Kellia (Egloff 1977). Adams classified this type under Ware U4 of Family T, Middle Egyptian Mud Wares (Adams 1986). These amphorae, with some variations in the shape and size, were produced at large worksopps in Middle Egypt, at Antinoopolis, Hermopolis, and Zawyet el Maietin (Ballet and Picon 1987, 38-39; Ballet et al. 1991, 134-39).

W. Godlewski (1990, 50-51) reported on the same two fabric variants among the pottery found at Deir el Naqlun in the Fayum Oasis. He noted that the red fabric with the black core was found in later contexts, notably in the hermitages which were in use till the end of the thirteenth century. The brown fabric was found in the seventh to eighth century levels. At Tod, the brown amphorae were found in the levels dated A.D. 750-900 (Pierrat 1991, 152, Fig. 4a). The stratigraphic evidence from Akhmim is in accordance with the Deir el Naqlun and Tod chronology. Also, the relative frequency of the brown fabric was much greater in Square One and in the lowest levels of Square Two.

b. Thick Walled Utilitarian Vessels (= Field Types B and I)

Fine grained paste (particles not visible under a 10x lens) with varying amounts of mica from only a few specs to over 20 grains per square centimeter. The large amount of vegetal fiber is the hallmark of this type. Impressions of the fibers can be seen in the paste and all over the surface. There are also varying amounts of large quartz sand with smooth and worn surfaces unevenly distributed throughout the paste. The density of the paste is very light compared to the amphora sherds of the Field Type A. The fracture is very crumbly, producing irregular grainy breaks. The surface exhibits a wide range of colors from 5YR to 10YR, while the paste is usually grey or black due to the thick vessel walls and the high vegetal content. Thinner vessels of this type are more evenly fired and tend to have a red paste. Carbon streaks are extremely frequent. The surface is roughly smoothed or not smoothed at all. Large amounts of fiber and seed impressions can be seen on the surface. The walls are usually over 1 cm thick.

The Field Type I resembles Type B except that it is burnished and somewhat better made. The paste is extremely coarse grained with low amounts of quartz sand but higher amounts of red, white, and other particles. There is the possibility of crushed sherds used as temper. The density is heavy and breaks are clean but along uneven planes. The color is dark brown but frequently the edges are sooted. Carbon streak is infrequent. The burnished surface on the interior or exterior is the hallmark of this type. Unburnished surfaces are roughly finished. In some cases, however, it is difficult to distinguish between intentionally burnished pieces and those which are burnished from continual scraping and wear.

Sherds of this category belong to various utilitarian, mostly storage vessels (water jars). Some of the thickest vessels are probably from portable ovens and cooking slabs, indicated by the flat surface or extremely wide circumference, indicated by sherd profiles. This ware is also used to construct thinner walled bowls and jars that occur in small amounts. Thick and thin walled vessels were not distinguished in raw weights. A significant number of painted sherds exhibited this fabric (classified under Field Type M). Some large and joining sherds have elaborate animal and floral motifs.

Utilitarian pottery of this category has been found throughout Egypt but only painted wares have received more attention in print (summary in Ballet 1990, Pierrat 1991). The closest analogies for the Akhmim painted wares are found among the material from Kellia (Egloff 1977, Ballet and Picon 1987, 41-43) and Tell Atrib in the Delta (T. Gorecki 1990). Further analysis of the Akhmim material in relation to the sherds of the very coarse fabric with vegetal inclusions, reported from the production sites in the region of Esna, may prove significant (Ballet et al. 1991, 139-40).

c. Thin Walled Utilitarian Vessels (= Field Type C)

The description of the fabric is the same as that of the Field Type A, but sherds belong to very thin walled vessels. They are always less than 0.5 cm thick and usually even thinner. Pottery in this category is usually better made and finer textured. The material is very fragmentary and only such general vessel shapes as pots and bowls can be identified. Thin walled pots reported from the workshop sites at Antinoopolis, Hermopolis, and Zawyet el Maietin are likely to have the closest parallels to the sherds from Akhmim (Ballet et al. 1991, 136-38).

d. Cooking Vessels (= Field Type P)

Fine grained paste with small white and black particles and larger specs of mica. Small amount of very fine grained quartz sand. The density is high. The fracture is slightly crumbly and uneven. The surface is always blackened from fire. The color of the paste is reddish brown with no distinctive core color. The outside surface is fairly smooth, while the inside is rough and feels like sand paper. It is very possible that several variant fabrics are present here, comparable to those summarized by P. Ballet (1990, 490). Further analysis may reveal distinctions between a more homogeneous Nile silt fabric, like that of the brown amphorae above, which seem to be predominant at Akhmīm and a more micaceous fabric with larger amount of quartz grains. The provenience of these cooking vessels is difficult to establish (Ballet and Picon 1987, 41-43). Local productions at many sites along the Nile, perhaps including Akhmīm, are most likely.

Typology of the shapes found at Akhmīm has not been done. Paralles should be sought with established types from Kellia (Egloff 1977, Ballet and Picon 1987, 41-43) The excavations at Deir el Naqlun in the Fayum have brought to light carrinated bowls, globular cooking pots, open bowls, and frying pans from the contexts of the sixth to thirteenth century (Godlewski 1990).

e. Fine Red and White Slipped Wares (= Field Type H)

These wares correspond to M. Rodziewicz's Group K and to J. Hayes' Egyptian Red Slip B. Detailed discussion of these wares follows in the next chapter.

2. Marl Clays

These clays contain high amounts of calcite and when fired exhibit light paste color - grey, beige or buff. The absence of organic matter and the abundance of carbonates are said to account for the light color (Butzer 1974, 377, with a reference to Lucas and Harris 1962). The same references place the sources of such clays in the lime-rich deposits of the desert wadis at Qena, Ballas, and in the area of Sohag. Recent research on kiln sites provided evidence for production at Abu Mina, Hermopolis, and Medamud (Ballet and Picon 1987, Ballet et al. 1991). Adams classified Egyptian wares made of marl clays under Family L or Egyptian Drab and Buff Wares ("drab-colored utility wares made from varying combinations of desert clay and Nile mud". 1986, 58). In Pierrat's classification of the Tod pottery marl clays are designated as "Pates M" (1991, 148-49 and 171-75). Vessel types belong generally to utility wares, like amphorae, water jugs, and pitchers (summary in Ballet 1990, 480, 490-92).

a. Fine Utility Wares (= Field Types D, K, and S)

Clossest parallels can be made with Adams' Sub-Family LB, the Ballas Ware (1986, 572-75). Typologcal study of the Akhmīm finds has not been done. The three distinctive fabrics will be described briefly:

1) Field Type D - very fine grained paste (particles invisible under a 10x lens) with large amounts (over 50%) of white and grey calcareous material. The density is very heavy and the fracture is very hard with clean and even breaks. The color of the paste is light red (10YR-2.5YR 6/8-5/8) or very pale brown (10YR 7/4).

Thin, uneven carbon streaks are occasionally seen. The thickness of the vessel walls is between 0.75 and 1.0 cm. The surface is carefully smoothed. Fine combed designs are characteristic of this type.

According to Adams' observations this fabric corresponds to his Ballas Drab Utility Ware, U12. Amphorae and kegs were typical vessel forms. This ware first appeared around A. D. 400 in Nubia, but became very common only after 1100 (Adams 1986, 575). The evidence at Akhmīm would place the major period of this ware at a much earlier date. It was noticed in 1978 that this type was extremely rare and infrequently recorded. It became more common in 1981, especially in Square One, when lower levels were excavated. At Tod jars of this fabric appeared in the levels dated 650 to 750, while kegs were found in the levels dated after 1000 (Pierrat 1991, 174).

2) Field Type K - the fabric is the same as that of Field Type D but with a thick greenish-white (10YR 8/3) slip on the outside. This ware possibly corresponds to Adams' Roman Ballas Ware, U16, used for large amphorae. It is very rare in Nubia and the possible dates are A. D. 400-500 (Adams 1986, 575).

3) Field Type S - the fabric is like that of Field Type K, but sherds are thin- walled. There are mall amounts of very fine quartz and small specks of mica. The density is high. The fracture is very hard with clean, even breaks. The color of the paste is orange-red with no distinctive core color. The outside surface always has white slip, like Type K. Both surfaces are smooth.

b. Water Jars and Pitchers (= Field Type G)

The paste is fine grained (particles barely visible under a 10x lens) with large amounts (over 50%) of very fine sand and small amounts of black and grey inclusions. The density is very light and the paste is porous. The fracture is usually crumbly. The most diagnostic attribut of this type is the greenish-grey color of the paste. Color range is around 5YR 7/3. There is no carbon streak. A wide range of surface treatment occur in this type. In most cases the surface is poorly smoothed with inclusions protruding through the surface. Some examples are very finely finished and even slipped.

This type seems to include several variant fabrics, what may be actually due to the variety in vessel function. Many of the thicker vessels are probably large water storage jars. The porous paste, which facilitated cooling, was obtained by mixing ash with the marl clay (Butzer 1974, 377). A subgroup of this type are extremely thin walled vessels which are water jars with filters. Indeed, many sherds of Type G are water filter fragments.

This ware could be equated with Adams' Sub-family LF, ware U13, which, according to him, was possibly made at Fustat (1986, 576-78). It was imported into Nubia from A. D. 550 and became very common after 1300. The earlier dates are more in aggreement with the evidence at Akhmīm.

3. Kaolinitic Clays

These are fine clays derived from lake beds deposits in the desert. They contain kaolinite and iron but no lime or magnesium (Ballet and Picon 1987, 43). The quality of wares made of these clays is superior to that of the previous groups. Evidence for a large scale production using such clays in the Aswan area has mounted during the past fifteen years. Recent research on kiln sites has produced significant new evidence (Ballet et al. 1991, 140-43, with up to date references). Major production seems to be located on the island of Elephantine, but other workshops were located inside and around the Monastery of Saint Simeon and at Nag' el-Hagar, north of Aswan. W. Y. Adams was the first one to introduce the term Aswan wares and has presented the most detailed classification of table and utility wares produced from A. D. 100 to possibly as late as 1500 (Adams 1986, 525-60).

a. Red Slipped Amphorae (= Field Type Q; see fig. p. 76)

The paste is fine, dense, and hard. The color varies from pinkish to light grey (2.5YR 6/4 and 7.5YR 7/4). Lighter core color is present in some sherds. Inclusions of black and red particles and quartz sand are numerous. The walls are thick. The outside surface always has a thin, matte, red slip. Both inside and outside surfaces are fairly smooth. The fabric and slip are very close to those of Aswan slipped table wares, Adams groups AIII and AIV, discussed in Chapter 8. No complete specimens were found at Akhmīm. Neck and toe fragments belong to ribbed amphorae with elongated and rounded bodies, thickened lip, loop handles, and rounded bases. The fabric and vessel shapes are comparable to those of Adams' ware AIII U8. It is likely that some sherds belong to his earlier ware AII U2. Some sherds have completely ribbed neck, like amphorae of the AIIU2 ware, although the lip is thickened like in the group AIII.

The production of these amphorae could be perhaps located at Nag' el-Hagar, just north of Aswan. Amhorae fragments constitute a significant portion of wasters on the site of workshops outside a Roman military camp (Ballet et al. 1991, 142).

b. Lamps or Oil Bottles (= Field Type J; see fig. p. 76)

The paste is very fine consolidated material which is almost vitrified. It has a high refractive index. There are high amounts of very fine quartz sand inclusions which is barely visible under a 10x lens. The density is very heavy. There are clean and even breaks at the fracture. The color of the paste and surface is a very dark brown or grey in the hue range around 7.5YR 3/2-4/2. The surface is slipped and burnished with a high refractive index. The interior is dull. Incised and stamped decorations are common on the shoulders.

This type is used for a distinctive vessel shape which has been variously identified as a lamp, oil bottle, and shipping container for precious liquids. The ware and vessel shape have parallels in Adams' Group AIV U6, Aswan Medieval Grey Utility Ware 1986, 559-60, Fig. 59, N 4-5, oil bottles and Fig. 65, P34-35, lamps). Adams noted that the grey burnished surface was apparently meant to simulate the appearance of iron. The sharp contours of the vessel shape also have a metallic appearance. Vessels of this shape and fabric have not been reported among the material found on workshop sites in the Aswan area. This ware appeared in Nubia in about A. D. 700, but the main importation period was from 950-1500.

c. Fine Red and White Slipped Table Wares (= Field Type H)

These wares correspond to M. Rodziewicz's Group O and W and to J. Hayes' Egyptian Red Slip A. Detailed discussion of these wares follows in the next chapter.

d. Glazed Wares

The Aswan fabric identical to Adams' groups AIII and AIV and some shallow bowls with flat base were also used for glazed wares found at Akhmīm. Adams classified these glazed wares as Group G.V and a rare variant of the utility ware AIV U6. The vessels are glazed on inside only, either with a monochrome yellow glaze or a runny polichrome glaze in yellow, green, and dark brown colors. M. Rodziewicz has shown that these glazed wares derived from the late Roman red slipped wares and named the "Coptic glazed wares" (1978 and 1983). D. Whitcomb has more recently published a detailed discussion (1989).

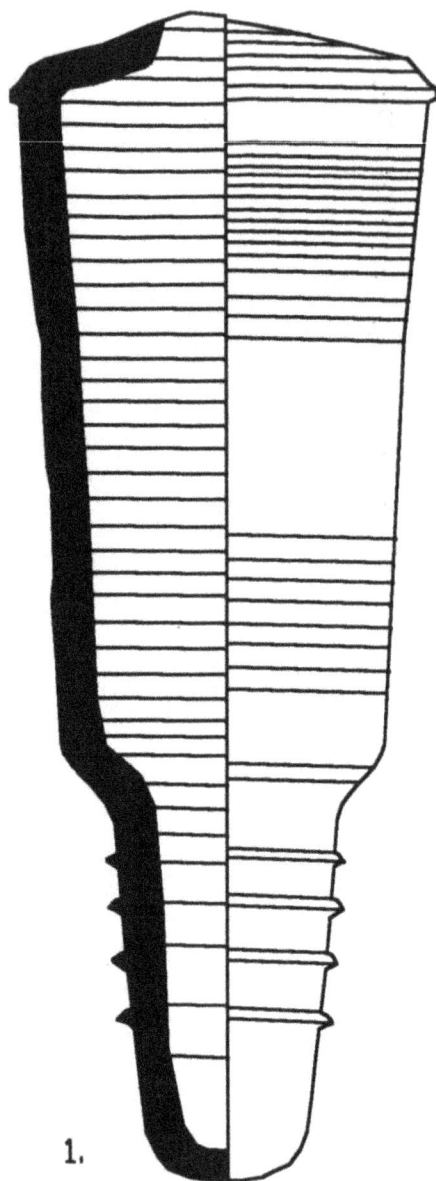

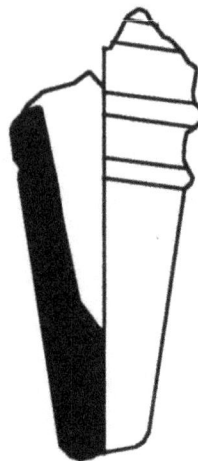

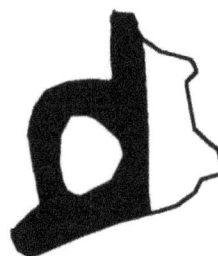

0   5   10 cm

1-2 BROWN AMPHORAE OF ALLUVIAL CLAY; 3-4 RED SLIPPED AMPHORAE OF KAOLINITIC
CLAY; 5 LAMP OR OIL BOTTLE OF KAOLINITIC CLAY

Chapter 8

EGYPTIAN SLIP WARES

Background

In the preliminary studies, conducted during 1979 and 1980 after the first season of excavations in 1978, red and white slipped sherds of the Field Type H from Squares One and Two were examined to subdivide this heterogeneous group. It was obvious then that imported Late Roman red slip wares were very rare and limited to only several pieces of African Red Slip Ware (see above). The bulk of the material represented several distinctive fabrics of Egyptian manufacture, two of them comparable with the wares previously classified by J.W. Hayes (1972), M. Rodziewicz (1976), and W.Y. Adams (1986). A computerized data base, using System 2000, which stressed relatively few basic attributes, was used for quick cataloging and easy retrieval of objects for diagnostic and quantitative analysis (see above p. 23). A collection of 610 sherds was analyzed from physical, quantitative, and chronological perspectives. A working typology of these fabrics was established to provide guidance to subsequent fieldwork and serve as a basis for future studies. The results of these studies were reported at the Annual Meeting of the American Research Center in Egypt (ARCE) in April of 1980.

During the second season in 1981 a great number of slipped sherds came from both excavated squares, which were enlarged in the course of excavations. Again all such sherds were conveniently classified as Type H because of the large amount of pottery that had to be processed at the site. Our initial working typology proved to be valid but had to be expanded to allow for a new type and for further subdivisions of two of the established types. The imported wares were still limited to African Red Slip Ware and only one more sherd was found, a total of five sherds from the two seasons of excavations. Phocaean and Cypriot Red Slip Wares, common in Lower Egypt, have not been found at the site. The studies following the excavations concentrated on the prevalent group, the Aswan ware, especially on the variations of the paste and surface finish of this ware and their fluctuation between levels within the excavated areas. A preliminary report on this research was presented at the Annual Meeting of the Archaeological Institute of America (AIA) in December of 1981. The progress in the study of the Aswan ware, including preliminary remarks on the painted, glazed, and utility wares of the same provenience, was reported at the Annual Meetings of the AIA in 1987 and the ARCE in 1988.

Classification

In the classification of Egyptian slip wares the type of clay was the basic determinant as described in the previous chapter. These attributes exhibit various degrees of variation and co-variation that determine their significance for the typology. Paste texture is almost consistently fine grained. The hardness of the clay varies between 2 and 8 on the Mohs scale and this variation proved significant for the diagnostic analysis. The fracture color and the material, size, and density of inclusions exhibit the most variability and are considered the essential attributes in this typology. Furthermore, the fracture color and inclusions consistently co-vary and are identified as key attributes. A distinctive core color is limited to a relatively small number of sherds that otherwise share the paste and inclusions with other sherds of the same type of clay. The essential and key attributes form the basis for classification into families of wares.

Attributes related to the slip also exhibit considerable variation. The variation is most noticeable in the color, thickness, and finish of the slip. Various shades of red slip are characteristic of all the families. Two families also have white slip and a bichrome combination of red and white slip. Consistent co-occurrences of certain fabric and slip attributes formed a basis for further subdivisions into types of wares. Vessel forms generally do not correlate with the variations in the fabric and slip. In all the families and wares and in all excavated levels there is a significant predominance of open forms, mostly bowls and plates, obviously used as tableware. However, some specific shapes of bowls and plates, which exhibit variations in their morphological parts, are associated with particular families or subdivisions thereof.

Three types of clay and five types of families can be distinguished on the basis of those analyses.

Slip Wares of Kaolinitic Clay

1. Aswan Ware (Adams); Egyptian Red Slip Ware A (Hayes); Groups O and W (Rodziewicz); Pates R (Pierrat)

Of the current classifications of the Aswan slip wares that of W. Y. Adams (1986), based on the evidence in Nubia, is the most relevant and detailed. Besides, the late chronology of the Nubian sites and the persistence of Aswan Ware, correspond well with the situation at Akhmīm. The major difference is the significant predominance of plain slipped sherds in the Akhmīm excavations, compared to the prevalence of painted sherds on the Nubian sites.

The Aswan Ware represents by far the highest percentage (60-80%) of recovered fine, slipped sherds in Squares One and Two. It also shows the most variation in the fabric and slip and is subdivided into five types of wares. These types correspond to Adams' divisions into groups according to the fabric and subdivisions into wares, based on the slip and the style of painting. Adams' nomenclature is followed whenever the correspondence in the fabric and slip is certain. The clay and production are discussed above in Chapter 7 (p. 72).

EGYPTIAN SLIP WARES

a. Aswan Byzantine Polished Red Ware — AIIR4

This type comprises red slip ware classified by Hayes as Egyptian Red Slip Ware A, Rodziewicz's Group O and Pierrat's Pate RII.

Paste: Fine grained, hard (5-6 on the Mohs scale), and dense. Color is in the range of light red to pink, mostly 10R 6/6 to 2.5YR 6/6.

Inclusions: Ground sherds, sand, and stone; abundant (density 20-40%) and fine to medium in size.

Slip: Thick, adheres well to the paste, and applied evenly to outer and inner walls; smooth and polished with glossy appearance. The color is a shade darker red than the paste (10R 5/8).

Decoration: Uncommon; occasional stamped design around the floor of plates: concentric circles (10 sherds) and rosettes (2 sherds). Stamped rosettes on the outside wall of a deep carinated bowl (2 joining sherds). Analogous decoration occurs on a fragment of a glass cup at Akhmīm. Such decoration, on both pottery and glass vessels has been found at Alexandria and Fustat in the seventh and eight century contexts.

Vessel forms: Mostly open forms, bowls and plates; commonest forms are bowls with various thickened, flaring, or flanged rims and ring feet (Drawings 3 and 4) and deep plates with thickened, molded, or flaring rims and high ring feet (Drawings 1 and 2). These shapes of bowls and plates are analogous to Winlock's types G, H, J, L, P, R, S, and V (1926) and to Hayes' types HH (1972). Closed forms are uncommon at Akhmīm and their shape cannot be reconstructed with certainty from the excavated rim, neck, or handle sherds.

Archaeological context: Found in all excavated loci of Square One. It is the prevalent ware (over 50%) when compared to all the Aswan slip wares in all levels where the same are found. In Square Two the same is evident in the bottom levels (Loci 60-64) and in the trash levels above them (Loci 34-59), which contained the Aswan wares.

b. Aswan Islamic and Medieval Plain Red Ware — AIIIR13 and AIVR13

Hayes, Rodziewicz, and Pierrat have not defined this ware as a separate variant. Adams distinguished two chronological groups AIII and AIV, but without clear distinction in the types of wares. The sherds found at Akhmīm also do not show two distinctive types of wares.

Paste: Fine grained, hard (5-6 on the Mohs scale, often 6) and dense. Color is in the range of grayish pink or buff, 5YR 7/4 or 5YR 7/6.

Inclusions: Ground sherds, sand, and stone; abundant (around 40%); medium to coarse in size; occasional granular size of ground sherds.

Slip: Thick, adheres well to the paste, and applied mostly on outer walls only; rough and dull on the surface, it feels like fine sandpaper. The color is dark red, 10R 4/6.

Decoration: Mostly undecorated vessels; occasional sherds with coarse rouletting or impressions on outer walls.

Vessel forms: Mostly bowls: plain and footed carinated bowls with plain rims (Drawing 6) and bowls with flaring walls, thickened rim, and flat base (Drawing 5). The former shapes are new, not in the Late Roman red ware tradition. Bowl shapes of the ware AIIR4 continue as well.

Archaeological context: In Square One there are few sherds in the bottom and low middle levels; occurrence increases in the middle and upper middle levels, together with the Fatamid glazed wares. In Square Two the occurrence is low in the bottom levels but increases in the trash levels above.

c. Aswan Byzantine White Slip Ware — AIIW3

This type corresponds to Rodziewicz Group W and to Pierrat's group WRII. Hayes records it as a variant of Egyptian Red Slip Ware A with orange or yellow slip. In Nubia painted pottery of this type is much more common than plain, as Adams' term "Byzantine painted cream ware" indicates.

Paste and inclusions: Same as AIIR4.

Slip: Thick, it adheres well to the paste; applied on inside and outside; smooth and polished with glossy appearance. The color is reddish yellow (7.5YR 7/8) or yellow (10YR 8/6).

Decoration: Mostly undecorated; there are occasional elongated impressions on the outside wall below the rim.

Vessel forms: Only open forms; mostly large and deep, footed plates with flaring and molded rims.

Archaeological context: In Square One there are few sherds, mostly found in debris levels above the floor 92 in Room 2. In Square Two they are found in the lower levels of dumping and industrial activity (Loci 50-64). In both squares they occur with pre-Fatamid and Fatamid glazed wares.

d. Aswan Islamic White Slip Ware — AIIIW22

This type at Akhmīm corresponds in the fabric to Adams' Group AII but in slip and vessel shapes to his AIIIW22 ware. Painted pottery of this type is again more common in Nubia and Adams calls it "white painted ware."

Paste and inclusions: Same as AIIR4.

Slip: Thin, flakes off the paste, applied on inside and outside; smooth and dull. The color is cream (7.5YR 8/4).

Decoration: Undecorated; one base sherd has stamped concentric circles around the floor.

Vessel forms: Only open forms; mostly small size bowls and saucers. Bowls are shallow, with a plain rim and flat base. Saucers have a narrow flaring, molded rim and flat base.

Archaeological context: Same as the previous type, but sherds of this type are more numerous in those levels.

e. Aswan Bichrome Ware

Rodziewicz reported on bichrome slip on later examples of his Group O at Alexandria, but did not specify the ware as a separate type (1976, 00). W. Kubiak classified such sherds from Fustat under his "Matte bichromatic type" and proposed the chronology of the 10th to the second half of the eleventh century (1990, 73-74).

Paste and inclusions: Same as AIIIR13.

Slip: Thin, it adheres well to the paste; smooth and dull. On the outside wall or just along the rim it is dark red, like that of AIII/AIV R13. On the inside or on the rest of the body it is light orange (10R 4/6) to reddish yellow (7.5 YR 8/4).

Decoration: Occasional impressed dots on the outside just below the rim.

Vessel forms: Only bowls; mostly shallow bowls with very thin walls, thickened rim, and flat base.

Archaeological context: Small number of sherds is found only in the top debris levels in Square One with Fatamid glazed wares.

Slip Wares of Alluvial Clay

1. Hermopolite Ware

a. Red slip ware = Egyptian Red Slip Ware B (Hayes); Group K (Rodziewicz); ERS H (Bailey)

Hayes grouped diverse products of alluvial clay under this type. He described them as regional fabrics made at more than one center (1972, 397; 1980, 530). Rodziewicz's Group K also seems to incorporate several regional products. Bailey's ERS H, whose manufacture he clearly locates at Hermopolis Magna, has a very distinctive core color. Identical ware was found at Tell Atrib in the Delta (Bailey 1990,4). The excavations at Akhmīm showed that this Hermopolite ware also reached Akhmīm.

Paste: Fine grained, soft (3-4 on the Mohs scale), and dense; so-called "sandwich" appearance at the break, with purple-red to black core color (7.5YR 5/6) and orange-brown (2.5YR 5/8) near the surface.

Inclusions: Abundant mica and some white stone particles of medium to coarse size, density about 40%.

Slip: Thick, adheres well to the paste; smooth, polished with glossy appearance. The color is dark red (10R 4/6).

Decoration: None found.

Vessel forms: Only bowls; mostly shallow bowls with thickened, molded rims.

Archaeological context: Represented with one to three sherds in all the levels in Square One, with the highest number in the bottom levels. Small number of sherds were also present in the bottom and lower debris levels in Square Two. The chronology of this ware at Hermopolis was not clear. Bailey believed that the

manufactre of the ware extended probably beyond AD 700 (1990, 5).

b. White Slip Ware

Bailey reported on "locally made white-slipped fine-ware bowls" at Hermopolis Magna (1990, 5).

Paste and inclusions: Same as above.

Slip: Same as above but the color is cream-white (7.5YR 8/4).

Decoration: None found.

Vessel forms: Large plates with molded rim and ring foot. Bailey noted only bowls at Hermopolis, which he said were copied from the white-slipped wares of Aswan (1990, 5).

Archaeological context: Only three sherds, one rim and two joining base sherds, were found. They may be fragments of the same vessel. The sherds come from Loci 121 (Room 5) and 125 (Room 6) in Square One. Bailey dates this ware from the sixth to eight centuries, based on the dates of the Aswan white slip ware (1990, 5).

c. Bichrome Ware

Paste and inclusions: Same as above.

Slip: Same as above, but various hues of red (2.5YR 5/8); 10R 5/8; 5YR 7/6) along the rim on the outside and reddish yellow (7.5YR 7/4) on the rest.

Decoration: Impressions on the outside wall.

Vessel forms: One rim sherd of a bowl with straight rim and one base sherd of a plate (?) with ring foot.

Archaeological context: The rim sherd comes from Locus 124 (Room 5) and the base sherd from Locus 121 (Room 5).

2. Red Slip Ware with Solid Brown Fabric = Middle Egyptian (Theban) Mud Ware — Family T (Adams); L7 Ware (Pierrat)

This ware is similar in the fabric to Hermopolite Ware but never exhibits a different core color. The slip is thinner and it is not polished. Vessels also show a different range of shapes, closer to the Aswan Ware shapes. Bailey equates this ware with Hayes' ERSW B and suspects its production in the Delta (1990, 4).

Paste: Fine grained, soft (3-4 on the Mohs scale), and dense. Color varies through the range of orange-brown to reddish brown (2.5YR 4/6, 5YR 4/6, 10R 4/6).

Inclusions: Abundant mica and some white stone particles of medium to coarse size, density about 40%.

Slip: Thin, adheres well to the paste, applied to inside and outside; smooth and dull. The color is red (10R 4/6).

Decoration: None found.

Vessel forms: Only open, bowls and deep plates; common are bowls with flaring walls, thickened rim, and flat base; deep plates have flaring, molded rims and ring feet. The shapes imitate Aswan shapes.

Archaeological context: Present throughout the excavated levels in Square One and in the lowest excavated levels in Square Two (Loci 61-64).

Red Slip Wares of Marl and Mixed Clays

1. Orange-pink Paste with White Inclusions

This ware does not correspond to any classification and was unfamiliar to both Adams and Rodziewicz. It is possible that it was produced locally as imitation of Aswan red slip ware.

Paste: Fine grained, soft (3 on the Mohs scale), and porous. The color is orange-pink to grayish pink (2.5YR 6/6, 5YR 6/4).

Inclusions: White inclusions (limestone) of medium to coarse size and some fine mica; density is about 20%; occasional ground sherds of coarse size.

Slip: Thick, flaking off the paste; smooth and dull; color similar to the paste color with a stronger red hue (2.5YR 6/4).

Decoration: Undecorated, but several sherds of large plates have painted decoration in the style of AIIW3 ware.

Vessel forms: Only open, bowls and plates. Most of the shapes imitate bowls with thickened molded rims or plates with flaring molded rims of the AIIR4 ware.

Archaeological context: Very common in all the excavated levels in Square One and in the lowest excavated levels in Square Two (Loci 61-64).

2. Orange Paste and Orange Slip

This could be another local product, since it is also unknown at other excavated sites that provided parallels for the material from Akhmīm.

Paste: Fine grained, soft (3–4 on the Mohs scale), and dense. The color is reddish brown (2.5YR 5/6).

Inclusions: White and black particles

Slip: Thin, adheres well to the paste, applied to inside and outside; smooth and dull; same color as the paste.

Decoration: None found.

Vessel forms: Only bowls of small size; imitation of the Aswan ware bowls with flaring walls and plain rim.

Archaeological context: Found only in Square Two in the lowest excavated levels (Loci 61-64).

BIBLIOGRAPHY

Adams, William Y. 1962. "An Introductory Classification of Christian Nubian Pottery." *Kush* 10:245–88.

Adams, William Y. 1964. "An Introductory Classification of Meroitic Pottery." *Kush* 12:126–73.

Adams, William Y. 1986. *Ceramic Industries of Medieval Nubia*, part 1 and 2. Lexington: University of Kentucky.

Adams, William Y. 1986/87. "Times, Types, and Sites: the Interrelationship of Ceramic Chronology and Typology." *Bulletin of the Egyptological Seminar* 8:7–46.

Bailey, Donald M. 1983. *Ashmunein*. British Museum Occasional Paper 46.

Bailey, Donald M. 1990a. "The local Roman Red Slip Ware of Hermopolis Magna." *Coptic and Nubian Pottery. Part I. Occasional Paper* 1:4-26. National Museum in Warsaw.

Bailey, Donald M. 1990a. "Late Roman pottery in the Nile Valley - a discussion." *Coptic and Nubuan Pottery. Part I. Occasional Paper* 1:27-28. National Museum in Warsaw.

Ballet, Pascale. 1990. "Ceramics, Coptic." *The Coptic Encyclopedia*. 480-94.

Ballet, Pascale, and M. Picon. 1987. "Recherches préliminaires sur les origines de la céramique des Kellia (Egypte). Importations et productions égyptiennes." *Cahiers de la céramique égyptienne* 1:39-47. Cairo.

Ballet, Pascale, and Fatma Mahmoud, Michèle Vichy, Maurice Picon. 1991. "Artisanat de la céramique dans l'Egypte romaine tardive et byzantine. Prospections d'ateliers de potiers de Minia à Assouan." *Cahiers de la Céramique Egyptienne* 2:129-43. Cairo.

Blackman, Winfred S. 1968. *The Fellāhīn of Upper Egypt*. 2d. London: Frank Cass & Co. Ltd.

Bourriau, J. 1981. *Umm el-Ga'ab. Pottery from the Nile Valley before the Arab Conquest*. Exhibition at the Fitzwilliam Museum. Cambridge.

Butzer, Karl W. 1974. "Modern Egyptian Pottery Clays and Predynastic Buff Ware." *Journal of Near Eastern Studies* 33:377–82.

Egloff, Michel. 1977. *Kellia: La poterie copte*. Recherches suisses d'archeologie copte, vol. 2. Geneva: Georg.

Emery, W.B. 1938. *The Royal Tombs of Ballana and Qustul*. Cairo: Government Press.

Emery, W.B., and L.P. Kirwan. 1935. *The Excavations and Survey between Wadi es-Sebua and Adindan 1929–1931*. Cairo: Government Press.

Godlewski, Włodziemirz. 1990. "Coptic pottery from Deir el Naqlun (Fayum)." *Coptic and Nubian Pottery. Part I. Occasional Paper* 1:49-62. National Museum in Warsaw.

Gorecki, Tomasz. 1990. "Coptic painted amphorae from Tell Atrib - introductory remarks on decoration." *Coptic and Nubian Pottery. Part I. Occasional Paper* 1:34-48. National Museum in Warsaw.

Hayes, John W. 1972. *Late Roman Pottery*. London: British School at Rome.

Hayes, John W. 1976. *Roman Pottery in the Royal Ontario Museum*. Toronto: Royal Ontario Museum.

Hayes, John W. 1980. *Supplement to Late Roman Pottery*. London: British School at Rome.

Hope, Colin A. 1981. "Dakleh Oasis Project - Report on the Study of Pottery and Kilns, Third Season 1980." *The Society for the Studies of Egyptian Antiquities Journal* 11:233-41.

Jacquet-Gordon, Helen. 1972. *Les ermitages chrétiens du désert d'Esna*, part 3: Céramique et objets. Publications de l'Institut français d'archéologie orientale, vol. 39, no. 3. Cairo: IFAO.

Johnson, Barbara. 1981. *Pottery from Karanis*. Ann Arbor: University of Michigan.

Kubiak, Władisław. 1990. "Roman-type pottery in Medieval Egypt." *Coptic and Nubian Pottery. Part I. Occasional Paper* 1:71-82. National Museum in Warsaw.

Kubiak, Władisław, and George T. Scanlon. 1973. "Fustat Expedition: Preliminary report 1966." *Journal of the American Research Center in Egypt* 10:11-26.

Kubiak, Władisław, and George T. Scanlon. 1989. *Fustat Expedition Final Report, Volume 2: Fustat-C*. Cairo: American Research Center in Egypt Reports.

Mason, Robert B., and Keall Edward J. 1990. "Petrography of Islamic Pottery from Fustat." *Journal of the American Research Center in Egypt* 27:165-84.

Matson, Frederick R. 1974. "Technological Studies of Egyptian Pottery - Modern and Ancient." *Recent Advances in Science and Technology of Material III*. Ed. Adli Bishay. New York.

Mond, Robert, and Oliver H. Myers. 1934. *The Bucheum*, vol. 3. Egypt Exploration Society Memoir, no. 41. London: EES.

Mond, Robert, and Oliver H. Myers. 1940. *Temples of Armant*. 2 vols. Egypt Exploration Society Memoir, no. 43. London: EES.

Myers, Oliver H., and H.W. Fairman. 1931. "Excavations at Armant, 1929-31." *Journal of Egyptian Archaeology* 17:223-30.

Petrie, W.M. Flinders. 1905. *Ehnasya*. Egypt Exploration Fund Memoir, no. 26. London: EEF.

Pierrat, Geneviève. 1990. "Poteries trouvées dans les fouilles de Tôd 6e-12e siècles après J.C.." *Coptic and Nubian Pottery. Part I. Occasional Paper* 1:29-33. National Museum in Warsaw.

Pierrat, Geneviève. 1991. "Essai de classification de la céramique de Tôd." *Cahiers de la céramique égyptienne* 2:145-204. Cairo.

Porat, Naomi and Joseph Yellin, Lisa Heller-Kallai. 1991. "Correlation Between Petrography, NAA, and ICP Analyses: Application to Early Bronze Egyptian Pottery from Canaan." *Geoarchaeology* 6:2:133-49.

Rodziewicz, Mieczyslaw. 1972. "Die Keramikfunde der Deutschen Nubienunternehmungen 1968/69." *AA* 4:643-713.

Rodziewicz, Mieczyslaw. 1976. *Alexandrie I: La céramique romaine tardive d'Alexandrie*. Warsaw: Éditions scientifiques de Pologne.

Rodziewicz, Mieczyslaw. 1978. "La céramique émaillée copte de Kom el-Dikka." *Études et Travaux* 10:338-45.

Rodziewicz, Mieczyslaw. 1983. "Egyptian Glazed Pottery of the Eighth to Ninth Centuries." *Bulletin de la société d'archéologie copte* 25:73-75.

Rodziewicz, Mieczyslaw. 1984. *Alexandrie III: Les habitations romaines tardives d'Alexandrie à lumière des fouilles polonaises à kôm el-Dikka*. Warsaw: Éditions scientifiques de Pologne.

Rodziewicz, Mieczyslaw. 1985. "On the Origin of the Coptic Painted Pottery in Kharga Oasis." *Mélanges Gamal eddin Mokhta*, 235-41. Cairo: IFAO.

Rodziewicz, Mieczyslaw. 1986a. "The Christian Pottery in Nubia and Kharga Oasis." *Nubische Studien*. ed. Martin Krause, 367-74. Mainz am Rhein: Philipp von Zabern.

Rodziewicz, Mieczyslaw. 1986b. "Contribution to the Pottery from Professor Dr. Dinkler Excavations in Nubia (Kulb, Tangur, Ukkina, Sunnarti and Turmukki)." *Nubische Studien*. ed. Martin Krause, 375-78. Mainz am Rhein: Philipp von Zabern.

Rodziewicz, Mieczyslaw. 1986c. "Mareotic Incised Pottery of Coptic Period." *La sité monastique copte de Kellia: Sources historiques et explorations archéologiques*. Geneva: Mission suisse d'archéologie copte.

Rodziewicz, Mieczyslaw. 1987. "Introduction à la céramique à engobe rouge de Kharga." *Cahiers de la céramique Egyptienne* 1:123-36.

Rodziewicz, Mieczyslaw. 1988. "Archaeological Evidence on the Chronology of the Sunnarti Church." *Beitrage zur Sudanforschung* 3: 56-95.

Roeder, Günther, ed. 1959. *Hermopolis 1929-1939*. Wissenschaftliche Veröffentilichung, no. 4. Hildesheim: Gebrüder Gerstenberg.

Scanlon, George T. 1990. "Ceramics of the Late Coptic Period." *The Coptic Encyclopedia*. 494-511.

Shinnie, P.L., and Margaret Shinnie. 1963. "A New Pot Fabric from Nubia." *Antiquity* 37:61-63.

Tobia, S. K. and E. V. Syre. 1974. "An Analytical Comparison of Various Egyptian Soils, Clays,

Shales and Some Ancient Pottery by Neutron Activation." *Recent Advances in Science and Technology of Material III*. Ed. Adli Bishay. New York.

Ulbert, Thilo. 1971. "Keramikstempel aus Elephantine." *Mitteilungen des Deutsches Archaologisches Instituts, Abteilung Kairo* 27:235–42.

Whitcomb, Donald S. 1989. "Coptic Glazed Ceramics from the Excavations at Aqaba, Jordan." *Journal of the American Research Center in Egypt* 26:167–82.

Whitcomb, Donald S., and Janet S. Johnson. 1982. *Quseir al-Qadim 1980:* American Research Center in Egypt Reports, vol. 7. Malibu: Undena Publications.

Winlock, H.E., and W. E. Crum. 1926. *The Monastery of Epiphanius at Thebes*, part 1. Egyptian Expedition Publications, vol 3. New York: Metropolitan Museum of Art.

Drawing 1, Plates
1. A.   OI.001.109.008.3112
1. B.   OI.001.060.001.0987
1. C.   OI.001.056.005.5851
1. D.   OI.001.060.001.0987

Drawing 2, Plates and Saucers:
2. A.   OI.001.10A.002.5547
2. B.   OI.002.059.025.6388
2. C.   OI.001.114.006.5370
2. D.   OI.001.191.002.8376

Drawing 3, Bowls:
3. A.   OI.001.158.002.7466
3. B.   OI.001.182.002.8328
3. C.   OI.001.164.002.7943
3. D.   OI.001.164.002.7945
3. E.   OI.001.168.003.7875
3. F.   OI.001.014.012.4164X
3. G.   OI.001.109.001.5352
3. H.   OI.001.151.002.7150

Drawing 4, Bowls:
4. A.   OI.001.151.005.7726
4. B.   OI.001.129.006.6164
4. C.   OI.001.099.001.4424
4. D.   OI.002.061.012.8693

Drawing 5, Bowls:
5. A.   OI.001.064.006.1503
5. B.   OI.001.093.001.4382
5. C.   OI.001.014.025.5624
5. D.   OI.001.062.005.1134
5. E.   OI.001.099.002.4452
5. F.   OI.001.100.003.4544
5. G.   OI.001.014.017.5459
5. H.   OI.001.150.003.1969

Drawing 6, Deep Bowls:
6. A.   OI.001.091.010.4116
6. B.   OI.001.091.010.4106A
6. C.   OI.001.151.002.7154
6. D.   OI.002.052.000.2437
6. E.   OI.002.061.081.9408
6. F.   OI.002.040.002.0392
6. G.   OI.002.039.004.0321
6. H.   OI.001.001.001.0001

EGYPTIAN SLIP WARE DRAWINGS:
List of Pieces Illustrated

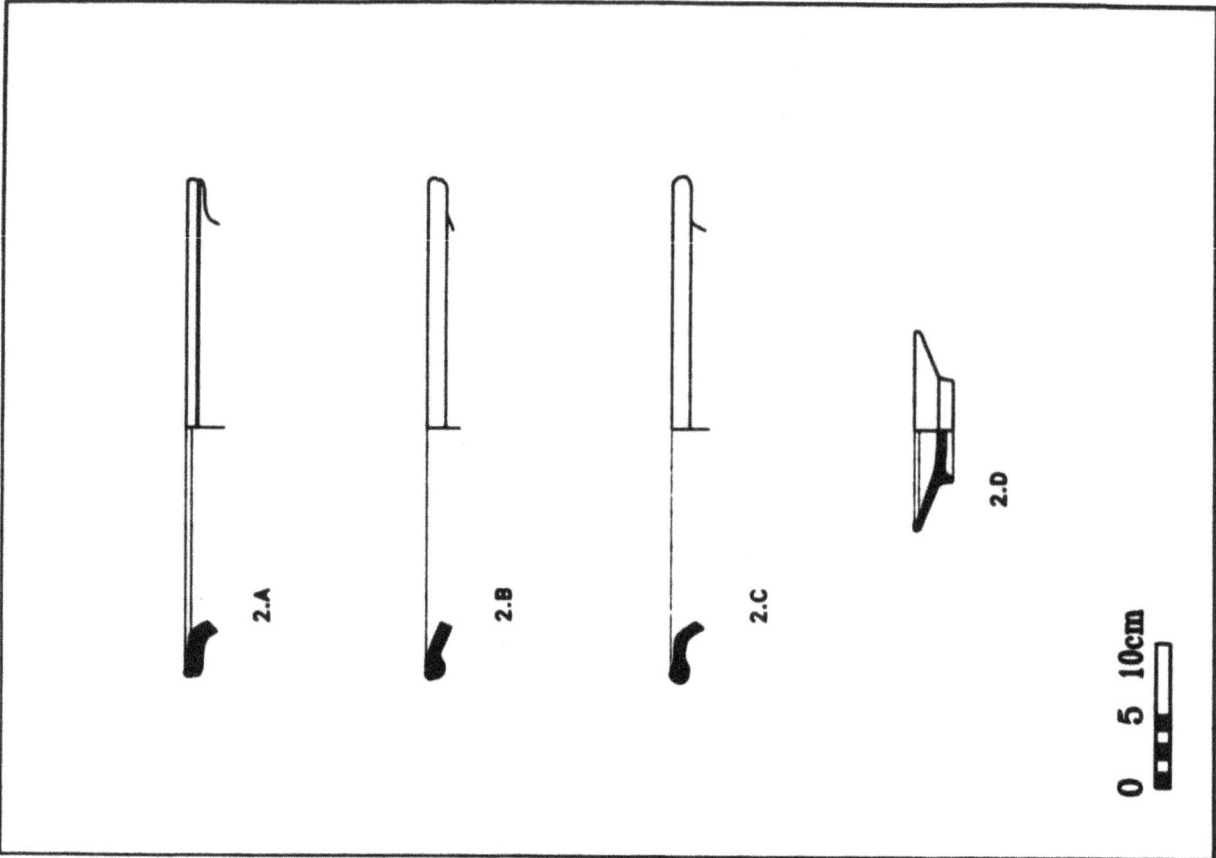

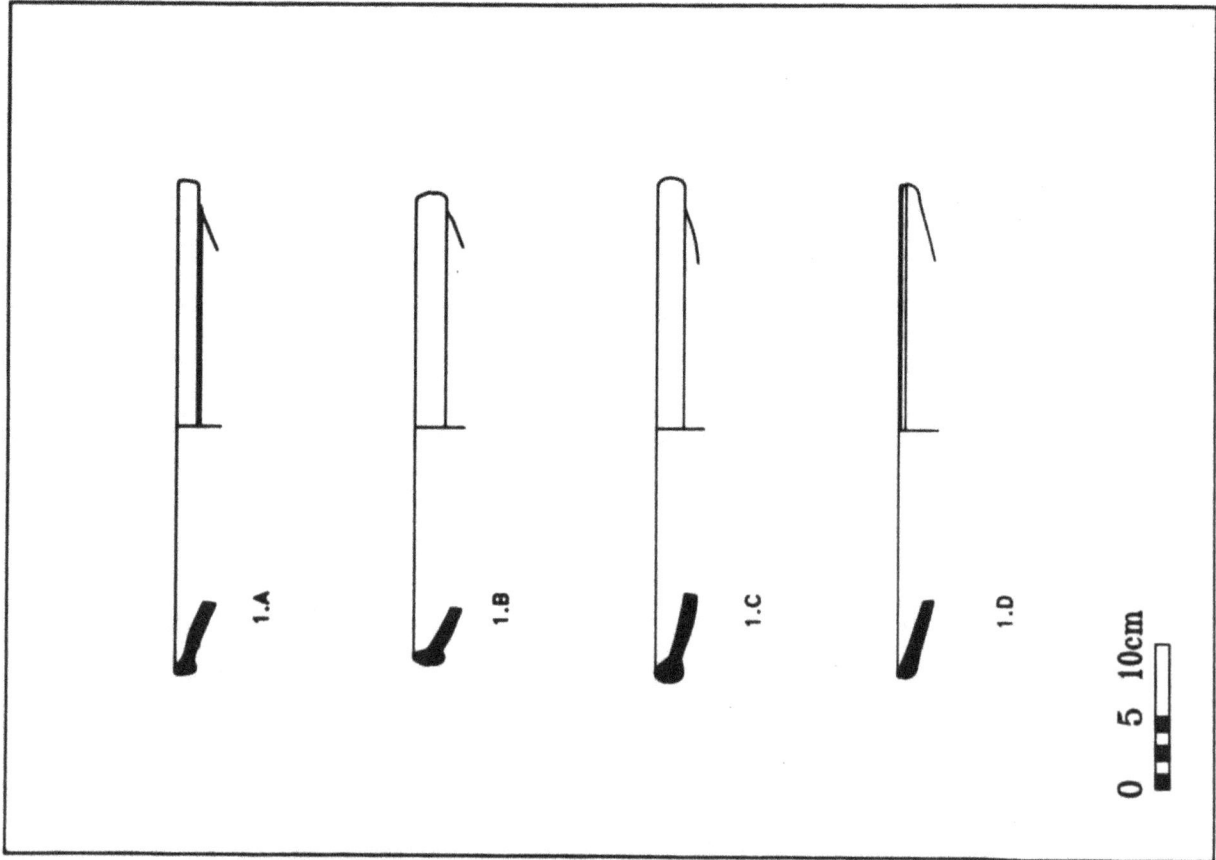

DRAWING 1, PLATES; DRAWING 2, PLATES AND SAUCERS

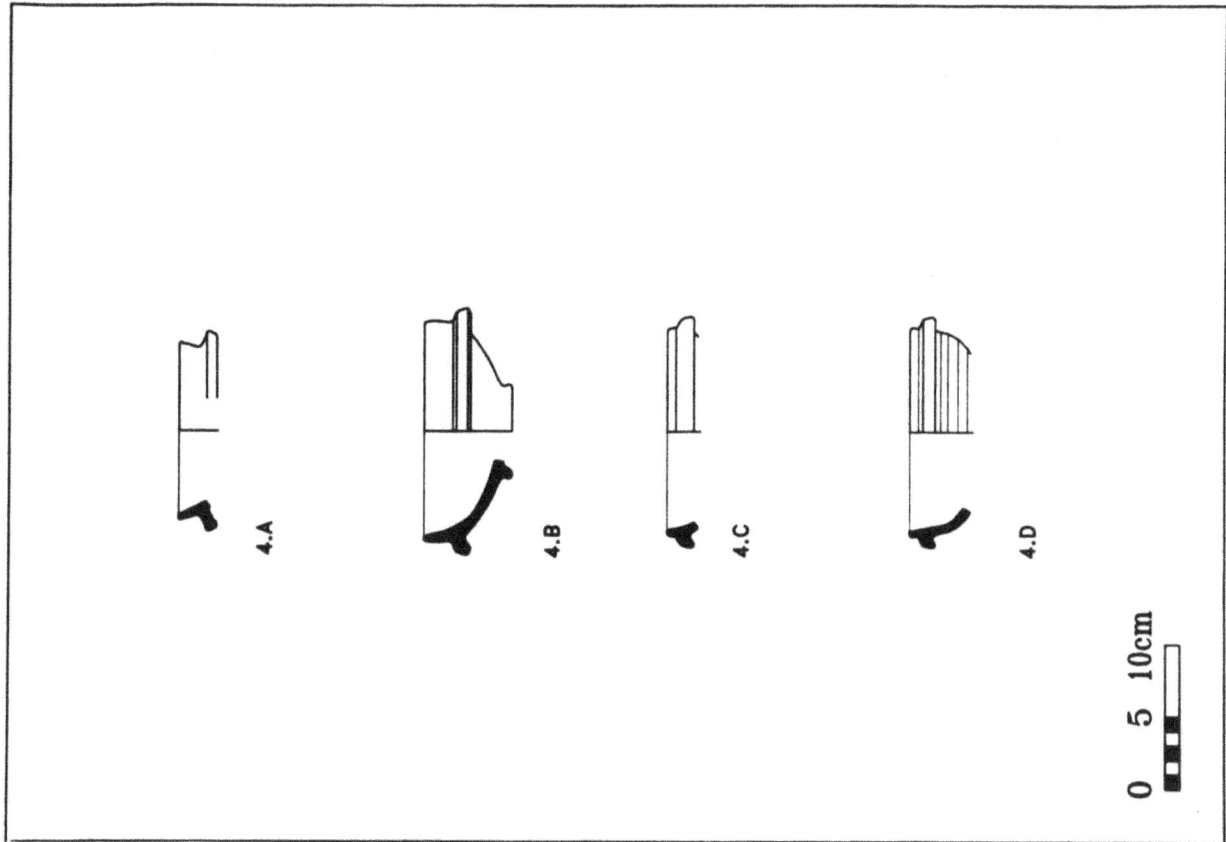

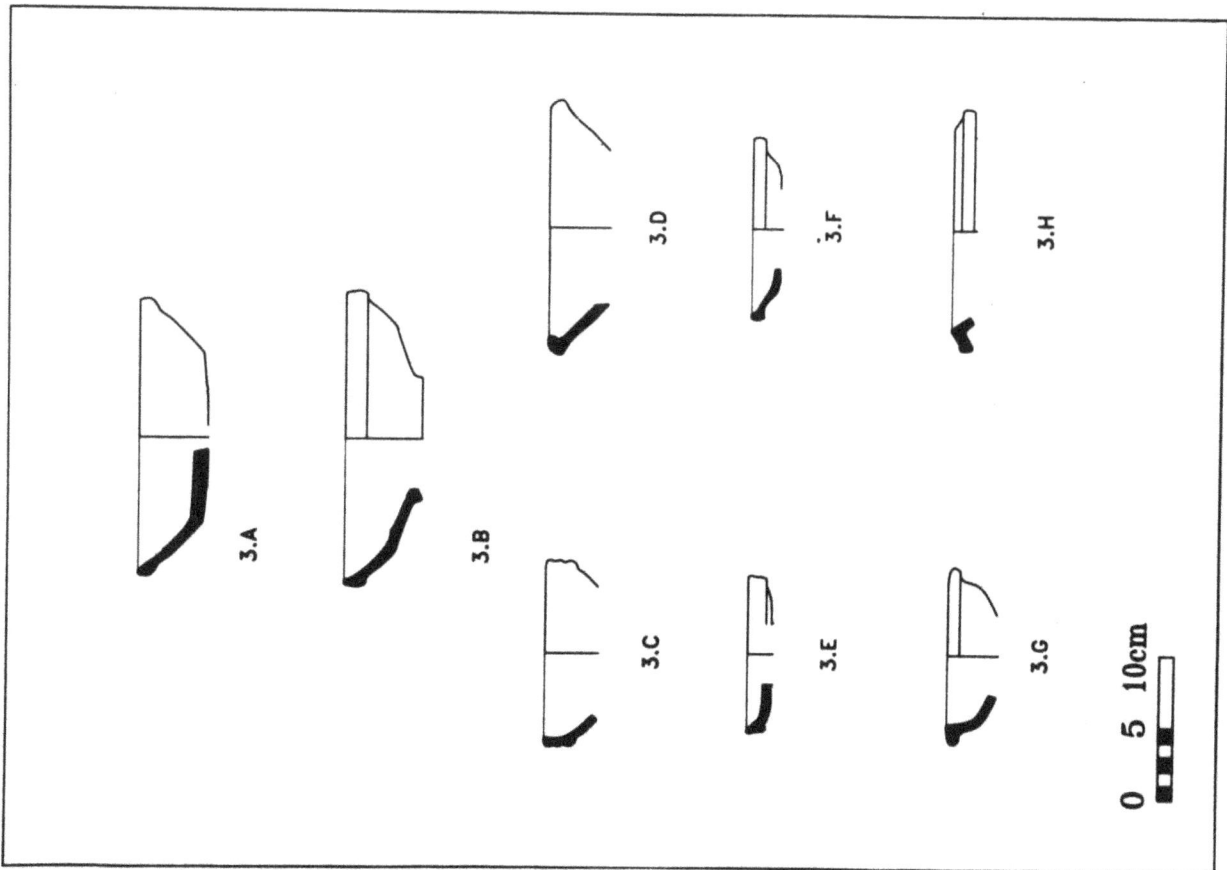

DRAWINGS 3 AND 4, BOWLS

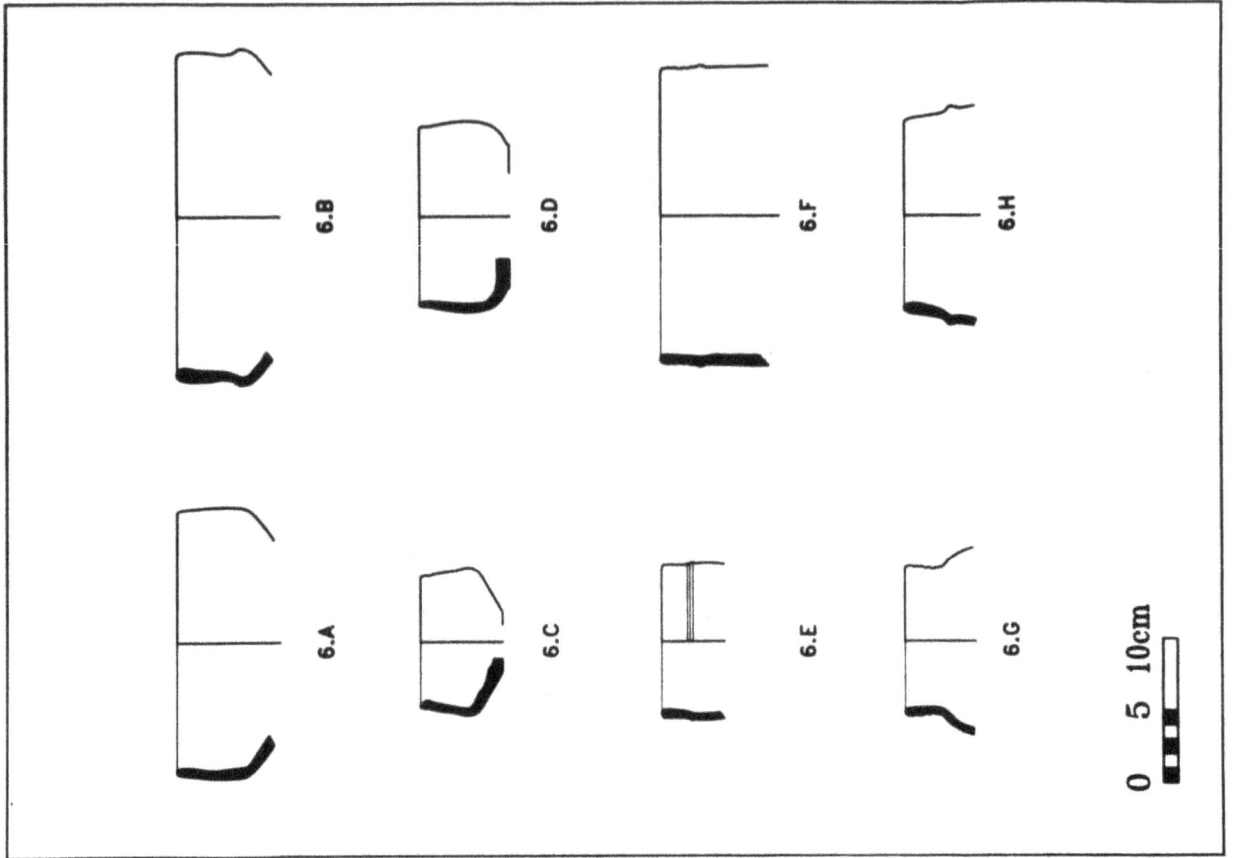

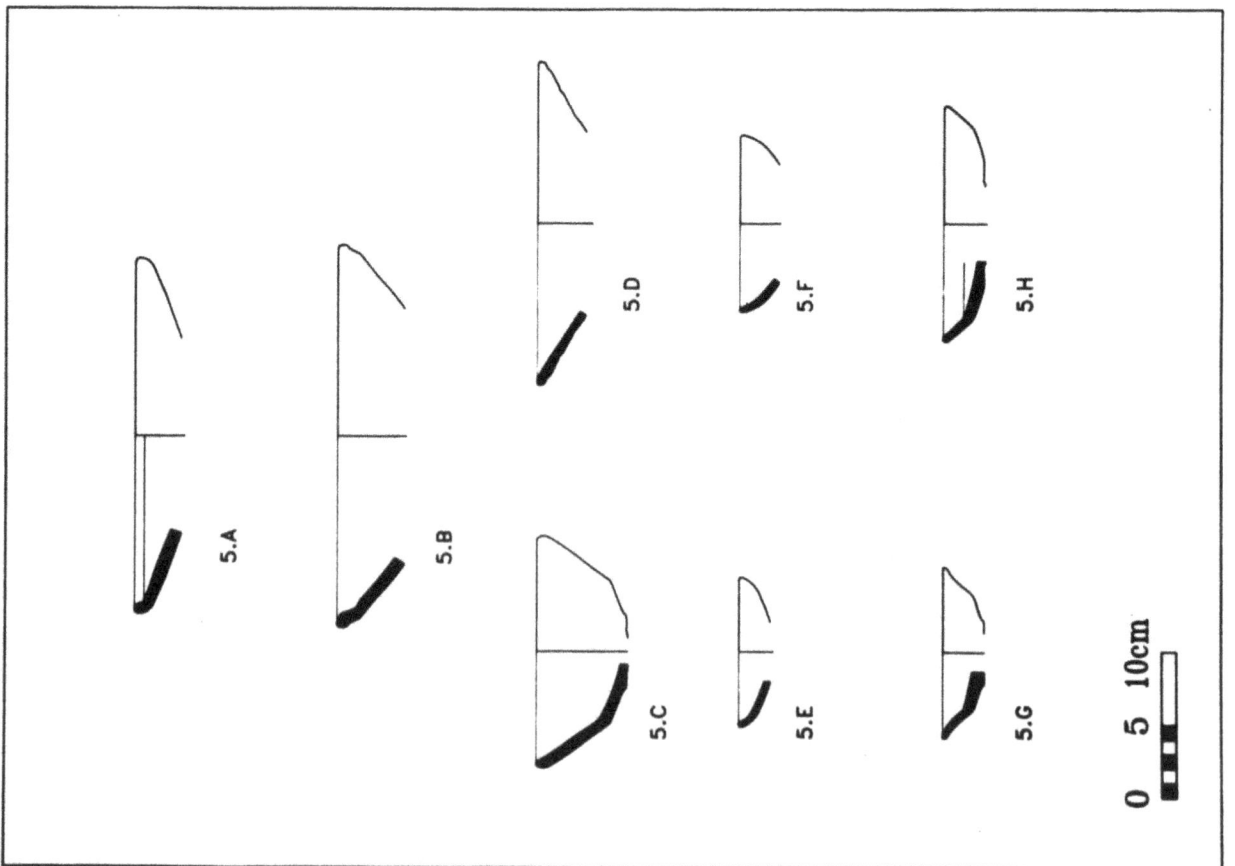

DRAWING 5, BOWLS; DRAWING 6, DEEP BOWLS

Chapter 9

SOME CHANGES OVER TIME:
THE POTTERY EVIDENCE

The graphs published here represent a modest beginning of statistical analysis. They indicate some overall changes during the history of the site as well as indicating problems for further study. The following discussion concentrates on suggestions that can be made about changes in city life, or at least life in this area. Methodological issues are kept to a minimum. They will be the focus of further discussion when more analysis has been carried out.

Two issues in interpretation concern the amount of earlier material one can expect to find in any level, and the relationship between function and time as an agent of change. Another type of issue concerns the usefulness of different types of statistics. Even the limited work carried out so far indicates considerable potential for future analysis of these issues.

The first sets of graphs represent the counting and weighing that occurred on site (see above, p. 66). First the categories are explained. Then an overall picture is described as it emerges from graphs showing the loci combined into larger groups as discussed above (pp. 25 and 85). Some tentative suggestions of factors that may be involved in these changes are presented as a basis for further consideration in studying the site. A more detailed analysis follows, based on graphs of individual loci within the larger groups. In this discussion, reference is also made to graphs of counts of catalogued rims. At the end of the chapter come brief discussions of the distribution of Aswan Painted Wares and Egyptian Slip Wares, based on graphs of the catalogued material.

Breakdown by Field Types[56]:

Five pottery types appear on these graphs

A: Mainly amphorae, but see below

B. Coarse ware, much of it local

C. Finer ware, often similar in fabric to A

H. Red and white slipped, unpainted fine wares, almost entirely Egyptian

Y. Glazed Ware

Of these, A Wares generally indicate trade in wine and foodstuffs: H Wares trade in fine table ware, and Y Wares trade in another form of fine table ware. Most of B wares are likely to have been locally produced. C wares probably include locally produced and "imported" (i.e., Hermopolite?) pieces. Fluctuations in amounts may have to do with fluctuations in the amount of trade, perhaps

indicating the level of prosperity: in the use of spaces: and in changes in taste.

All remaining types (see note 55) are grouped as "Other," because the amount represented of any one is seldom sufficient to show up on a chart.

In the main set of charts, statistics from the lower square, Square One, are presented only for one room, Room 2, so that the coherence of the sequence is assured. Room Two was entirely in the Statistical Zone (see above pp. 21, 23). The overall chart shows the percentages from the five groupings discussed above (Ch. 3, and chart p. 36):

Bottom Habitation: Loci 195, 189, 181, 180, 177, 174.

Middle Habitation : Loci 182, 172, 166, 164, 158, 155, 68, and 14 baskets 18-24.

Top Habitation levels: Locus 14 baskets 1-17.

Debris: (mainly deliberate filling): Loci 20, 18, 13, 12, 8, 7.

Contaminated: Loci : 1,5.

The charts for Square Two represent the whole area within the Statistical Zone (see above p. 23), that is, all loci except the enlargements of the square at the top. They are presented in the five groupings discussed above (Ch. 5).

Bottom (byproducts of industrial activity): Loci 64, 63, 62, 61.37,38,39,40,41,42,50,51

Dumping: Loci 60, 59, 58, 52, 51, 50,38,34.

Varied activities : Loci 32, 31, 27, 26, 24, 23, 21, 20, 19, 18.

Cemetery: Loci 17, 16, 15, 14, 13, 12, 8, 7, 5, 4.

Recent: Loci 11, 10, 6, 3, 2.

Charts based on weights are used, because weights were obtained in both 1978 and 1980. Some charts of counts are included for comparison. The patterns remain substantially the same. They are, however, markedly different from the charts based on counts of rims, in which the distinction between open and closed vessels makes itself felt.

1. Overall Picture

The first four charts show distributions by weight in the large groupings in the two Squares.[57] In Square

---

[56]Schrunk outlines the Field Typology on pages 66-67 above, and then discusses its subsequent modification.

[57]The next eight charts, showing counts when they were available, and counts of registered rim sherds, are included for comparison but not discussed here.

One, B Ware predominates in the Bottom Habitation levels,[58] constituting about 50% by weight. A Ware is the next largest group, constituting about 47%. The remaining wares, including both local and imported table wares (H and C) form very small percentages, less than 10% in all. No other group of loci on these two charts shows such a dominance of A and B wares, and B ware only reaches the same dominance once again (in the "Varied" loci of Square Two).

In the Middle Habitation levels, the percentage of A Ware remains about the same, but the percentage of B Ware drops and percentages of the remaining wares increase, most notably the percentage of H, or Egyptian Slip Ware, which doubles.

In the Top Habitation levels, the percentage of B Ware shrinks notably, and the percentage of A Ware increases. The percentages of other wares also change, less significantly. The percentage of H ware falls, although not as low as in the Bottom Habitation levels.

In the Debris or dumped fill over the abandoned habitation, the percentage of A Ware remains almost exactly what it had been in the Upper Habitation levels. The percentage of B Ware continues to drop, accompanied by an increase in the percentage of Other. C Ware remains about the same. H Ware all but disappears, replaced by a very similar percentage of Glazed Ware. A modified view of the relative importance of H and Y, Egyptian Slip and Glazed Wares, emerges from graphs of rim sherds in these levels, see Detailed Analysis below.)

The supposedly Contaminated levels break drastically with the patterns found in the preceding loci, or those in the upper square. "Other" constitutes the largest percentage, followed by Glazed Ware. A and B both shrink drastically. Although it is hard to see why this change would occur as a result of the recent building activities (see above p. 21), it nonetheless seems best to conclude that these loci have indeed been contaminated, and not to try to find a historical reason for the changes. The total amounts of pottery are in any case very small.

The lowest levels, i.e., the grouping called Bottom, in the Square Two end at about the level of these Contaminated levels in Square One (i.e., at c. 60.32 m ASL: excavation in the Square One began at 62.39 m ASL, see above p. 23). All of the groupings of loci in Square Two contain larger amounts of pottery than those in Square One, because in Square One the bar graphs show information from only one part of the Statistical Zone. In the upper square no major horizontal divisions appeared within the Statistical Zone, so the total statistics are presented.

In the Bottom, the percentage of A Ware rises In the Square One: Debris levels it formed under 20%, and now rises to over 65%. The percentage of B Ware

declines. All the remaining wares together form about 15%, a little less than they do in the Debris levels of the lower square. A surprising break in the apparent pattern of continuing change however is that the Glazed Ware becomes statistically invisible, and the C ware also shrinks notably.

The Dump levels remain very similar to the bottom levels in the latter respect. Percentages of H Ware, C Ware, and Other remain constant, and Glazed Ware remains invisible. The amount of A Ware however declines by almost 10%, and B Ware fills the gap.

In the Varied levels marked change occurs. A Ware drops to its lowest percentage so far in either square, under 20% of the total. B Ware assumes the most dominant position so far, about 70%. H Ware and C Ware both disappear, and Glazed Ware reappears in a percentage double that in the Debris levels of the lower square.

The Cemetery levels contain a slightly smaller percentage of Glazed Ware, and a higher percentage of A Ware. The A Ware in these levels however is no longer primarily amphorae. In the Recent levels Glazed Ware again shrinks slightly, A Ware rises slightly, and B Ware remains the same.

2. Considerations for Interpretation

The earliest habitation levels reached are notable among all these groups for the predominance of wares that may have been locally made, and the small amount of fine table ware, that is H or Y. These characteristics seem to indicate relative impoverishment. All dating is so far highly tentative, until the finds have been further studied and the site further explored, but these loci must belong to either the latest Roman or the immediate post-Conquest period. Impoverishment in either one would be understandable, and interesting. It should however be noted that these levels are in or near a storage bin. If the loci accumulated while this part of the room was being used for storage, rather than being brought in as make-up for a floor, the apparent poverty of their composition may reflect that use.

The succeeding Habitation levels, both Middle and Top, consisted mainly of material brought in to create a succession of floors. Therefore the pottery mixtures probably accumulated during dumping outside the house rather than living inside the house. (There are exceptions to this principle, see above p.26.) Fine table ware forms a respectable percentage in these levels, and the amount of A Ware relative to B Ware increases, probably an indication of modest economic improvement.

Much of the material in the so-called Debris levels was probably dumped into the room at one time, after the house had been abandoned and partly demolished. The material indicates continued economic improvement, and change in taste. A Ware remains at the same level as in the last phases of habitation, i.e., Top Habitation, but Glazed Ware now takes the same position that Egyptian Slip had held in that phase. Glazed Ware coexists with a small amount of Slip Ware (represented by the small space between Y and C on the bar).

---

[58] I am using the term "levels" here when I refer to groupings of loci. These groupings are intended to represent phases, but the degree to which the discrete phases could be clearly separated differs in different cases as discussed above in Chapters 3 and 5. "Phase" is used here only to refer to what seems to be a clearly defined set of activities.

If the small remnants of construction found in and above the Debris levels of this square have been correctly interpreted as part of new housing, then the new housing may have been prompted by a rising standard of living, and perhaps a change in taste (but see above p. 48). The Glazed Ware seems to place this phase in the Fatamid Period.

The relationship between the highest level in this square and the lowest ones in the upper square remains enigmatic. In one respect, the Bottom levels of Square Two seem to continue patterns observed in the Debris levels of Square One, suggesting that they may form a chronological sequence. (The Contaminated loci are discounted in this assessment.)

The Bottom levels in Square Two have been interpreted as relating to nearby industrial activity, possibly glass making (see above p. 59). There is a continued rise in A Ware, or amphorae. This rise certainly relates to the use of the area rather than simply to increased trade in foodstuffs, since the secondary use made of amphorae was one of the principal indications of the industrial activity in these levels.

But if there is a strong element of apparent continuity with developments in Square One, there is also a notable break, i.e., the virtual disappearance of Glazed Ware and the reappearance of Egyptian Slip Ware. H Ware appears in a percentage equal to its place in the Middle Habitation phase of Room 2 in Square One. The decline in Glazed Ware by itself might be an indication of impoverishment, or simply a result of the industrial use of the area. The resurgence of Egyptian Slip Wares is harder to explain. Just conceivably, it could be a sign either of impoverishment or of conservative reaction in taste, causing people to stop buying glazed pottery from the North and increase buying more old fashioned, presumably cheaper, fine table ware produced in the South.

Another possibility to consider is that the material deposited in these Bottom levels may come from a period considerably earlier than that represented by the Debris levels in the lower square. In the context of an Egyptian city tell, such a discrepancy between absolute levels and dates, presupposing something in the nature of a hillock rising beside the houses in Square One, is unlikely but not impossible. Only further excavation can shed light on this problem.

In the Dump levels, the material dumped above the industrial area after it had gone out of use, a decline in the percentage of A Ware amphorae reflects that changed use. The odd prominence of Egyptian Slip Ware and lack of Glazed Ware continues.

In the period of time during which the space was being used in a variety of ways (i.e., forming the loci called "Varied"), two changes linked to chronology occur. Amphorae become relatively unimportant, and Glazed Ware reappears as a strong component. Most of the glazed sherds may be tentatively dated to the Mamluke Period.

In the Cemetery and the Recent accumulations, A Ware makes a recovery, but it no longer represents amphorae, which have all but vanished. The percentages of Glazed Ware shrink, partly because of the use of the

site, and then more recently because the wares imported in the Nineteenth and Twentieth Century from England and Japan are much lighter than the older wares.

In summary then it may be suggested that there a steady rise in prosperity characterized the habitation in the house in the lower square. Finally that prosperity is accompanied by a change in taste that coincides with, and may have prompted, a reuse of the site. The changes in the upper square may have more to do with land use than with chronology, the exception being the decline of amphorae roughly coinciding with the disappearance of Egyptian Slip Wares and the appearance of Mamluke Glazed Wares.

3. Detailed Assessment

Square One: Bottom Habitation

The amount of pottery in the bottom habitation levels is about 60.30 kilos. The smallest amount is in locus 181, between 2 and 3 kilos, and the largest in locus 177, about 22 kilos. The percentages of weights show a fluctuation of A Ware from over 70% in Locus 189 to under 25% in Locus 180, of B Ware from under 20% in Locus 189 to about 70% in Locus 180, and of H Ware from invisible in Locus 180 to about 3% in Loci 189 and 174. Generally, A and H Wares rise and decline together, but probably no significance should be attributed to these variations since they involve small amounts of sherds. A Ware dominates at the bottom, but then falls abruptly. It should be noted that Locus 189, which has the highest percentage of A Ware, is roughly equivalent to 180, which has the least. The sustained drop in A Ware in the next three loci may be more significant.

Square One: Middle Habitation

The amount of pottery in these loci totals about 95.16 kilos. The largest locus, 158, has over 26 kilos; the smallest had less than 3. A Ware varies from just under 28% in Locus 166 to almost 75 % in Locus 68. B Ware varies from about 59 % in Locus 166 to about 21% in Locus 68, and H Ware from about 7% to 3%. The percentage of A Ware is low in the two lowest loci, then rises. The sharp rise in Loci 182 and 172, which overlap Locus 164, is less significant than the sustained rise in Loci 158, 155, and 68, and the similarity between 155 and the bottom baskets of Locus 14, called 14B here. Changes in the percentage of A correlate with the fluctuation of both B Ware and "Other." They correlate negatively, if at all, with the percentage of H Ware. Joining sherds have led to the conclusion that much of the material in these loci may have been deposited at one time, so these variations may not be significant.

Square One: Top Habitation

This grouping is by far the smallest, consisting of 17 baskets from Locus 14, a total of (under 20 kilos) kilos, varying from well under a kilo in some baskets to 6.94 kilos in the largest one. The excavator believed that this material constituted two floors, one comprised by baskets 1 through 7, and the other by baskets 8 through 19 (see above p. 26, note 46). Nineteen has been reassigned to the Middle Habitation. No change in overall distribution can be noted between the two supposed floors, but the upper group of baskets contains a larger amount of Glazed Ware, concentrated in Loci 2 and 3.

Square One: Debris

The total weight of pottery from the debris (or deliberately dumped fill) is 163 kilos. Weights from different loci varies from just over 16 kilos from Locus 12) to about 47.50 from Locus 18. A Ware fluctuates from about 44.43 % in Locus 8 to 67. 31 % in Locus 13. B Ware fluctuates from 14.24 % in Locus 13 to 34.72 % in Locus 8. A Ware is notably more important, and B Ware correspondingly less important, in the lower loci, 20, 13, and 12, compared to the upper loci, 8, 7 and 18. Somewhat surprisingly, if one expects a steady decline over time, H Ware is more strongly represented in the upper three loci, although it is a minimal presence throughout. Glazed Ware is present in fairly constant amounts, fluctuating from under 1% to slightly under 2.50% in Loci 12, 8, and 18. Other Wares are strongly represented toward the bottom, and decline in the higher loci except Locus 18.

Rim counts, not illustrated here, clearly indicate the continued presence of H Ware along side Y Ware. Rims of Egyptian Slip Wares equal or exceed the number of glazed rims in most loci.

Square Two: Bottom (related to industrial use)

These loci vary greatly in size. The small final locus, 64, yielded only a little over 65 kilos of potsherds. The deposit of ash and slag, Locus 62, yielded 80.68 kilos. Locus 63 yielded almost 422 kilos, and Locus 61 slightly over 769 kilos. Nevertheless, the distribution of pottery wares remains consistent throughout. A ware varies only from 59.93 to 70.78 %, B ware from 16 to 24.59% %, C Ware constant at about 2%, H ware from just under 3% to 6.63%.

Square Two: Dump[59]

These loci decline in total content from 237 kilos in Locus 60 to about 75 kilos in Locus 38, before rising again to almost 193 kilos in Locus 34. All the loci below 34 however are quite similar, and resemble those in the Bottom. In these loci, A Ware dominates, fluctuating from 65.63% in Locus 51 to 55.91% in Locus 50, but usually usually between constituting between 60% and 65%. B Ware fluctuates from 19.98 to 26.91%, constituting about 20 to 22 % in most loci. H Ware fluctuates between 2.03% and 5.75%. The percentage of H Ware declines in the upper loci, at the same time that a small percentage of Glazed Ware appears.

The uppermost locus assigned to this grouping, Locus 34, presents a markedly different picture from the others and should probably be seen as representing a distinct phase. A Ware drops precipitously to just over 38%, the amount of B ware increases to just over 54%. Fine wares of any kind almost disappear, but Glazed Ware at 1.26% dominates H Ware at 0.51%

---

[59] A number of small loci, all part of one tip, have been omitted from this chart. They resemble the other loci below Locus 34.

Square Two: Varied Activities.

The amount and distribution of pottery in these loci fluctuate considerably, reflecting the various procedures of formation. Most of these loci are small, containing from five to forty-five kilos of pottery. The lowest sabah layers, Locus 32 and 31, closely resemble most of the loci in the Dump (except Locus 34) in the percentages of A and B wares. Loci 31 and 32 differ mainly from the lower ones mainly in that H ware is absent. In the next sabah layer, Locus 27, and the pit-like formation, Locus 26, the amount of A ware drops precipitously, probably reflecting the declining use of this ware for amphorae carrying wine or foodstuffs. The percentage of B ware increases greatly, as does the percentage of Glazed Ware. A small amount of H ware appeared in the supposed pit. The small ashy deposit, Locus 24, contained more A Ware and less Glazed Ware. Locus 23, larger than Locus 24 in extent but only slightly larger in pottery yield, consists almost entirely of A Ware and a small amount of B ware. The upper four loci, on the other hand, although differing markedly in sizes, present a consistent picture in distribution. Loci 19, 20 and 21 are poprobably one deposit. Locus 18is probably results from a distinct, later action, but remains similar in pottery types. In all, B Ware forms the predominant ware, from 70 to 80%. A Ware varies from 5 to 25%, rising in the uppermost locus, Locus 18. Glazed Ware varies from 5 to 3%, first increasing and then declining in amount. A Ware amphorae have ceased to be an important factor: the A Ware sherds found in Locus 18 probably came from different pot types.

Square Two: Cemetery.

The total amount of pottery from the cemetery loci is small, with the exception of Locus 12. Loci 17, 16, 14 and 5 were mud brick walls and Locus 7 a packed surface, probably a floor. All contained small amounts of potsherds broken before this construction occurred. Nevertheless, they present a pattern of pottery usage consistent with that in the adjoining levels that formed after the walls had been built and while the burials were occurring. This pattern carries forward the developments that begin in the upper four loci grouped under "Varied." A Ware represents between 20 and 40% of the pottery in most of the loci, excluding the very small Loci 8 and 16. B Ware fluctuates from just under 50% to just above 60%. B Ware drops drastically in Locus 4, but this Locus, although large in extent, yielded very little pottery.

Aswan Painted Wares

The bar graphs of Aswan Painted Wares show counts of registered sherds. No sherds with painted decoration were discarded, so these represent all the Aswan Painted Wares found during excavation within the areas on which the preceding charts are based. The Aswan Painted Wares (a subtype of M in the field typology) have been classified according to Adams' system into types A2R14, A2W3, A3R12, A3W22, A4R24, and A4W12 (Adams 1986, cited above, p. 80). In Nubia Adams found the two

A2 types preceded the two A3 types, which in turn preceded the A4 types. The distribution of sherds at Akhmim indicates that Adams' typology, at least as far as it could be applied to these sherds, does not follow the chronological sequence he observed in Nubia.

A4W12 is the dominant type in all phases (i.e., locus groupings) from which more than a couple of sherds were recovered.[60] In the lower square, A3W22 is the next most strongly represented, followed by A2W3, and then A4R24. In the upper square on the other hand, A3R12 is the second most popular type, followed by A2R14 and A2W13. In Square One, White Slip types greatly predominate in all phases. Red Slip types form less than 10% of the painted Aswan sherds. In Square Two on the other hand, Red Slip forms close to 50% of painted Aswan sherds in the Bottom levels, and over 30% in the Dump levels.

A2R14: In Square One this type is not well represented. Sherds appear only in the Middle Habitation levels. They reappear in the same small number, but a slightly higher percentage of the whole, in the Bottom levels of Square Two, and in slightly larger quantity and percentage in the Dump levels

A2W3: A single A2W3 sherd appeared in the Bottom Habitation, in the lowest locus, 195. Sherds of this type appeared in all the other phases. There were few in the Middle and Top Habitation, but a larger percentage in the Debris levels above the supposed houses in Square One. In the Bottom and Dump levels of Square Two they occupied about the same place as in the Debris of Square One.

A3R12: In the lower square, sherds of A3R12 appeared only in the Debris levels, and only in small numbers. In the upper square on the other hand this type jumps to form the largest segment after A4W12. It is almost equal to A4W12 in the Bottom levels, and then falls slightly.

A3W22: This was the most popular type after A2R14, but always very much less well represented. In the Bottom and Dump levels of Square Two the amounts decline.

A4R24: Sherds of A4R24 constitute a small percentage of Aswan Painted sherds in the Middle Habitation, a larger percentage in the Top Habitation, and a small percentage again in the Debris levels of Square One. In the Bottom levels of Square Two, sherds of A4R24 form approximately the same percentage as in the Middle Habitation. In the Dump levels of Square Two this type declines slightly in popularity.

A4W12: Sherds of this type form about 70% of the Aswan Painted Wares in the Middle Habitation, Top Habitation, and Debris levels in Square One. In the

[60]Only a single Aswan Painted Ware sherd, type A2W3, was found in the Bottom Habitation levels. Substantial numbers of sherds come from the other phases in Square One, and from the lower phases in Square Two. In the later levels of that square they are almost entirely missing: The levels designated as Varied, Cemetery and Dump in Square Two are therefore omitted from the following summary, as are the Contaminated loci from Square One.

Bottom levels of Square Two they fall down to about 30%. In the dump levels the prcentage rises again, but does not equal what it had been in the lower square.

Egyptian Slip Wares.

These bar graphs, like the last, show counts of registered sherds. Some sherds were discarded, so these graphs do not represent all the Slip Ware found within the areas cited. The Egyptian Slip Ware (H in the field typology) was further divided into Hayes' Egyptian Red Slip Wares A and B, and three previously unrecognized other types, D, E and F, distinguished by Ivančica Schrunk. D is the designation used here for one marl or mixed clay fabric (see above p. 79, no. 1). F designates another marl or mixed clay fabric (see above p. 80, no. 2). E designates alluvial clay fabrics (see above p. 79, nos. 1 and 2).

The divisions here reflect fabric type, rather than an attempt at chronological typology like the divisions in the last graphs. Type A, the Aswan fabric, is always dominant. The small amount of Egyptian Slip Ware found in the Bottom Habitation levels of the houses in Square One occurred mainly in the uppermost loci of that grouping. Type A makes up about 60%, and it rises to between 70 and 76% in the later (Middle and Top) Habitation and in the the Debris levels. Type D, well represented in the Bottom and Middle Habitation, declines thereafter, a decline matched by the rise in the amount of Type E. Type B fluctuates more. Type F is only statistically visible in the Debris levels.

In Square Two Egyptian Slip Wares almost completely disappear above the Dump and Bottom levels. In the Bottom, i.e., the material around the upended amphorae (see above p. 59), very few sherds of Egyptian Slip Wares appeared. Almost all of those were in the uppermost locus in this group, Locus 61. Type A dominates to an even greater extent than in the levels of the lower square.

In the Dump levels, the amount of Egyptian Slip Ware found greatly exceeded the whole amount from Room 2 in the lower square. Most of this pottery came from the lower loci, loci 52 to 60. This concentration of Slip Ware and some joining sherds suggest that the top locus assigned to Bottom, locus 61, and these loci of Dump may represent one activity even though Locus 61 was notably different in color. Similar distinctions between Loci 52 to 60 and the remaining loci were not observed in the Aswan Painted Ware, or in the broader field types.

The percentage of Type A declined slightly from the percentage in the Bottom, but remained higher than in any of the groupings in the lower square. Types E and D continued to be next most frequent, although not well represented. Type B, as usual, was only a minor presence. For the first time, Type F appeared in some quantity.

Although there must be much mixing of materials first in the debris from which some of this material was brought to form levels, and again by contamination within the loci, it is striking that this large amount of Egyptian Slip Ware appears in loci that have very few Glazed Ware sherds.

As soon as those become numerous, in the loci formed by Varied Activities, the Egyptian Slip Ware almost totally disappears.

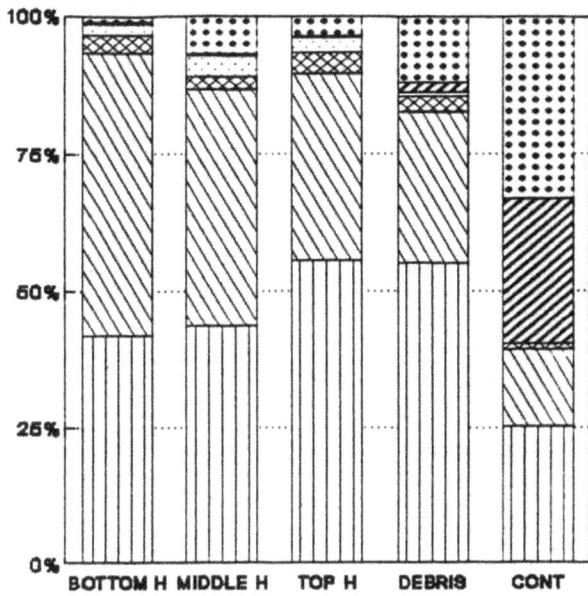

SQUARE ONE: ROOM TWO
PERCENTAGES

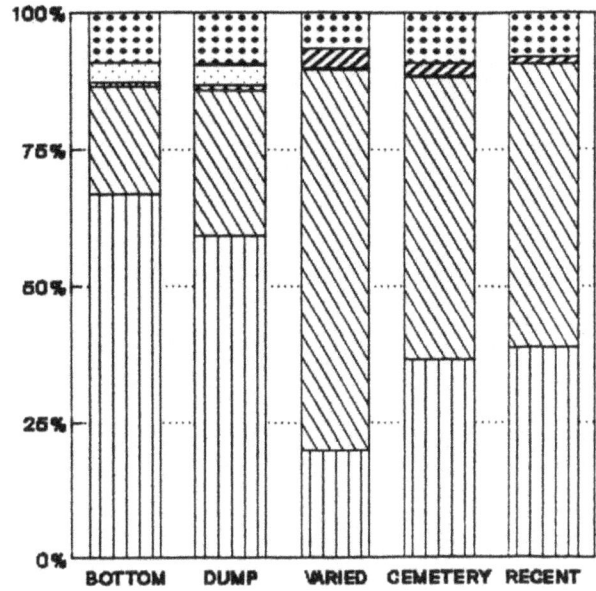

SQUARE TWO
PERCENTAGE

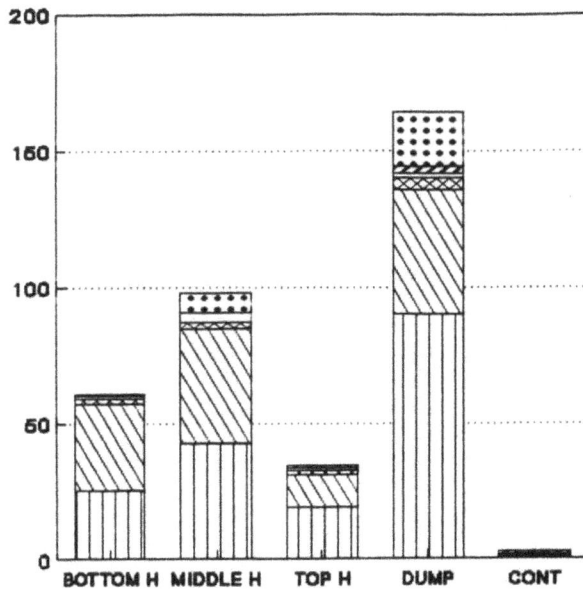

SQUARE ONE: ROOM TWO
KILOS

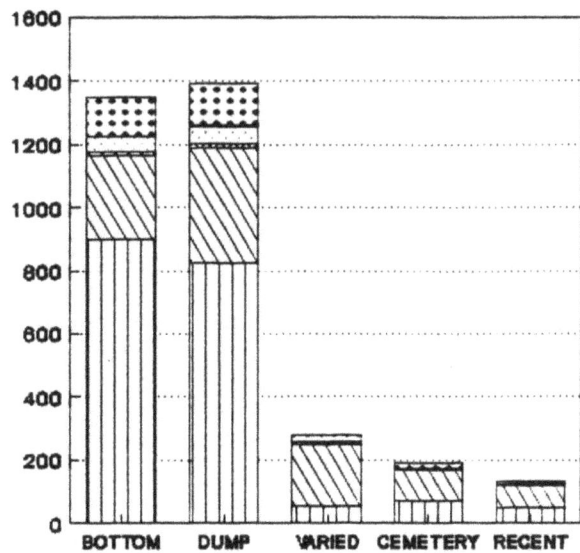

SQUARE TWO
KILOS

KEY

A B C H Y OTHER

OVERVIEW: WEIGHTS

CHANGES OVER TIME: THE POTTERY EVIDENCE

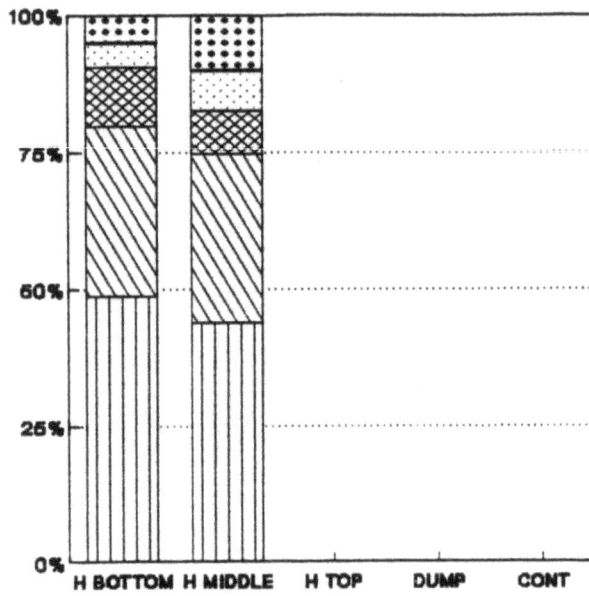

SQUARE ONE: ROOM TWO
PERCENTAGES

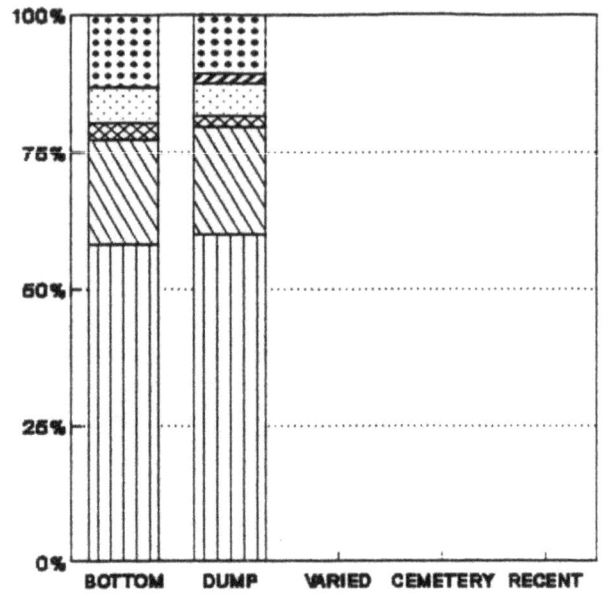

SQUARE TWO
PERCENTAGE

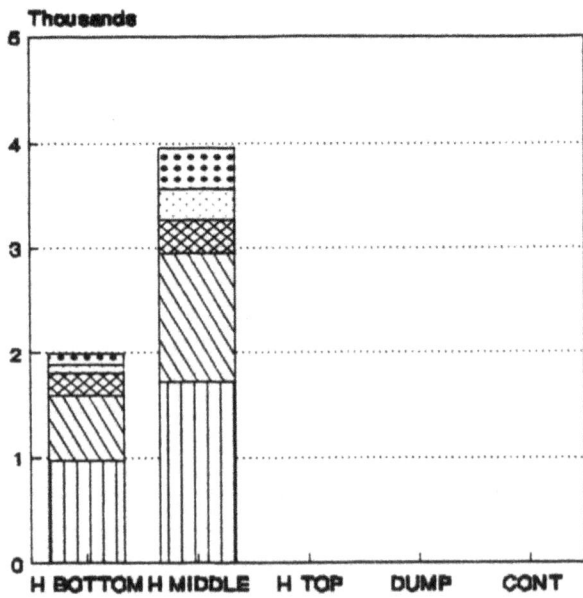

SQUARE ONE: ROOM TWO
THOUSANDS

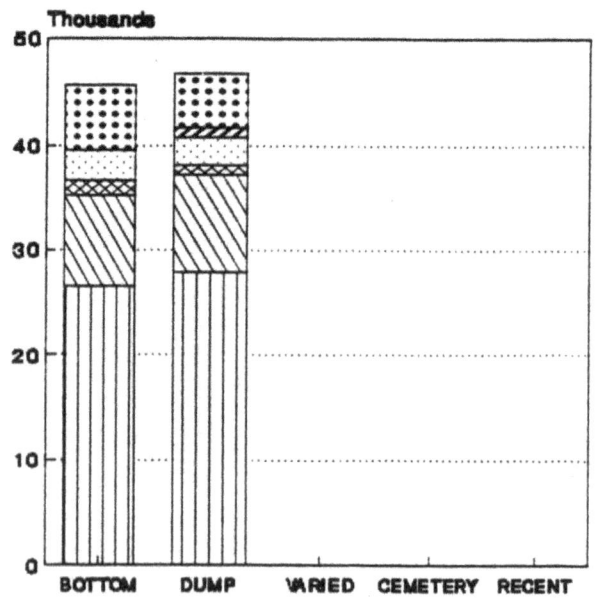

SQUARE TWO
THOUSANDS

KEY

A   B   C   H   Y   OTHER

OVERVIEW: COUNTS

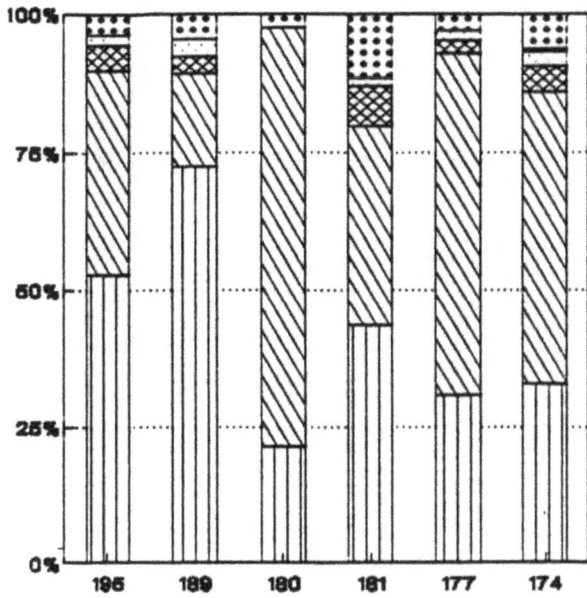

BOTTOM HABITATION

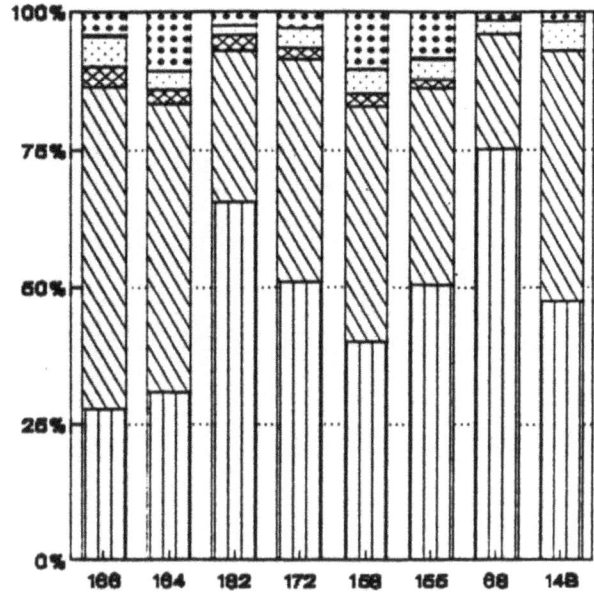

MIDDLE HABITATION

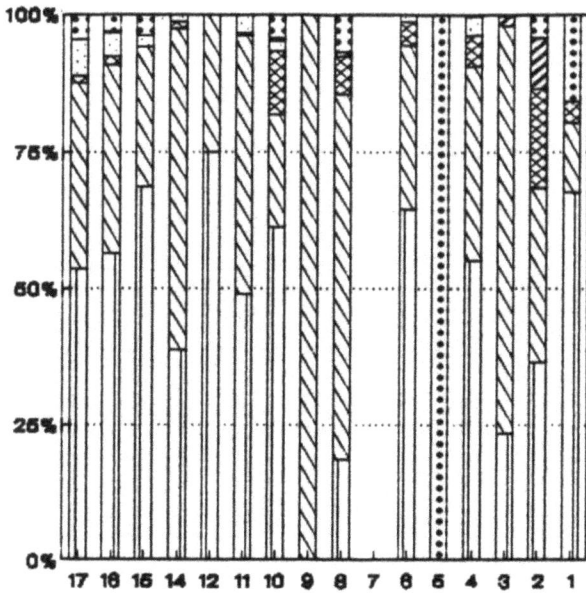

TOP HABITATION

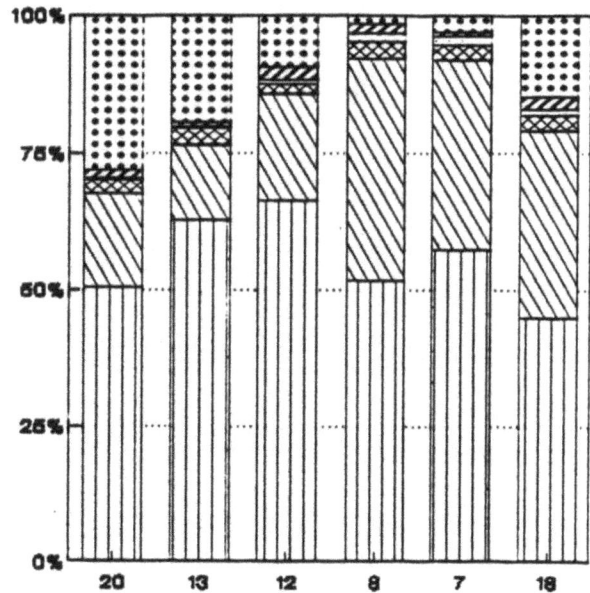

DEBRIS

KEY

A   B   C   H   Y   OTHER

DETAILED ANALYSIS:WEIGHTS
SQUARE ONE, ROOM TWO

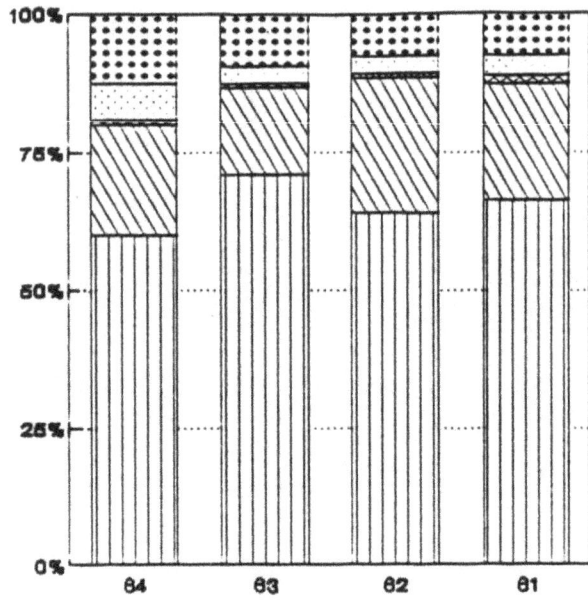

BOTTOM

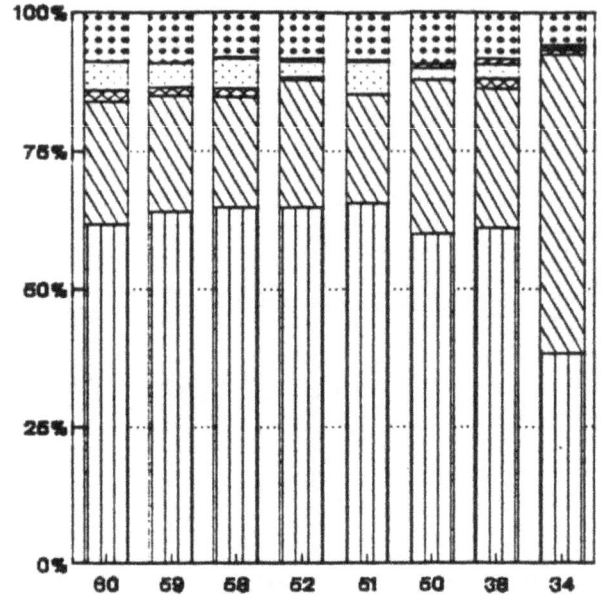

DUMP

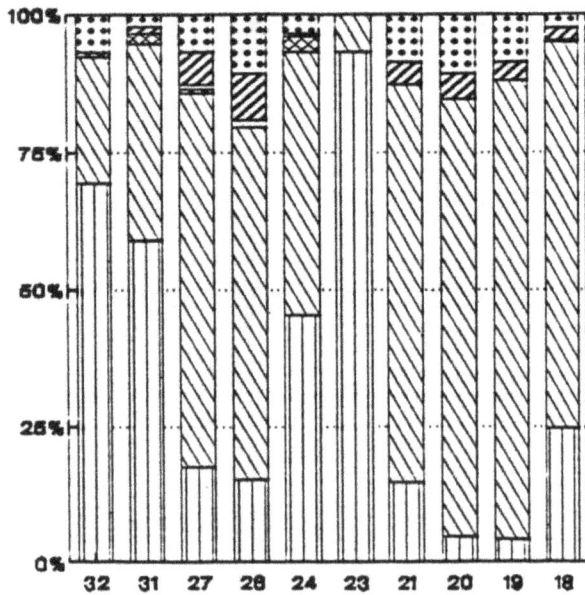

VARIED

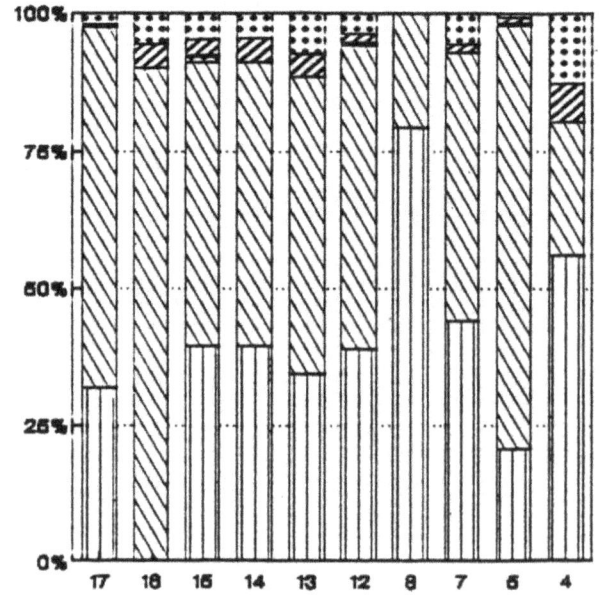

CEMETERY

KEY

A B C H Y OTHER

DETAILED ANALYSIS:WEIGHTS
SQUARE TWO

DETAILED ANALYSIS
Weights by Percentage

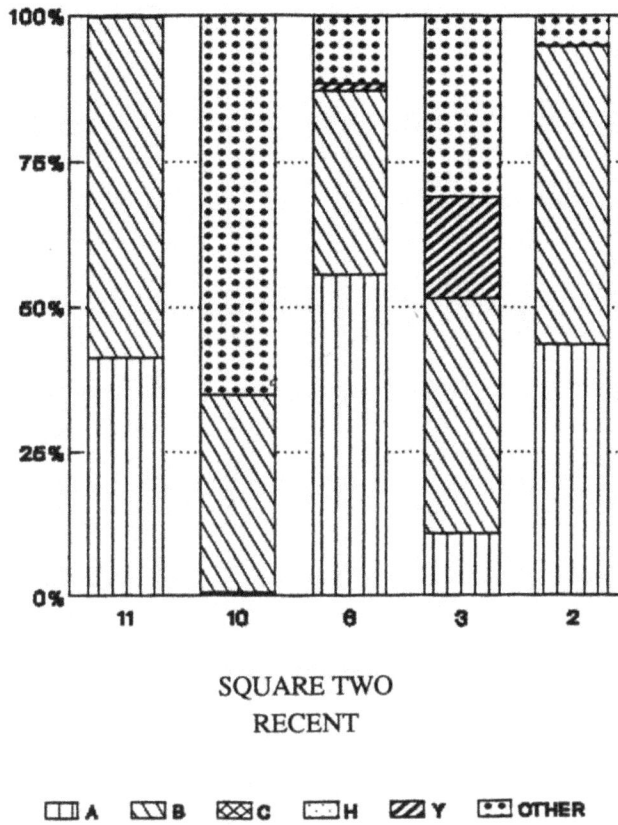

SQUARE TWO
RECENT

▦ A ◨ B ▨ C ▢ H ▨ Y ⊡ OTHER

97

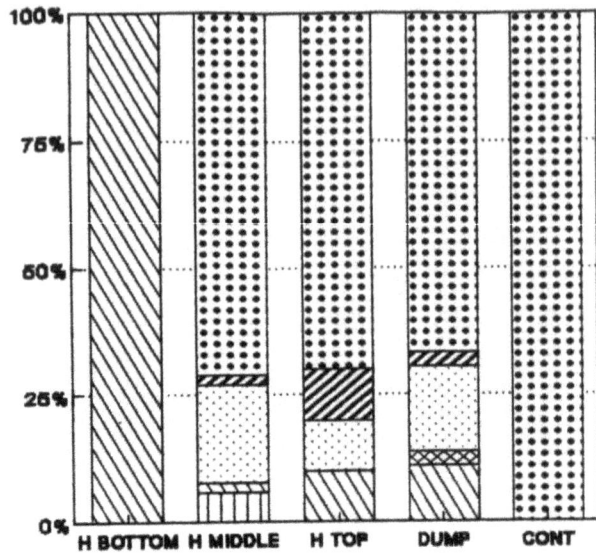

SQUARE ONE: ROOM 2
PERCENTAGES

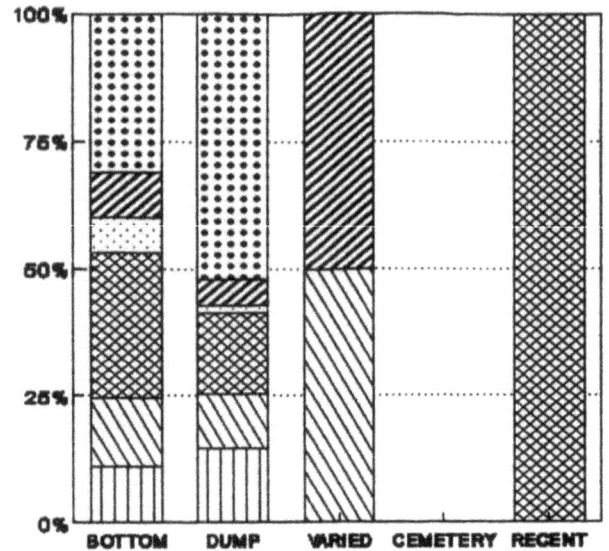

SQUARE TWO
PERCENTAGES

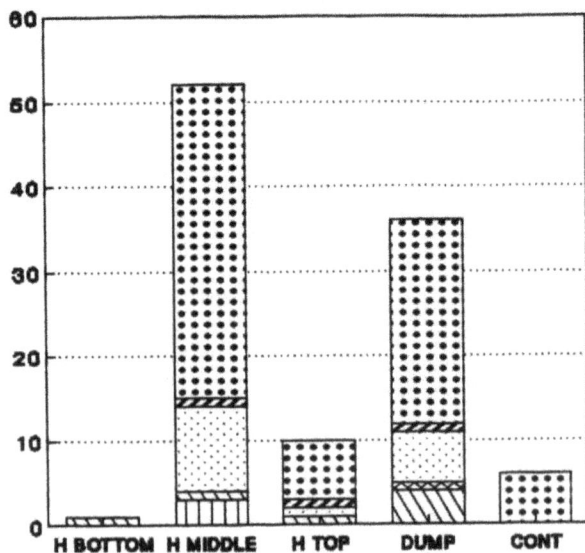

SQUARE ONE: ROOM 2
NUMBERS

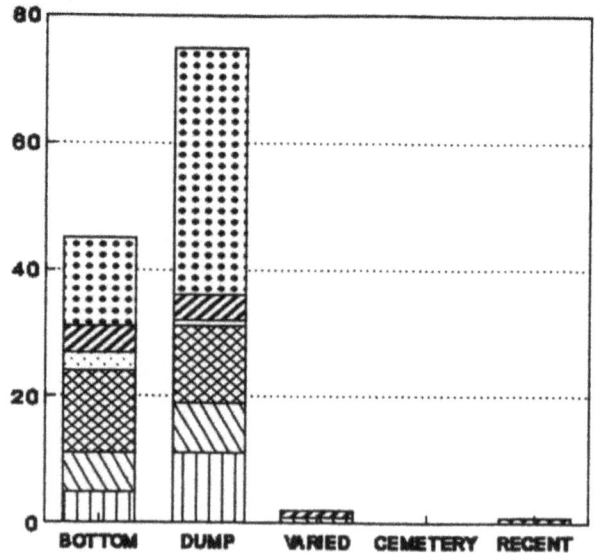

SQUARE TWO
NUMBERS

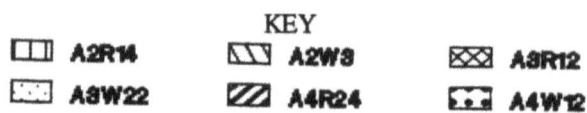

KEY

A2R14   A2W3   A3R12

A3W22   A4R24   A4W12

ASWAN PAINTED WARE: COUNTS OF REGISTERED SHERDS

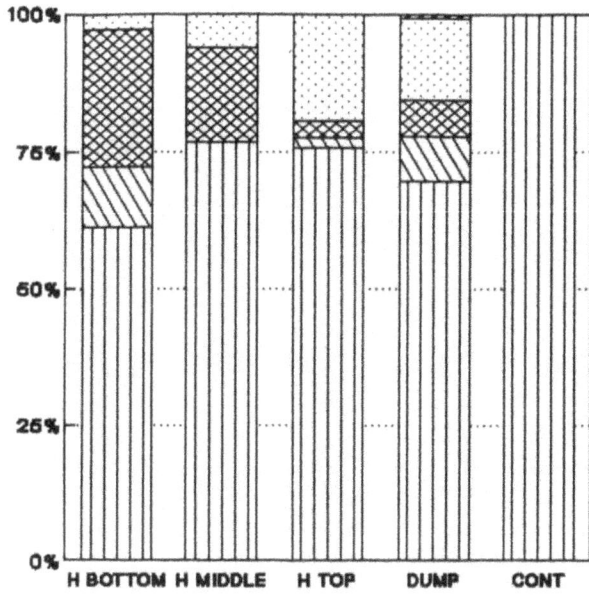

SQUARE ONE: ROOM 2
PERCENTAGES

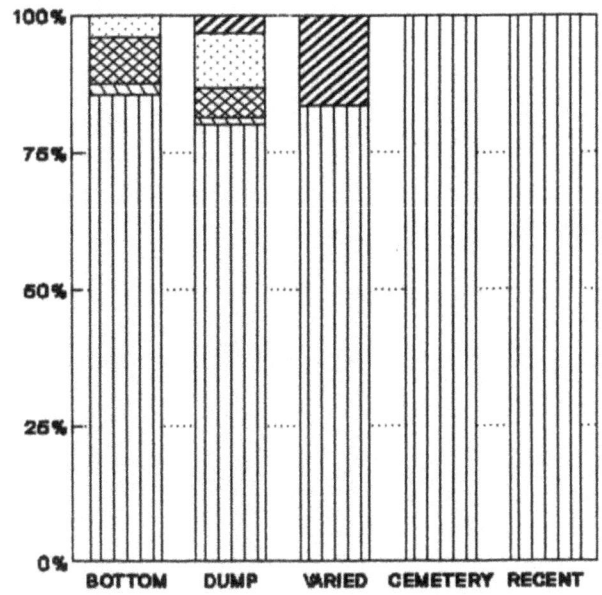

SQUARE TWO
PERCENTAGES

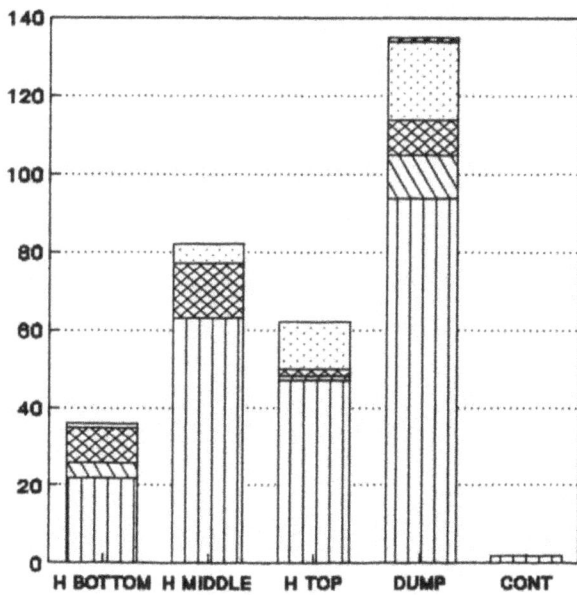

SQUARE ONE: ROOM 2
NUMBERS

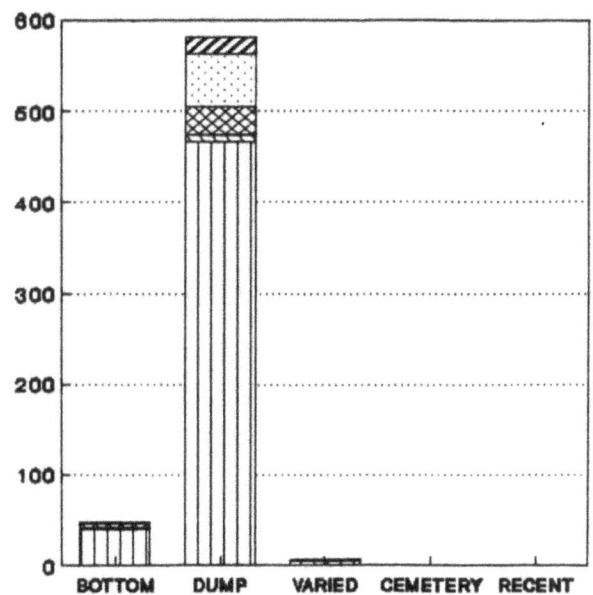

SQUARE TWO
NUMBERS

KEY

A   B   D   E   F

EGYPTIAN SLIP WARES: COUNTS OF REGISTERED SHERDS

CHURCHYARD OF ABU SAYFAYN (SECTOR ONE)

MARKET PLACE (SECTOR TWO)

BEGINNING OF EXCAVATION

OVERVIEW AT END OF EXCAVATION
SECTOR ONE: SQUARE ONE

ROOM 2 AT END OF 1978 EXCAVATION

STORAGE BINS IN ROOM 2
SECTOR ONE, SQUARE ONE

103

FLOOR IN ROOM 2

WALL A IN ROOM 2
SECTOR ONE, SQUARE ONE

WALL B IN ROOM 2

WALL C AND STEPS FROM ROOM 3 TO ROOM 2
SECTOR ONE, SQUARE ONE

105

BINS IN ROOM 3

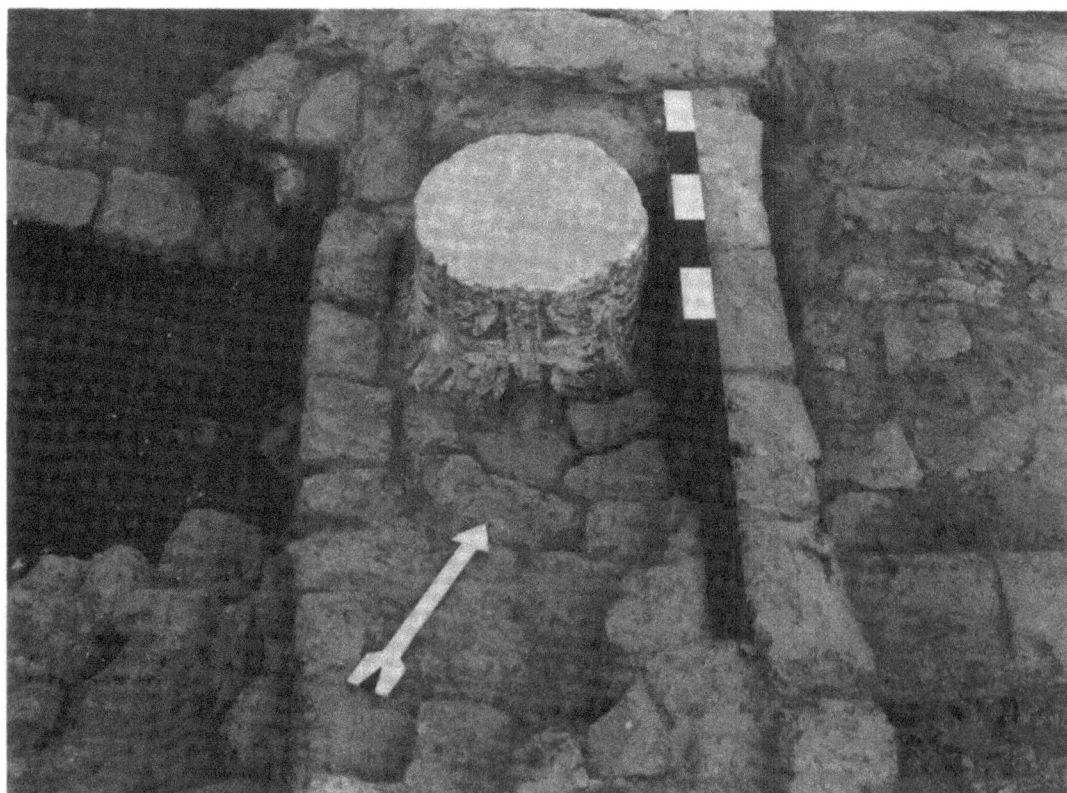

BLOCKED DOORWAY IN WALL E
SECTOR ONE, SQUARE ONE

ROOM 4 AT END OF EXCAVATION

POTTERY IN FLOOR OF ROOM 4
SECTOR ONE, SQUARE ONE

NORTHWEST BUILDING AND PIT

UPPER WALL REMAINS
SECTOR ONE, SQUARE ONE

BEGINNING OF EXCAVATION

COFFIN

COFFINS

SECTOR ONE: SQUARE TWO

109

BURIAL CHAMBER

ROW OF AMPHORAE *IN SITU*
SECTOR ONE: SQUARE TWO

www.ingramcontent.com/pod-product-compliance
Lightning Source LLC
Chambersburg PA
CBHW061300270326
41932CB00029B/3417